D1562529

THEATRE
IN MY BLOOD

*Some people think a commercial success
is wrong; that somehow there is more prestige in
attracting only a tiny audience, in order
to prove how artistic you are. I could never agree
with that. It must be because I have the
theatre in my blood — I always want
people to enjoy themselves.*

John Cranko

THEATRE IN MY BLOOD

A biography of John Cranko

JOHN PERCIVAL

A GROLIER COMPANY

FRANKLIN WATTS
NEW YORK 1983

Library of Congress Card Catalog Number: 83–50083

ISBN 0–531–09800–1

First published in Great Britain in 1983 by
The Herbert Press Limited

First United States publication in 1983 by
Franklin Watts, Inc., 387 Park Avenue South,
New York, NY 10016

Printed and bound in Great Britain

6 5 4 3 2 1

WHY did so many people assume that John Cranko's sudden death must have been suicide?

It is easy to see how the sleeping pill he had taken could be misunderstood as an overdose, but an airliner full of his friends would be an unlikely place for anyone to kill himself. Besides, what motive would he have had? On the surface, none. He was a man of forty-five, at the top of his profession, fresh from new triumphs in an international career, with further possibilities just opening ahead of him. A man who had made his name by his own imagination and energy, not in just one skill but three: as choreographer, as deviser of revues and other shows, as director of a company that he had brought from obscure provincial competence to world-wide acclaim. A man surrounded by colleagues of exceptional talent, who treated him with a uniquely loving respect, whom he in turn loved more dearly than a family.

True, he no longer had any real family with blood links or domestic ties: separated from his mother since adolescence, so far as any real communication went; his father dead; himself disappointed in love. Those who knew him best saw the melancholy that went hand-in-hand with the gaiety he showed the world, and because he lived every emotion intensely, his misery went deep. Anyone could see that there were times when he drank far more than was good for him. There were whispers, too, about an earlier time when several of his close friends died suddenly and sadly, when he was full of self-doubt, and his despair had become more than he could bear.

For all that, there is no faintest shadow of doubt. His death was nothing but an absurd, ludicrous accident. It was also highly theatrical, as his whole adult life had been: an airliner diverted to an unexpected destination, the body found dead on arrival, people already waiting at his destination to greet him before they heard the shocking news, grief and incredulity on all sides as the story spread around the world.

John Cranko lived in the theatre, for the theatre, and like the theatre. The outlines of his life are familiar but, because it fell into three parts separated by place as well as time, it is obscure in detail even to those who were closest to him at any given time. I can safely claim that nobody at all can read what follows without learning something new about him, any more than I could have imagined, when I began preparing it, how much unrecorded information I would find. It does not fundamentally change our view of him: his character was already vivid enough, his achievements large and firmly based. But it is possible to understand better the man behind those achievements.

There was nothing in his early childhood to hint at the extraordinary life he would lead. Growing up in a South African mining town, the son of a reasonably successful lawyer, he might easily have settled down to an ordinary, respectable career, following his father into law, perhaps, as one of his cousins did, or becoming an architect like another of them. But as an adolescent he developed a passion for the theatre, first in the form of puppets, then ballet. Even before he reached his nineteenth birthday, he had begun to make a name as a choreographer, and one of the works he made then is still danced: only a trifle, but full of the wit that was one of his gifts. The precociousness of his talent now seems to have been just as well, because by time he left his native land, aged eighteen, more than a third of his life was already gone.

He never went back, because he loathed the way the black people there were treated. But it was ambition, not politics, that drove him to England. London was the place to prove himself as a choreographer, and he spent almost exactly the next third of his life there, fifteen years, doing that and much more besides. Success came quickly, thanks to a happy mixture of talent, determination, enterprise and luck. At twenty-two, he was already recognized within the ballet world as the most gifted dance creator of his generation, and George Balanchine commissioned him to make a work for New York City Ballet. At twenty-three, he had his first big hit with the general public: *Pineapple Poll*, still a crowd-puller after three decades. At twenty-four, he first ran his own small company. But success at Covent Garden and Sadler's Wells, invitations from the Paris Opéra and La Scala, Milan, the chance to collaborate with leading composers and painters — all this was not enough to satisfy him or occupy his energies fully. So he turned to other forms of theatre, directing operas, writing and staging revues and musicals, to which he brought new ideas and methods that were widely admired.

Then came a sudden reversal of fortune: flops (some, but by no means all, deserved) in ballet and the theatre; his father's death; a scandal arising from a prosecution for homosexual activity. His fame made criticism sharper and more wounding. His standing as an accepted figure, even a friend of the Queen's sister, Princess Margaret, made him vulnerable to attack.

So at thirty-three he seized the chance of a fresh start. He pulled up his roots a second time and moved to another new land, Germany, where during the twelve years that were left to him he accomplished a "ballet miracle", building not merely a repertory and a company in Stuttgart, but a whole new public attitude that affected other theatres throughout the country. Dancers flocked to him; he in return developed their abilities wonderfully and gave them roles to show off their gifts. As he did all his life, he also found and encouraged new designers and composers. His own qualities as a choreographer blossomed in this setting. He became a supreme story-teller in dance, but kept his passion for experiment, too, often disconcerting his admirers and yet still gaining their acceptance.

His achievements alone would have won admiration, but John Cranko had another quality besides. Everything he did was enriched by a warm concern for other people that inspired affection from even slight acquaintances, and love from his closer colleagues. No wonder his sudden early death caused such grief. Yet this man found himself unloved, in that he demanded so much from his friends that he could not find a close, enduring relationship to satisfy him. That was one cause of the melancholy that dogged him.

So he swung between extremes of mood, darkened towards the end by the death of cherished friends. Hence the alarmed thought on the part of many that he might have taken his own life. Far from it: he had come out of the darkness and was full of hope and plans. He died as active as ever and, although only forty-five, had already crammed more into that space of time than most people manage in a far longer span.

His was a hectic life, becoming more so as it went on. It was full of extremes: a success story that left the winner dissatisfied, a source of pleasure to many thousands of people while he experienced misery as well delight. But to be sorry for him would be a mistake: he lived his life to the full, and in all his deeds he enriched the lives of others. What I have tried to do in this book is to tell how he did it.

SOUTH AFRICA

Scene One
ORIGINS

Scene Two
BEGINNINGS

Scene Three
CAPE OF GOOD HOPE

ORIGINS

JOHN Cranko was puzzled by his surname; amused, too. He made a pun on it for the title of his revue *Cranks*. More seriously, he thought that it was probably a corrupt version of some such name as Krankovitz or Krankovsky, indicating that one branch of the family had come from eastern Europe. John's father had told him vague stories about a grandfather who was said to have spent his time in mysterious pursuits of his own, returning home at intervals to sire another child before disappearing again. He might be the hypothetical Slav ancestor: a Russian, Pole or Czech, perhaps. I am not sure whether John was aware of a tradition among some of his distant cousins that the family originated from Poland, possibly in a Count Cranko, romantically supposed to have been descended from the founder of the city of Krakow.

Not long before he died, John visited London. While there, he looked for the first time through papers which his father, Herbert Cranko, had left: two notebooks and a number of typescripts. Among the confused jottings in the larger notebook he found this:

Grandpa must have arrived early in 19 Century about Napoleonic times —
? When did British occupy Cape?
Assuming he was born 1850   Married 1880—1
His father 1820 settlers?   Huguenots

The "he" born in 1850 must have been Herbert's Pa, not Grandpa. The argument is not very logical but the notes were enough for John to decide that the family origins must, after all, have been French. He deduced that the name might formerly have been Craingeau, Graingeau or Gringaud, any one of which would be pronounced sufficiently like Cranko to become transformed. He told this to Dr Schäfer, the Intendant or general director of the theatre at Stuttgart, who published it after John's death, spelling the hypothetical name differently on various occasions. Obviously John had no time to investigate the theory, and probably he would not have bothered anyway, since it looks convincing and he was given to quick enthusiasms. If he had enquired into it, he would have discovered that there are examples among Huguenot families of names changing in that way, but that nobody named Craingeau or

3

Gringaud or anything else that might sound like Cranko is listed among the Huguenot settlers in South Africa.

Since John's death, however, one of his younger cousins, Robin Cranko, has made it his business to search out the beginnings of the family. His father, like John's, had been still young when their father died, and consequently could not remember him, only the "very Victorian mother" who brought them up, and the tales she told about him. So Robin Cranko, who wanted to know more about his ancestors, began looking through public and church archives. He also consulted old copies of the *Cape of Good Hope Almanac and Annual Register* which, among other practical information, recorded the names and addresses of residents. Gradually he pieced together the story, visiting or writing to members of the family in several continents to confirm details. What he discovered caused the jottings by John's father to fall into place, separating fact from speculation, and what follows is based mainly on collating those two sources. The truth turned out to be stranger than the legend, and it throws light on the qualities of character which John inherited.

The first people to bear the name Cranko were two brothers, James and William, and their sister Miemie, all living in Cape Town in the middle of the nineteenth century. Their father's name was Theunis Krankoor, and it is probable that either he or his father was the first person to take that name too.

Krankoor is as odd a name as Cranko. It means, in Dutch, a sick or defective ear. If you want a colloquial equivalent in English, Thickear might be as good as any. There are many such names in Dutch and Flemish, dating from Napoleonic times. Until the Netherlands came under Napoleon's rule, many of the inhabitants had managed perfectly well without surnames. That did not suit Bonaparte's desire for order and was inconvenient to his need for conscripting recruits to his army. So those who had no family name were required by law to adopt one. Resenting this, and probably thinking that the requirement would be as short-lived as the fortunes of war, many of the peasants took derisive and ribald names. Examples among families who settled in South Africa are Klerenbesem, Koevoet and Krombeck, meaning respectively clothesbrush, crowbar and crooked muzzle. Krankoor must almost certainly have been another such.

On that assumption, Theunis Krankoor's arrival in Cape Town can be placed within a period of about fifteen years, after the implementation of the full Napoleonic legal code in the Netherlands and before the birth of his first child, James, who, according to his wedding and death registrations, was born in the Cape Colony about

4

1823 or 1824. At that time the settlement of Cape Town, which had been just a small staging post on the voyage between the Netherlands and the East Indies, was beginning to grow, but although the English had occupied the Cape in 1806, the white population remained mainly Dutch until the arrival of many new settlers from Britain in 1820.

The supposition that Theunis — or maybe his father — invented the name Krankoor shortly before emigrating comes from the fact that no surviving Krankoors, nor records of such a family, have come to light in Holland; two Crankos live in The Hague but they are recent arrivals from South Africa. Theunis, whose second name was probably Carel or Carl, had a wife, Maria Dorothea, whose maiden name was Rubenden, but little is known about either of them. Records of their two sons, however, and of their daughter, also named Maria Dorothea but known as Miemie, remain in the form of wills and marriage or death certificates. The wills are written in Dutch; their weddings were solemnized in the Dutch Reformed Church. That they spoke Dutch among themselves is also suggested by the fact that the longest surviving member of that generation, William's widow Sarah (née Weiss, of German origin), continued to speak Dutch or Afrikaans until her death in 1922. Even so, the beginning of an English influence is suggested by the brothers' first names and by the fact that William's second name, Justavus, is spelled that way, indicating an English pronunciation, instead of the more usual Gustavus.

For obvious reasons, many of the Dutch settlers in Cape Town found it expedient under English rule to become anglicized, although those who had moved inland maintained their national identity. The *Annual Register*s record the gradual transformation of the Krankoor family name. A change from Krankoor to Kranko came between the 1847 and 1848 volumes, soon after Theunis's death. As you would expect, the change in pronunciation was made once and for all, but either the brothers or the editors of the *Register* seem to have had difficulty making up their minds how to spell it. The version Cranko first appears in 1850, but the two versions competed with each other at least until the end of the decade. (Details are given in Appendix A). Eventually, the more English-seeming version of the family name, with the initial C, prevailed. Later generations of the family spoke English as their first language and went over to the Anglican church.

Theunis Krankoor's elder son, James Cranko, married twice. His first wife, Helena, died in 1845 giving birth to a daughter. In 1847 he married Fredrica Schoukerk, daughter of an usher in the Cape

Town Supreme Court. They had two sons, the elder of whom, Fredrik Jacob Willem, was born about 1848. This Frederick (he adopted the English spelling) was the mysterious grandfather that John Cranko was told of, who was supposed to spend much of his time visiting the fleshpots of Cape Town.

James Cranko died in 1852, aged about 28; some say he was poisoned. His widow married again in 1854; she and her new husband, Hendrik van Blerk, lived on a farm at Kuils River, Cape Town. Frederick was apparently brought up there with the daughter, Hester, of the new marriage, but he ran away to sea. He went for a time to Australia, then jumped ship in Cape Town (which caused a scandal) and was subsequently cared for by his uncle Willy, Theunis's younger son.

Since becoming sole owner of the family tailoring business, William had built it up very successfully. He had his coach and horses, lived in comfort in a fine house and bought property all over the town. When his sister Miemie (who had married a carpenter, Hermanus Dempers) was widowed, he took her in as companion for his wife and housekeeper to the family. William travelled in Europe and had an account with a London bank. He sent his son, William Johan, also known as John, to school in England. (This earlier John Cranko, incidentally, married a Scottish girl, Annie Scleater, and later settled in England. He did not die until 1951, five years after his namesake and distant kinsman, our John Cranko, arrived in England. Two of his daughters were also living not far from London throughout the time the younger John Cranko was living there, but there is no indication that the latter was aware of these kinsfolk).

Old William Cranko and his nephew Frederick both seem to have been fond of feminine company. Robin Cranko thinks that one of them, if not both, must have been responsible for some branches of the Cranko family whom he came across during his researches. The name is now widespread in South Africa. Many of those who hold it live in poor areas and some are Coloured, that is, of mixed European and African descent. Herbert Cranko used to tell a story about a very dark-skinned man named Cranko turning up one day in his Johannesburg office, calling him uncle and announcing that he was short of money. Herbert, who had no colour prejudice but a careful attitude about money, was proud of his reply: "My dear sir, this is a legal office, not a money-lending office."

Frederick Cranko in 1876 married Susannah Solomon, a member of a famous Cape legal family, but soon divorced her. In 1881, in his early thirties, he married again. His second wife, Bilhah Solomon Jacobson, known as Belle, was a remarkable woman. She was born in London in 1863, one of the eleven children of a Jewish family. Old Mr Jacobson emigrated to the Cape in 1880 after a quarrel with his wife, taking with him two of his four sons and all but one of his seven daughters. He set up in business as an antique dealer but, according to Herbert Cranko, "seems to have loved his stock more than his customers, often refusing to sell a cherished piece to a disliked buyer". One may be sceptical about that "often". His grandsons remembered him as a very old man, fond of reading the *Encyclopaedia Britannica* and so failing in his memory that, when he dozed over one of the volumes, the boys would turn over several pages and he never noticed but read on from there when he woke up.

Herbert's notes give only tantalizing hints of what happened to the other Jacobson children. Charlie became a "jeweller, pawnbroker, fisherman" and Dave was a "poverty-stricken philanthropist". Most of the daughters (except Rose, who lost an eye) soon married, but Minnie's marriage to Abe Greenbaum came to an abrupt end when she did a "bunk with Claud" — a doctor she met on a visit to London. The Jacobsons, like the Crankos, were an adventurous family, tending to be foot-loose and adaptable.

In 1885 Frederick Cranko (who, after starting as a sailor, worked as a tailor, an engraver and a clerk) joined the gold rush to Pretoria and thence to Johannesburg, a thousand miles from Cape Town. South Africa was a big, thinly populated country, its interior only just being opened up as its mineral wealth was discovered. Frederick went on the new railway as far as the railhead at the diamond mines of Kimberley, and had to join an ox-wagon train the rest of the way. Belle followed later with their daughter Muriel and their first son, Samuel, known as Toy; the younger children were born in Johannesburg. Belle's sister Lil went with her as a companion for the long journey. One of the first houses in the goldfields was built to welcome them and the two children; the roof was not on by the time they arrived but many miners joined in helping to complete it, the sight of two young Englishwoman being a delightful rarity.

In Johannesburg, actually in the mining camp at Ferreira's Town, Frederick and Belle opened an hotel, which according to Robin Cranko was the first in the locality. It seems to have thrived. Before leaving London, Belle had been secretary to an hotel keeper and wine merchant, which should have provided useful experience for the venture. Its success must have been largely through her efforts if it is true that Frederick was often away from home.

We may wonder what was behind those absences. Belle gave her sons the idea that it was capricious irresponsibility. Robin Cranko has the impression that his grandfather was "rather over-fond of life

7

and living... quite an arty person... an unusual, warm being, fond of the good things". Some of those qualities appear to have been inherited by Frederick's youngest son Herbert and, as already mentioned, sone of them may have been present in Frederick's uncle William. Belle, on the other hand, was described by Robin's father as something of a martinet.

In October 1899 the Anglo-Boer War broke out. All uitlanders, or non-citizens, of British stock had to leave the Transvaal Republic, and in spite of their Dutch antecedents the Crankos had by then become fully anglicized. So they had to abandon the Ferreira Hotel and most of their possessions. Mother, father and six children set off first by train in open cattle trucks. Muriel, the only daughter, was in her early teens, the boys all younger, down to Herbert aged just four. As they travelled through territory held by Dutch settlers, nobody was willing to sell food to the "English". Belle devised the trick of waiting by a food stall at a halt until the train was just pulling out again. Then she hurled some money at the stallkeeper, grabbed loaves and other food, and jumped on the moving train. The railway took them hundreds of miles east (further away from Cape Town) to Delagoa Bay in Lourenço Marques; from there they were taken by ship to the Cape. Either Frederick became ill because of their privations, or he may already have been suffering from pneumonia, which was worsened by the hard journey. In any event, he died in Cape Town during December 1899.

Frederick Cranko's family, who had disapproved of his marrying a Jew, would have nothing to do with his widow. That may have been one factor in causing her subsequently to bring up the children in the Jewish faith. Although she was the dominant parent, she had made no attempt to do so until then; Robin's father remembered being circumcised after his father's death, when he was seven. Presumably other members of the Jacobson family must have given Belle some help, because in spite of having left most of their possessions in Johannesburg, they achieved a state of gentility during the year or two they lived in Cape Town, according to Herbert's notes.

In 1901 Belle went to England for a year, taking the children with her. The older boys attended a Rabbi's school at Ealing to learn about the Jewish faith. During 1902 Belle was able to return to Johannesburg and retrieve at least some of her possessions. In 1906 she moved to Krugersdorp where she ran the Swan Hotel and, according to Herbert, achieved prosperity. About that time she was married again. Ten years or so later, she moved to Rustenburg, where she ran the Grand Hotel, which her eldest son took over when she retired. During the nineteen-twenties she spent some time in London, and after her second husband, Maurice Platner, died in 1929 she moved to Johannesburg, where she died in 1932. So her former connection with Rustenburg, and the presence there of his brother, may have been among the considerations that prompted Herbert Cranko to choose that town when he found it necessary to settle down after a roving life.

A photograph taken in 1908 shows Belle, strongly matriarchal among her children. A family likeness can be seen among all the boys, every face dominated by a long curved nose. It is at least possible that their features came from their father's side of the family, judging from an anecdote which Herbert told of having been on holiday at the Cape as a young man. He was on Muizenburg Beach, then a popular resort, when a stranger came he up and asked him in Afrikaans "Is your name Cranko?" When he replied that it was, she told him "Come this way, your auntie wants to have a talk with you." The aunt (actually great-aunt) who had known him from his appearance was Sarah, widow of old William Justavus Cranko, and the companion she sent to fetch him was Miemie Dempers, William's sister. They had a long chat in Afrikaans; Herbert specially mentioned the language because it was only the survivors of the family's oldest generation who still habitually spoke it.

The Crankos seem to have included more than their share of wanderers. As well as the journeying already mentioned, others of the family settled in the United States, New Zealand and Australia. Herbert, too, visited Australia when he was about sixteen. Five years later, in 1916, he qualified in law, and about that time went through a phase which prompts the single word "Bolshy" in his notes. Then he went to fight in France from 1917 to 1918. Back in Johannesburg after the war, Herbert began to practise law in partnership with one of his elder brothers, James, but later went off to Europe for a year to study law in Vienna. His notes say that it was in 1924, but it must have been sooner, probably 1921 or 1922, because he was back in South Africa in time to get married in 1923. Herbert Cranko, like his son, was often very vague about dates. Herbert's papers include an uncompleted short story about living in Vienna as a postgraduate student which, like other stories he left, is evidently only thinly disguised autobiography. He says that "wanderlust and chance" brought him to the city which he associated particularly with Mozart, Strauss and Lehár, also with Freud and Einstein. He describes lodging in the beautifully furnished house of a respectable widow with artistic tastes, who had been impoverished by inflation. That inflation enabled students with money from abroad (English pounds in his own case, he says) to rush from one currency dealer to another, taking advantage of different rates to make a profit.

The story's climax, had he reached it, was obviously to have been the outcome of his meeting with the widow's beautiful and gifted daughter. In real life, too, there was an intention (perhaps stronger on her side than his) that he should marry his landlady's daughter, but nothing came of that because, on returning to Johannesburg, Herbert met Grace, who was in fact to become his first·wife and John's mother. Herbert was then twenty-eight and no doubt set in his carefree ways. Grace, who had a daughter, Peggy van Druten, by an earlier marriage, was twenty-six.

Her family's history, although nobody has recorded it in such detail, seems to have been almost as adventurous as that of the Crankos. On her father's side, she was descended from Thomas Hinds (thought to come from Essex), who had been shipwrecked off the coast of Port Elizabeth in 1821. He and his brother George survived by swimming ashore. Thomas's son, also called Thomas, was Grace's father; she was born on his farm, The Junction, at Magaliesberg, Transvaal, and baptized Hilda Grace in the Anglican church there. Grace's mother, Alice Jennings, also traced her ancestry to England, in her case to Wiltshire. Alice's grandfather had been about to embark for Cape Town with the 1820 settlers when he became ill, was taken to hospital in Portsmouth and died before sailing. The ships in harbour had to leave because of a storm; they sailed away bearing his new widow and her son, aged two, who grew up to become a big game hunter in central Africa. Alice Jennings was his daughter.

Grace met Herbert through Major Chaplin Court Treatt, the husband of her sister Stella. He was working for an engineering firm and met Herbert in the course of business. Grace was staying with her sister and brother-in-law and went with them to have dinner with Herbert at the end of August 1923; her account of the meeting is that "lightning struck" and three weeks later they were married.

Marriage did not immediately cause Herbert to settle down. Court Treatt had long dreamed of making the hitherto unattempted journey by car from the Cape to Cairo, and had already surveyed the route by air. Herbert caught his enthusiasm for the idea. Neither had much money, so they decided to go to London with their wives and look for sponsors. They set off in November 1923 and it took a year to set up the expedition. When Court Treatt returned to Cape Town, Herbert remained in London to organize supplies, including petrol, which had to be delivered along the route, then a wilderness without roads or bridges. The successful Cape to Cairo Expedition, in which Grace's young brother Errol also took part, set out in 1925, but the journey was a long one, and after that there were many arrangements to be wound up, so Herbert's work in London was not complete until late the following year. During their time in London, which was a happy one, he and Grace went to see the Diaghilev Ballet and also Pavlova's company. Grace's daughter Peggy had ballet lessons from Seraphina Astafieva, whose most famous pupils were Alicia Markova and Anton Dolin.

Late in 1926, Herbert returned to South Africa to give lectures about the expedition, illustrated by still photographs and moving pictures. He left Grace and Peggy behind with the intention of travelling for a while in Europe, but he had only just landed in South Africa when Grace realized that she was going to have another child. She let Herbert know, and he cabled her to cancel all other arrangements and catch the next ship back.

Deciding now to take up the practice of law again, Herbert thought that the best opening would be to build up a country practice. Rustenburg, where his brother was running the Grand Hotel, offered the right sort of opportunity. They stayed first in the hotel and were still living there when John was born. About sixty miles from Johannesburg and the same distance from the provincial capital, Pretoria, Rustenburg's prosperity was based on mining, especially for platinum, but it is surrounded by good farming land in a warm, beautiful valley. In this sleepy little town, Herbert Cranko set up his business and awaited the birth of his child.

BEGINNINGS

JOHN Cranko was born at about six in the morning of 15 August 1927, a Monday. He was a big boy, weighing nine and a half pounds at birth. His mother writes that he was

> a strangely good baby, always laughing and talking to himself in his own fashion, kicking in his pram, talking to the trees. He was strong, crawled about for a short while and walked quite strongly at ten months. As a child he was always adventurous and found everything a huge joke... From the time he could say words, he always spoke correctly, no baby talk... He always adored animals, he had pets all his life. He was a good horseman from the age of seven.

There was even a time, John said later, when his one ambition was to devote himself to horses, but his father was not especially enthusiastic about that idea.

His mother's collection of family snapshots shows that, whereas most babies look much like any other babies until they begin to grow up a little, John looked recognizably himself at a very early age, thanks largely to his big smile, almost a grin. In many of the pictures he is accompanied by his half-sister Peggy, about ten years older than he, who was devoted to him. John may have reciprocated that feeling when very young, but the warmth, at any rate on his side, did not survive into adult life. At one time he also had a nanny, who came from the German-speaking part of Switzerland.

At six weeks old, he was baptized with the names John Cyril at Holy Trinity Church, Rustenburg. His godparents came from his mother's side of the family, her brother Errol and Florence Court Treatt, who Grace thinks may have been Major Court Treatt's mother; also a friend, a government official named John Keith, after whom John was named. His mother says he would never own to his second name, which was that of a friend of Herbert's living in London.

Grace had been brought up in a very religious household and she maintained strict standards for herself but, she says, "was not allowed to check or discipline John in any way". In that we see Herbert's more easy-going temperament. He too had been strictly brought up but seems to have shrugged off his mother's influence in that as easily as he resisted her attempts to make him a practising Jew. Grace insists that for most of his life Herbert's associates, girl friends and other friends were not Jews. In his fifties, he became involved in an airline flying to Israel, which was later absorbed into El Al, the official airline of the new state of Israel. At that time, from all accounts, he must have become more outwardly Jewish in his attitudes. This able and likeable man was admirably adaptable to circumstances and had something of an eye to the main chance. Robin Cranko tells a story illustrating Herbert's sense of business opportunity. When Robin had newly qualified in law, Herbert strongly recommended Rustenburg as a place to start practising, and offered to allow his name to be used in return for a small interest in the practice, on the grounds that many people would remember it. He was somewhat taken aback when Robin pointed out that he was entitled to use the name anyway.

When Herbert came to put paper on his ideas about where his son's gifts had come from, he started trying to develop a theory about "mongrelization", or the mixing of racial and cultural traditions, with some countries such as the United States, Australia, Canada and South Africa acting as crucibles or melting pots. He wrote of a fusing point at which the mixture becomes homogeneous, like an alloy, but thought that "some intransigents never fuse — Jews, Scots". From that, and from the way his notes keep returning to her, it appears that he regarded the Jewish influence, through his mother, as important in his life and John's. Yet when John eventually went to make a ballet in Israel, there were arguments among people who had dealings with him about whether or not he was a Jew. Some were convinced one way, others were equally sure of the opposite.

As an adult, John did not follow any religious observances. He had a large menorah, the traditional Jewish seven-branched candle holder, in his living-room at Stuttgart, but that was a souvenir of his work in Israel. Equally, he had a peasant cross, made of embroidered material, hanging on the wall of his bedroom there; he had bought that in Bulawayo when there with a visiting company in 1953. He sometimes claimed Jewish blood, sometimes denied it, and there is evidence that feelings about how Jews had been treated under the Nazi regime troubled him after he had settled in Germany. However, in early days he seems to have led a sunny existence.

As a small boy, he did the usual things that boys do. His mother tells an anecdote about his wanting to join the Cubs, the junior branch of Boy Scout movement, when he was only four or five: much below the permitted age, but he was so insistent that the Cubmaster let him in. The Governor-General, the Earl of Clarendon, went to

13

Rustenburg and reviewed the Scouts at a garden party. Overcome by the regalia worn by this very tall man, John went up to the august personage, slipped a small hand into one of his, and asked "are you the king?" Lifting him up, the Earl replied "No, son, but I am the next best thing."

Rustenburg when John was a boy was a small town, or large village, in an area inhabited by many races. Herbert Cranko enumerated them. He had gone there expecting "to suffer the tedium of a few years living in the backveld, in order to make some very necessary repairs to the fortunes of myself and my small family" but found that "against all expectations I had wandered into a bewilderingly interesting, exciting and varied World". The district covered by his law practice ranged "from the middle veld north of the Magaliesberg Mountains to the bank of the Crocodile River bordering Bechuanaland". The oldest inhabitants were black, though they were not one people but quite a variety. Many of Herbert's clients were Africans. Then there were Coloured people of mixed racial descent, and the whites, also "of many different origins and races, and also bitterly divided". They included the Boers,

> highly individualistic, unwilling to accept any authority and already out of touch with Europe, save for their devout and passionate adherence to the Bible (Old Testament) as the sole instructor and guide in all matters. But even in their religion they could not keep together... In my village there had been historic upheaval over such questions as whether it was right that hymns should be sung in the House of God. Some considered that the Psalms, as part of the Holy Book, were fitting, but hymns the work of mortals... a strong faction condemned their performance in church as blasphemy.

Other settlers included "stray Italians, Greeks and other Europeans, Syrians and many odd mixtures... escaping from tyranny or crime, or just on the look-out for adventure or fortune" and, more recent arrivals, many English ex-servicemen, "particularly of the officer type, unemployed, with reasonably substantial cash bonuses and other means. They had discovered the possibilities of cotton growing in the district" and they puzzled their Boer neighbours by their zest for games (cricket, golf, polo) and for such strange, unnecessary luxuries as electricity or water plumbing in their homes, or even wrought iron gates instead of the traditional wire strands which had to be laboriously fastened with primitive devices. The development, of platinum, chrome manganese and iron ore mines had brought new white technicians and black workers, and there were Indian and

Jewish communities, engaged largely in commerce, who kept themselves to themselves.

The ox remained the chief means of transport, Rustenburg had been built

> in a beautiful valley where a kloof gave abundant water. This was led through the streets in furrows so that each burger could have his turn at the stream to irrigate his garden, with its vegetables and flowers. The houses were built of home-made brick, whitewashed, and roofed with ugly imported galvanized iron or occasionally with the smooth thatch of the native crafts-man. They were high, cool and comfortable, and surrounded by spacious stoops. In the middle veld, the climate is hot to discomfort in summer, with warm, pleasant winters, and much of the life of the family was spent on these stoops.

This was where John passed his early years, absorbed in a largely outdoor life. Even such dancing as he saw there was out of doors and quite different from what was later to occupy him. He said that, travelling with his father to the kraals, he had the chance to watch the religious dances of the black tribes; Grace thinks it was later, after the family had left Rustenburg, that John first saw the dancing at the Johannesburg mines. Either way, in later life he looked back on that experience as evidence that dancing could be part of everyday life in a way that it is not for most Europeans. But for the time being, dancing meant little to him. If his parents had not separated, and if they had remained living in Rustenburg (two big ifs, not necessarily related), it is likely that we should never have heard of John Cranko.

In fact, the family moved to Johannesburg in 1935, when John was about seven or eight. Herbert, deciding that he had had enough of provincial life, set up in partnership again with brother James. By then, his marriage was under strain, but in any event the family's way of life would have been greatly changed in this new environment. By international standards, Johannesburg is not a great city — about the same size as Stuttgart, in fact — but it has to be remembered that South Africa is a large country, almost half a million square miles in area, with a population that even today is only about 16 million. The Transvaal is the most northerly and the most populous of its four states, with the capital, Pretoria, and main business centre, Johannesburg, its only towns of any note. Johannesburg, at that time, was expanding and gaining many new buildings. Not only were the surroundings very different from Rustenburg, but the climate, too, in spite of being not many miles removed; its elevation caused bitterly cold winters in contrast to the hot summers. Being a prosperous town, thanks to the surrounding mines, with an ambitious but isolated population (inclined to snobbishness — and, incidentally, to anti-Semitism), social and artistic life was active, and one effect of moving there was that Herbert had the chance to indulge his interest in amateur dramatics. Herbert did not actually perform, but he produced shows (John specifically mentioned revues) and was quite knowledgeable about the theatre. He became chairman of the repertory club, and his business sense helped set it on its feet. John, as a child, loved dressing up; he and his friends played with old clothes kept in a big trunk, and his cousin Petrie writes that the costumes of his father's club gave him opportunities to indulge in this game.

Already, even before the move, Herbert was "going his own way", and there had been a period of separation the previous year when Grace took the children to stay in Cape Town for six months or more. While they were there, Peggy (who had been at a boarding school in Pretoria) was able to resume her ballet classes. She studied with Helen Webb, a noted teacher, and later with Madge Mann in Johannesburg, but she never danced professionally. Grace describes John going to watch her class, and how he sat entranced. She also has a story of how he disappeared during the dress rehearsal of a performance by Miss Webb's pupils, to be found later "in the wings, sitting perched on a pedestal, in a dream world of his own".

There was a strong influence from his parents pushing John towards an interest in ballet. From an early age, his mother and father showed him the illustrated books on the subject which they had brought back from London, and described at length the wonders of the ballets they had seen danced there by the Diaghilev company, "when they were young and in love", as John put it later. They used to talk to him endlessly about it, he said, so he grew up hearing about "this enchanted world" which became for him rather like fairy stories for other people. He suggested that one reason his parents had talked so much about it was that "they really were like oil and water, and the only thing they really agreed about was the ballet. Sometimes I think I grew interested in it because it was the only common ground we had." But it was to be some time before he began putting his interest to any practical application.

After a short time in Johannesburg, Grace and Herbert started living apart. She took a flat with the children, but then Herbert bought a house for them to live in. After about a year, however, for some reason he sold the house again. At that time Grace sent John, aged nine, to a boarding school, St John's College. She writes that it was "one of the best, but it did not suit John, as he was accustomed to

16

follow his whims, and invent or discover for himself, and therefore did not like the regimentation of doing things at a given time. He had no time for school sports and would rather interest himself in planning and building a village on the school grounds." His unhappiness should not have been any great surprise, as St John's was known as a high Anglican school, elitist and exclusive. Things grew to the point that he ran away and, not having the bus fare, walked the five or six miles home. On being taken back, he ran away again a few days later and this time was not forced to return, nor permitted to do so. The headmaster thought him a prime example of naughtiness, but Herbert responded that if the staff were doing their job properly, little boys would not want to run away.

Nowadays, that sort of conduct could lead to a social worker's being asked to take an interest in the child. It is easy to imagine the conclusion that would be drawn: that the broken home had caused the child to become emotionally disturbed. There might indeed be truth in that assessment, but it would be far from the whole truth. The absence of a conventional, stable home ultimately had a beneficial effect on John in two important respects. It encouraged him towards early independence and self-sufficiency without which he would not have got his career off to so quick a start; and it must have contributed to the ease with which, to further that career, he uprooted himself first from South Africa and later from his adopted second homeland in Britain. Doubtless he paid a price for that, too, in the misery that darkened his later life, but if he had not felt that misery he could never have created the works he did.

Actually, John nearly went to England much sooner than turned out to be the case. After he had been withdrawn or expelled from St John's College, Grace sent him to the local government school, Highlands North. However, in 1937 Herbert had the idea of sending John to Summerhill, a school in Suffolk which had been founded by A. S. Neill, a teacher famous (at that time many would have said notorious) for his views on freedom in education. Neill had just visited Johannesburg as part of a lecture tour in South Africa. So that John would not be alone in England, Herbert suggested that Grace should take him there, her daughter Peg also accompanying them. Grace agreed, with the proviso that she and Herbert should make their break permanent. A divorce was therefore sought and granted on grounds of incompatibility; Grace initially had custody of John. But by the time the decree came through, Herbert had discovered that no place was available at Summerhill.

Neill's system of education would have suited John. One of his principles was that children should not be forced to attend lessons unless they wanted to do so. With Herbert's support, John seems to have applied that principle to his own education, even in an ordinary school. Hanns Ebensten, who met John when he was about fourteen and quickly became his best friend, first heard of him from one of John's fellow pupils, Inge May, who with her mother was a lodger at the Ebensten home (they were all German refugees). Inge told fascinating stories about this boy

> who refused to wear the stuffy school uniform but came to classes in a grubby khaki shirt and shorts, would not sit properly on his chair but cross-legged on it, yawned during lessons and often stayed away from school altogether. When the headmaster telephoned the boy's father, he was told by that unusually permissive parent that, if the teachers could not hold his son's attention, it was better for the boy to educate himself at home.

John showed high intelligence in the subjects that interested him, such as geography, history and music, but would not bother with anything that bored him. Highlands North was really rather a good school for him: a new state high school set up by what was a remarkably progressive Transvaal Education Department. It was the first co-educational school of its type, breaking a barrier of sexual segregation as rigid as that of the English 'public' (i.e. non-state) schools. St John Nitch was a good and popular headmaster, who inspired his staff and had the same courtesy for everybody. The staff were young, enthusiastic and of high quality — many of them went on to high positions. The school was well equipped, too: the geography room, for instance, more like a laboratory than a traditional teaching cell.

Also, the pupils were of high quality. The catchment area was a growing, upper-middle-class suburb of Johannesburg which attacted a large number of refugees from Hitler's Europe. John's contemporaries among his fellow pupils were cosmopolitan European as much as South African, with a background of culture which perhaps only Johannesburg, in those special circumstances, could then provide in South Africa. As often happens, being a group of good intelligences together, they spurred each other on, and John easily held his own among them. He was enlisted into the running team, too, when an excellent runner was unavailable to compete on Saturdays, and to his own surprise did well.

By now, John had developed several artistic interests which competed with school subjects for his time and attention. While he was still a child, the family's black servants had taught him to make clay models of animals, using thorns for their horns, and how to paint on stones using natural colours.

There is some divergence of evidence about how far his relationships with black people affected him. In later life, John put some emphasis upon South African treatment of the black population as an important reason for his leaving that country and refusing ever to return. It is probable that in retrospect he gave that factor more weight than it carried at the time. But he gave an account of having grown up being looked after by black servants because both his parents worked, and he claimed that, after they had separated, a black housekeeper named Evelyn became almost a mother-figure to him. His mother insists that John spent much of the time at the house of his aunt Kay (wife of Grace's brother Errol, then a prisoner-of-war), or in the company of her children, who came to use the swimming pool attached to the flats where Herbert and John lived, so that John was never left to the care of black servants. But John's remarks are quite specific. As he told the story, probably with some exaggeration, Evelyn is supposed quite often to have gone out, perhaps only as far as his aunt's house nearby to borrow some sugar, and to have failed to return. Then, John said, he would know that she had been arrested because she had forgotten her pass, which all blacks had to carry, and would automatically telephone his father to go and fetch her from prison.

John also described an incident when he was about ten or eleven which seems to have had a traumatic effect on him, the horror of which, bottled up for many years, can be felt in ballets which he made long afterwards. He had gone to stay during the school holidays with the children of a farmer who was one of his father's clients. One night he heard a loud noise in the yard, looked out and saw a black person apparently being whipped — as he thought, to death. He possibly over-estimated the severity of the treatment, but what he saw horrified him. The next day he rang and begged his father to fetch him home, but without explaining why. Herbert said no, you must stay there, they are nice people. No, John insisted, I must come home, and home he went, but never told his father about the experience. His mother says that he talked to her about it and she tried to convince him that he was misinterpreting what he had seen and heard, but as far as I can learn John never mentioned it to anyone else until late in life, when telling Dr Schäfer about the thoughts which led him to make his ballet *Spuren*.

Such an episode would affect any sensitive child, all the more one who had mixed happily with black people and, as already mentioned, received his first lessons in handicrafts from them. John acquired many other manual skills. He learned to knit clothes for himself and others, and on the wall of his Stuttgart home there hung a big, beautifully designed and stitched carpet which he made in 1952 while recovering from an illness. From quite an early age, his mother told me, John's interest in theatrical things, and specifically in ballet, manifested itself in setting up cardboard boxes as stages, with pipe cleaners for dancers.

At one point, John decided that he wanted to learn about music, although in fact he never acquired much technical knowledge of the subject, and could not read a score. Grace, who played the piano herself, writes,

> I could see that he would not enter that field by long hours of practice, as he had an impulsive nature. At that time in Johannesburg an exceptionally artistic conductor of the Colosseum Theatre, named Charles Manning, interested me greatly. His hand movements were a perfect poem of grace and expression. I asked him if he would teach John music, and explained the difficulty, as John wanted to know too soon and would not have the patience to practise. He fortunately knew exactly what was wanted and would talk to John for hours on end, about the making of music, history, composers etc., to such good effect that, when John wanted to put music to ballet, he knew exactly what he wanted.

Petrie Cranko adds that, even if Grace had prepared the way, "Herbert told John, who was quite young, to telephone Manning and make the arrangements himself" for the lessons. John also travelled into town alone by bus for the lessons; Herbert made him very independent. Petrie's recollection of Charles Manning is less rosy than Grace's: "He had long white hair, was billed as the 'Svengali of Music' and pranced around, stooping and conducting with hair and fingers dangling as he gesticulated comically and did a little dance on the podium". Manning and his orchestra used to rise from the pit of the Colosseum, playing Chabrier's *España*: his concerts brought the popular classics to a large audience.

John also began building up a collection of gramophone records; Herbert gave him pocket money to buy one a week. He first acquired a great deal of Gilbert and Sullivan, because his father was keen on the Savoy operas, but eventually John turned to ballet music because of the tales his parents had told him about the Diaghilev Ballet. One of the first pieces of music he bought then was Stravinsky's *Firebird*. Playing records like that and *Scheherazade*, another early purchase, John tried to imagine what could be happening in the ballet. In an interview shortly before his death, he said, "I think it was these imaginings and wonderings to music — that sort of fantasizing to music — that started me off to wish to be a choreographer." But before choreography, he developed another passion, for puppets.

John took up with puppets by about the age of twelve. His interest in them, foreshadowed by the pipe-cleaner dancers on their cardboard stages, was provoked by the gift of a puppet theatre from a friend of his father's. As John's enthusiasm grew, so did his productions, soon outgrowing the original theatre, which he rebuilt and enlarged. It was this that brought about John's separation from his mother. Grace, as I mentioned, at first had custody of John but, as she wrote, she had always been very proud and independent and refused maintenance. She was working but had only a small salary and "soon found that it would be impossible to care for John's upbringing satisfactorily. I therefore approached Herbert for an allowance for John which he refused." The outcome was that John moved in with his father, who was now living in a pleasant flat at Houghton Heights, Johannesburg. His mother writes that "it was just a comfortable flat with no frills", but Hanns Ebensten says that "it was one of the most prestigious block of flats in Johannesburg at that time". It was intended that John would spend six months at a time with each of his parents, but when Grace was due to have him back, Herbert took her into John's room, which was the larger of the two bedrooms in the flat. There, to her amazement, was a huge structure built in the form of a stage. Herbert asked whether Grace could provide similarly for John to develop his ideas and she, "absolutely flummoxed", replied of course not.

John's skill in puppetry was greatly advanced by help and encouragement from John Wright and his wife Zoë, professional puppeteers from Cape Town. When a tour brought them to Johannesburg, Herbert took John to a performance and afterwards asked whether they could be shown how everything worked. John was then no more than fourteen, perhaps younger, but John Wright says that his interest in ballet and in puppets was already apparent. Herbert invited the Wrights to a meal and they became friends. After that, Herbert sent John to Cape Town to stay with the Wrights during school holidays, and he started to learn to carve puppets properly. John Wright remarked to me that he met some strange friends through John who, while still a teenager, was obviously finding friends of a congenial bohemianism akin to his own. But John Cranko profited most from his meeting with the Wrights, because John Wright acted as stage director for the Cape Town Ballet Club and was consequently much involved with the whole ballet world at

21

the Cape, into which John eventually gravitated after his puppet phase.

John carved his puppets himself from wood, sewed the dresses for them, wrote verses to accompany the shows and (with his aunt Kay as assistant) manipulated the strings to give performances for his friends and relations. Hanns Ebensten describes the puppets as "marionettes, on strings, about fourteen inches high. They were delightful, with carved heads and limbs of dowel sticks, very cleverly dressed and bejewelled." John told Myfanwy Piper, after he came to England, that the successes of his puppet repertory had been a version of *The Little Mermaid*, performed to Ravel's Introduction and Allegro for harp, strings and wind; a dance for three ballet girls on one string to music from *The Nutcracker*; and a series of adventures for two invented characters, a small boy named Pee Wee and his aunt, Anunziata. Hanns, who became John's collaborator on the puppets once they had met, mentions also *A Midsummer Night's Dream*, some fairy tales and an oriental play by Daniel Varé, which they presented to schools and at fêtes for various charities. Hanns, when he joined in, "did all the décor for the performances and designed costumes, handled the light and sound (and fire!) effects" and thus presaged their cooperation on John's first ballets.

Herbert's magnanimity in making do with the smaller bedroom, so that John might have plenty of room for the puppets, made Hanns envious; the more so, as he had to sleep on a couch in the dining-room of his parents' boarding-house. A further example of Herbert's tolerant disposition came when John found, as he grew up, that his sexual interests were exclusively homosexual. When his mother found out about this (which was not until much later), it was a cause of great heartbreak to her. But Herbert, for all his bourgeois, very respectable Victorian background and his own tendency to womanizing, made no attempt to dissuade his son. Instead, he told him he must live his life his own way, and advised John, when he spoke of having fallen in love with a "straight" boy at school, to try to save his love for someone who could return it. Herbert may have been the less surprised since Robin says that one of Belle's brothers was homosexual, and so was one of Herbert's brothers although, in his case, married and the father of three children. John, however, had no sexual dealings with women (although he always, from schooldays on, had close female friends); Hanns told me that John never had any doubt about where his inclinations lay.

Another example of Herbert's attitude is that, although he advised John to go into business rather than art, he raised no objection when John insisted on becoming a dancer, and in fact helped him.

Whatever John's mother may have thought about his likely lack of application when he wanted to study music, once he decided to learn ballet he took it seriously and must have worked hard to make up for a late start. He often said that he never really wanted to be a dancer, and his only purpose was to acquire the knowledge of dancing necessary to become a choreographer. Certainly he never became an outstanding dancer, but as a performer he did have a feeling for movement and character that enabled him to make a theatrical impact in some roles not needing much technique or classical style. More important for his choregraphy, he had an eye for what other dancers could achieve.

Grace had tried to persuade John long before to go to ballet classes, because she thought him small for his age and hoped the exercise might encourage growth, but he refused, saying "Oh no, mummy, the boys will call me a sissy." When he was about thirteen or fourteen he decided he would like to take classes provided that he could go to private lessons. Grace writes that he studied first with a teacher he had met named Nina Runich (an Austrian married to a Russian); she used the stage name Nina Pavlochieva. Once John had made a start, he went to study with Marjorie Sturman, one of the leading ballet teachers in Johannesburg. All his early interests in music and the theatre, even his puppets (if manipulating them is thought of as a kind of preparation for choreography) came together in this new activity.

Ballet was not well established in South Africa at that time. There has been hardly any interest until Anna Pavlova took her company at the end of December 1925 — less than two years before John's birth — for seasons at the Opera House, Cape Town, and afterwards at the Standard Theatre, Johannesburg. It was the first time professional ballet was seen in South Africa, and the performances caused much excitement. As happened on Pavlova's tours all over the world, many little girls were fired with the wish to dance, and many mothers encouraged their daughters in that ambition.

Some dancing schools already existed in South Africa, and others soon opened to meet the demand. Among the pioneers teaching before Pavlova's arrival, the most important was Helen Webb (whose father was famous as the first man to swim the English Channel). She was the teacher with whom John's half-sister had studied in Cape Town. Miss Webb arrived in South Africa in 1912, intending to start a school in Johannesburg, but was captivated by Cape Town and settled there instead. Her activities were at first regarded with suspicion by headmistresses of local schools, so, to placate those who did not outright forbid their pupils to attend, she described her lessons as rhythmic exercises to music. However, she was successful enough to be able to present annual displays by her pupils from 1916 and to show them in other towns, too, from 1923.

Among those pupils were the two women who were chiefly to pioneer ballet in South Africa. Dulcie Howes was the first of them. She has recorded how Miss Webb's classes were initially "a matter of party frocks and sashes, tambourine dances with decorum. Later she began to weave the dances of her young pupils into ballet form and gradually accustomed the audiences in South Africa first to accept, and then to appreciate, the combination of music and dance in its more sophisticated form."

Even so, it was natural that Dulcie Howes, having shown talent, should travel to London to extend her studies. She danced for a time in Pavlova's company, and returned home in 1928 with the ambition of developing ballet in her native land. She began to teach, opened her own school in Cape Town in 1931, and soon began presenting her pupils in occasional public performances, with members of the staff taking the solo parts. In 1934, on the recommendation of Professor Bell, Dean of the Faculty of Music at the University of Cape Town, her school was given a studio in the College of Music and she was taken on the staff of the Faculty of Music. (Helen Webb had taught at the college earlier, but not since its incorporation into the university.) Thus began what developed into a full Department of Ballet at the university, offering, from 1941, a three-year certificate course for which pupils were required to attend lectures, read widely and study music appreciation as well as their dance classes. It was one of the earliest examples anywhere of a ballet faculty attached to a university, and that affiliation meant that students of white and non-white races could be accepted together.

While Dulcie Howes was active at the college, another of Miss Webb's pupils went to Europe: Cecily Robinson, who danced with Ballet Rambert in London, in the opera season at Covent Garden, with Woizikowsky's company and de Basil's Ballet Russe. While appearing with them in Berlin in 1937 she tore a ligament and had to give up further hope of dancing. During her short career she ambitiously taught herself the principal and solo roles as well as the corps de ballet parts of the various ballets by careful attention during rehearsal and performance, and by assiduously watching even the works in which she did not appear (such as *Le Spectre de la Rose*). On returning to Cape Town in 1938 she could remember many of the standard ballets. Wanting to use that knowledge to help form a permanent company, she persuaded several dance teachers to cooperate in letting their best pupils learn *Les Sylphides*. The management of the large Alhambra Theatre agreed to put this on for a week as a curtain-raiser to a horror film starring Boris Karloff. It was given without scenery, and the music was played on the Wurlitzer theatre organ. A male dancer volunteered for the partnering but it was thought tactful to omit his solo. Audience reaction was mixed.

That venture was rapidly followed by the founding of the Cape Town Ballet Club in August 1938. Its first "season" (two successive Saturday nights at City Hall) added to *Les Sylphides* another of Fokine's ballets, *Carnaval*, again staged by Cecily Robinson. For the second season, in July 1939, several specially created works were given, with choreography by various dancers and teachers. Among them was *Danse macabre*, staged to music of Saint-Saëns by a young dancer, Alfred Rodrigues, who was to make his career, like Cranko, mainly as a choreographer in Europe.

Thus Cape Town acquired two ballet companies that were professional in their attitudes, if not their finances, with high ideals and the best standards practicable at the time. They had no competition from overseas: only two companies followed Pavlova's example and visited Cape Town, one established by her former impresario Alexandre Levitoff in 1934, and René Blum's Ballets de Monte-Carlo in 1936 (this latter particularly stimulated local enthusiasm). But standards of teaching were good; just how good is shown by the large number of South African dancers who won leading positions in British companies before and after the 1939 war. Naturally, it was mainly the best dancers who went abroad to work. That caused a shortage, especially of male dancers, which was worsened when others were called up for military service during the war. Some male roles had to be played by women; for instance, Pamela Chrimes was the original Pierrot in Dulcie Howes's ballet *St Valentine's Night*, and Delysia Jacobs danced the title part in a production of *Le Spectre de la Rose*. Actors took some mimed roles, and any available male recruit was eagerly seized upon to dance with both companies, the University Ballet and the Ballet Club. Cooperation between the two organizations was close.

David Poole, who came into ballet in Cape Town a few months before John Cranko in 1944, described his beginnings: how he saw his first ballet performance on a Saturday night at City Hall, spoke to friends there of his desire to dance, and on the Sunday was told by them that they had arranged with Dulcie Howes for him to attend classes at the University Ballet School. "By the Monday evening I was doing classes with Cecily Robinson... In that first week, Dulcie was planning a programme of ballets with the school, and I was immediately cast as Kostchei — almost entirely a mime role — in her own version of *The Firebird*, called *Russian Tale*. This only illustrates how very scarce male dancers were at the time."

So it is hardly surprising that John Cranko, already a ballet pupil, although of very limited experience, was able to make himself useful when the two Cape Town companies had seasons in Johannesburg towards the end of 1943. The University of Cape Town Ballet had been there before, in 1941 and 1942, building up local support to the extent that on their third visit, in September 1943, all six performances in the Great Hall at Milner Park (the theatre belonging to Witwatersrand University) were sold out before the opening night. John hung around the theatre and lent a hand in any way he could. Dulcie Howes first met him backstage at one of the performances, given in aid of a war charity. "I was aware of the presence of a stranger and asked the stage manager to 'see him off'. The stage manager told me of John's background and interest in theatre and that he 'was making himself useful'. During the war years we were very short of backstage staff" so John was allowed to continue. He said that he had been allowed to go on stage as an attendant to a goddess in Howes's *Pastoral*, a ballet to Beethoven's Sixth Symphony. That was presumably his stage debut, because although his teacher Marjorie Sturman started the Johannesburg Festival Ballet Society about that time, it did not give its first public performance until the following year, when he was already in Cape Town and unable to get away. Among the cast of *Pastoral* was Pamela Chrimes, who was to be important in John's early career.

It was clear to John that the opportunities in ballet, both for training and performance, were far better in Cape Town than in Johannesburg. But to move there would involve a drastic break with his home. The journey of almost a thousand miles took more than two nights and a day by steam train, along track of narrower gauge than is usual elsewhere, and therefore with slower speeds. The terrain was so difficult that for part of the journey three locomotives were needed to pull one train. You left one afternoon and arrived on the morning of the third day. The intermediate day was spent travelling across the Karo, a desert landscape, hot and dusty, and the trains did not have the benefit of air conditioning.

Herbert Cranko asked to see Dulcie Howes and discussed John's training with her. She writes that he was not keen

> to allow his adored sixteen-year-old son to live alone in Cape Town, so I offered to take John into my home... He started his training at the University of Cape Town Ballet School in August 1944. Recognizing his potential ability — not as a

26

dancer, but someone with a great deal to offer to theatre — I obtained permission from the Senate and the Dean of the Faculty of Music (of which the ballet school was a part) for John to be a registered student on the three-year Ballet Certificate course. This gave him the opportunity to study Ballet, Pas de Deux, Repertoire, History of Ballet, Stagecraft and Lighting, and Ballet Music. John made full use of all the tuition provided.

Another advantage of being enrolled in the University Ballet School was that his tuition was free. John described it to many interviewers as if the free lessons were a concession in return for taking part in performances, but it would be more realistic to regard the performances by the University of Cape Town Ballet as a valuable part of his ballet education.

Before joining the Cape Town school, John had seen performances by the Cape Town Ballet Club, which paid its first visit to Johannesburg for a week at the Empire Theatre from 6 December 1943. It had only one skilled male dancer on its strength, Lionel Luyt, and in the first of their two programmes he had to partner the ballerina in the second act of *Swan Lake*, then dance both the Prince and Bluebird in *Aurora's Wedding* (with just three minutes to change costumes) and finally lead the cast of *Prince Igor*. Cecily Robinson brought her three leading dancers, Patricia Murphy, Lillian Graham and Luyt, to Johannesburg four days early, so that they could become used to the high altitude, which would affect their breathing, and to the steep rake of the stage. They stayed at the Carlton Hotel, the best in town, and Cecily Robinson was astonished by her first sight of John, who arived for dinner with a leg-warmer he was knitting, much to the amusement of all the other diners.

During this season in Johannesburg, John unexpectedly had the chance for the first time to dance a real role in public. That came about because one of the dancers had fallen ill just before they all set out from Cape Town. There was nobody else available to take his place in the Chinese dance in *Aurora's Wedding*, and John cajoled his way into being allowed to dance it at three performances. The dance is a comic interlude, quite short and making no great demands on technique. The music is actually from *The Nutcracker* and was first put into *Aurora's Wedding* in the Diaghilev Ballet's production. In this version, the man carried a parasol, and the most memorable sequence is when, brandishing it in front of him like a cross between a broom and a weapon, he opens and shuts it in time with the steps. A sense of comic character and timing are the main requirements, and John carried it off successfully. Hanns and another friend, Anne Sproat, made a costume for him out of dyed calico, on which Hanns painted huge chrysanthemums.

In later years, when explaining how he got to Cape Town, John always mentioned having appeared in one or two small parts when the ballet from the Cape came to Johannesburg. He seemed to think that his success played some part in the invitation to go there to study, but Dulcie Howes's account, already quoted, of her discussions with Herbert Cranko does not bear that out, and anyway people connected with the Ballet Club had forgotten all about John's having danced with them so early, and denied Hanns's account of it until Lionel Luyt, going through old scrapbooks, found a slip in the programme announcing the change of cast. John was not always a reliable source of information about his own past: he combined a poor memory for dates with an imaginative flair for making the best of any story.

The Ballet Club paid a second visit to Johannesburg in July 1944, and John wrote to Hanns, exclaiming jubilantly that "We arranged for me to have meals at the Carlton, so I have been dining in style this week!" He was by then on friendly terms with several of the dancers, and had made a pact with Jasmine Honoré "that we are now brother and sister". Lionel Luyt told me that John quickly tagged on to him when they met during those Johannesburg seasons, and was eager for discussions which went on, after performances, into the small hours. Luyt met Herbert, whom he remembered as more like a friend than a father to John. He was shown the puppets too, and the performance cannot have gone entirely without excitement, because he mentioned to me explosions backstage and things falling down.

John's letter to Hanns about the second Ballet Club visit, just before he himself left for Cape Town, ends with the remark "You will soon be back to gossip and see my new nose!" Cosmetic surgery was rare in those days, but John had needed an operation on his nose because he suffered from a condition (apparently a deviated septum) which hampered his breathing. That would be a severe handicap for a dancer, and while he was having it corrected he asked for his nose to be straightened too. Unfortunately the result was disappointing, and years later, in about 1955, he took the trouble to have a second operation to improve its appearance. Even after that, few people noticed the difference, and his mother confirms that both operations on his nose were a great disappointment to him. His face was never conventionally good-looking. It was still dominated by the long nose and wide mouth, also by eyes of an intense pale blue, which always seemed to focus sharply and penetratingly on whoever he was talking to. The strength of the individual features set in a long thin face gave him a striking and attractive appearance. Other people found his looks so engaging that it is sad to think that he was deeply conscious of noses, especially when he was worried about Jewishness. At one time when he had been going out a lot with a Jewish couple he wrote to Hanns "I have become a regular ghetto-yid", going now to a stately home "to ride their circumcised horses, now to a vile villa of Bellevue to hear real kosher recordings of Beethoven which none of them liked or understood, though they pretended they did, and now to a café which is inhabited solely by people who look like Schnozzle Durante." Characteristically, after this burst of bitter humour he added that "it was quite nice" even though he found his host "about as intelligent as a mule and as human as a boa-constrictor".

The prime purpose of John's nasal operation was remedial, now that he knew he wanted to make his career in ballet. He had to be able to perform even though already "at this young age he had a realistic approach to his future and with his 'banana feet' realized that he could not become a danseur noble and that his great interest was in choreography. He was persuaded that the only entry to this was to join a company as a dancer." Dulcie Howes, who wrote that comment to me, had told the Cape Town critic Denis Hatfield at the time that John would never really be a dancer but that he had "such a remarkable eye for balletic pattern, an imagination so vivid, and such an ear for music in relation to movement" that she was certain he would make a choreographer.

Herbert had at first been reluctant to believe that it was better for John to study dance in Cape Town than to return to high school in Johannesburg. According to Robin Cranko, he consulted John's headmaster, St John Nitch, and the advice he received was that John would not be suited to a rigid academic life, or work in an office or commerce. So, just before his seventeenth birthday, a thin, gangly boy, but (as Lionel Luyt remarked) completely unselfconscious, with a nose still red from his operation, John Cranko began to work full-time at ballet.

___CAPE OF GOOD HOPE___

"I DON'T have much time for visiting, parties, etc., just work damn hard and collapse at home", John wrote in August 1944 to Hanns Ebensten, back in Johannesburg. Even so, he managed to spend a Sunday sailing in a friend's boat, had met a potter who was throwing a dinner service for him ("will you phone my father and ask him if he wants a coffee set as well?") and had found "some beautiful corduroys. I have bought some dark blue-black ones — complete heaven and I adore them." In the circles where he was now moving, a mixture of the artistic and homosexual worlds, corduroy was the smart thing: working-men's clothes adopted as a badge of nonconformity and made fashionable, just as happened years later with blue jeans.

However hard he was working, John was happy in his work:

> Now that I am here in Cape Town, I realize more than ever how vitally necessary it is to study down here. Every moment I am conscious of those little differences which, although appearing minute to the layman, to the dancer constitute the difference between the amateur and that *je ne sais quoi* which makes him professional. Here the ballet is a vital living thing — the classrooms are where the pigments for the choreographer's art are made, whereas in Johannesburg — oh shit!

That weekend found him in a sunny mood. Dulcie Howes was in hospital with appendicitis, so he had gone to stay again with his puppeteer friends, John and Zoë Wright. Clearly he found the familiar atmosphere in their house, Glamorgan, more congenial than staying with his director. He wrote that Cape Town was

> so very beautiful. There are three pines outside the house which spring tall, slender and black out of the watery green grass and are silhouetted against an angry battleship grey sky... Glamorgan is way up on Devil's Peak, and the sight of misty blue clouds hovering over its rocky peaks, so low that you feel that you could touch them, is so awe-inspiring that one feels all it needs is God's voice thundering from the sky to make you fall flat on your face and worship. Then there is the sea, the cold grey ever-moving winter sea — but you must see it for yourself!!!

Already he was beginning to get roles in the ballets by Dulcie

30

Howes which were being rehearsed. He had previously written listing them: "Pierrot in a wishy washy thing called *St Valentine's Eve* a man in *Our Lady's Mercy*, a grasshopper in *Carnaval des Animaux* and a man in some Russian thing." Hanns must have replied teasing him about them, because he now wrote indignantly, "My parts are definitely not all 'A Man' — one (Pierrot) is a *lead*, the fisherman is a big part and so is the Russian; the other (the owl, not the grasshopper) is not so good." The fisherman (not mentioned in John's earlier list) was in a ballet called *I Pescatori*. The Russian ballet was *Pliaska*, a ballet to music by Liadov about the romps and romance in a Russian village; the gaiety of his dancing that impressed one local critic, Dennis Hatfield.

Even more exhilarating was the fact that already his ambitions as a choreographer were making progress: "I have been in such a state lately! There has been a possibility of my doing the *Soldier's Tale* here in December, but it is still very much *en l'air*, as we balletists would put it — so don't get excited *yet*." This was just five days after his seventeenth birthday, and in the first weeks of his first term in Cape Town, so there was cause for excitement.

The letter ends with gossip about rehearsals for the opera season in Cape Town ("It really is pathetic") and about people with whom he had dinner and drinks. Instead of a signature it finishes "here endeth the epistle of the apostle St Cranko." Almost every letter he wrote to Hanns has a different affectionate greeting. The tone of his correspondence varies from self-mockery to flights of fancy, and the handwriting changes almost as much: angular or rounded, neat or sprawling. Perhaps that is a reflection of his enthusiastic, volatile nature. The spelling is frequently eccentric, and remained so all his life, although he read widely and voraciously. In transcribing, I saw no point in keeping his errors, and I have slightly amended his hasty punctuation too, when sentences dragged on clause after clause, separated only by dashes. But the letters reveal an intelligent and lively young man, full of ideas and able to express them vividly. They include frequent recommendations of new books he had found, and much comment on painters he had come across.

He was not often as cheerful as the example quoted. Here is the opposite extreme, three or four weeks later, when he was still struggling hard to become a dancer but already working hard on his first ballet:

> In Johannesburg we have a good, good life; stick to it! I don't know if you realize what hell it is to leave the life one leads, and go to a new city where one knows no-one and nowhere to go.
>   I don't know if you know what it is to work every day as if

your life depended on it, to work until you feel you are going to bust a gut, until you want to cry or howl at yourself because your own body is so stubborn.

And yet in spite of all this work they cry "More, John!", "Harder, John!", "John, you're not *trying*!" and you look at your feet in the mirror, ugly, unable to do the things which you want them to do, or see your body collapse in the middle when you know that it should be firm and rigid — and see them all, even the children, doing something, following what you cannot follow. And just when you think it is coming right they cry "No John, not like that!"

I have lost confidence in myself. With every step I take I say "See those knees! See how they turned in they are, you will never make the grade!" It is all so much *work* and nothing may come of it.

The task of writing *Soldier's Tale* looms so large in front of me — I hear voices calling

"No no you can't cast *her*!"

"How many yards of red?"

"The setting is disgusting,"

"Will you be able to finish it in time?"

"Who is this John Cranko anyway?"

"Work John — twelve hours a day is not good enough!"

It's maddening — like voices in a dream, I can't sleep at night, they taunt me

"You're so inexperienced!"

"Those steps don't fit!"

"Who *is* your designer?"

until I want to go away, but I can't because I have to do my job. As well as this, I have to remember

"Eat regularly, you cannot dance on an upset stomach."

"Keep your back up!"

"Don't flap your arms!"

"Keep your hips square!"

until I just think that suicide is the quickest way out.

No, do not change that lovely, almost dreamy life we had in Joh'burg — I haven't been to any *real* parties since I've been here — had no fun, but even so, I have lost the desire for them. I am alone here with a task I must carry out!

I am glad that you have had orgies at Jay's — I am jealous, but I cannot hope to play if I want to work. Go to the ball, go to Henry's party, and laugh at all the queens sitting round (I could almost name them). But I feel that never can I join you, for I have found that I have left my training so late that it is "work or else!"

_____

This all (this morning) seems a highly coloured raving — but I hope it lets you see how dazed and alone I feel just at present.

What I *really* wrote to tell you is that the Ballet Club Committee says that the Scarlet Woman must be changed — so please do *two* new designs for me to choose from — and help me! (Send as soon as possible).

All my very deepest love to you,

John

PS After reading this through, I have come to the conclusion that I am a racehorse.

John had conceived the idea of staging *The Soldier's Tale* even before he left Johannesburg for Cape Town. Stravinsky had for some years been his favourite composer, and he had worked with Hanns on ideas for the setting and costumes. The designs were displayed in an exhibition of stage designs held in Johannesburg in June 1944 in connection with the second visit there of the Cape Town Ballet Club, although the ballet was not actually commissioned and produced until later that year. It was not to be the work as originally written by Ramuz and Stravinsky for musicians, actors and a dancer, but a ballet with a plot of John's own devising to the suite of Stravinsky's music. Hanns described the plot:

> Soldiers, returning wearily from war, reach a village where they are warmly welcomed by maidens, and their leader succumbs to the charms of the Scarlet Woman. A Devil, mischievous, destructive but lovable, appears and contrives by various ruses, such as that of disguising himself as a beautiful girl, to amuse himself in causing havoc and death among the soldiers and finally, by playing furiously upon his violin, to force the villagers to dance to death. Only the chief soldier, stopping his ears, is able to escape — to fall exhausted in front of the dropcloth at the end of the ballet.

Before the end of August 1944 John was able to write to Hanns:

> As the days go by, the chances of my writing *Soldier's Tale* seem to get stronger and stronger. I think therefore it would be advisable to make the necessary adjustments in the costumes and send them to me as soon as possible. The adjustments are:
> 1. The set is perfect — leave it.
> 2. The two devil costumes are perfect — leave them.
> 3. The scarlet woman is perfect — leave her.
> 4. The soldiers *must* be changed; what about jaunty

33

tricorne, blue chin, military jerkin, one sleeve torn from shoulder, bare arm, one sleeve tattered, belts, striped culottes torn just below knee, hessian leggings, gartering. Do not forget gun.

5. The women must be changed — the skirts remain, but a *redder* red — the bodice *must* be changed — no cross garterings as men have these — head fine.

6. The buffoons are cut out.

The notes about the soldiers' costumes are scribbled all round the edge of a sketch showing what he wanted.

Because Hanns was still living and working in Johannesburg, their collaboration had to be conducted largely by correspondence. So for once the sort of comment John would make face to face with other collaborators is actually recorded. Note how specific his criticisms are, and how he always, even so young and immature, boosts the designer's confidence by throwing in praise too.

Later in August, John wrote that "Pat Murphy is co-producing with me in *Soldier's Tale* and on Saturday morning we got the march written. It hideously complicated music and it needs a lot of concentration... My idea is to get the whole ballet worked out as a mere skeleton, and then embroider it when the cast know it." That is the only mention of a "co-producer" and Lionel Luyt suggests that John was probably using Patricia Murphy to work out steps and phrases on her. One of the leading dancers with the Ballet Club, she is described by Luyt as having a brilliant technique, and he says she "was compact and a dream to do double-work with, and was fearless in trying out death-defying lifts". The idea that John was trying out his ideas in private first, getting them carefully developed before he actually faced his cast, is confirmed by another letter to Hanns in which he wrote, "I have written the first record, and am starting rehearsals for *S.T.* tomorrow." David Poole, who was to play the leading soldier, told me that "I thought sometimes he worked out his ideas for ballets on his puppets, then simply transferred them to people". One point to remember, incidentally, is that in those days all recordings were played at 78 rpm, so each side ran only a few minutes.

One who had faith in him from the start was Dulcie Howes. She wrote to me that

the choreographic ideas poured out of him. We would sit deep into the night in my sitting-room while he played the music he had chosen and he explained his ideas for its interpretation. At times my sleepy little daughter was brought down from the nursery and stood on a stool while John draped pieces of

34

material on her and showed me how he wanted the costume to move and flow, and so help illustrate what he wanted to express and convey to an audience. We argued and discussed — and in the morning he had scrapped that idea and had several others to offer in its place.

All details of the ballet had to be approved by the Club as he went along. On 9 September he sent Hanns a telegram: "Committee says redesign Scarlet Woman", an instruction repeated in the depressed letter already quoted. About a week later he explained at more length that the committee had seen all the drawings and liked them with this one exception. He also quoted John Wright, who was stage director for the Ballet Club, as saying that "if the two low side roofs... were omitted, the design would be far pleasanter and less chaotic. Don't do anything yet, I shall get John to write you a long technical letter. As to fees — how much do you think? John suggests £10 — £15 has been allowed me for costumes."

Later that month (most of his letters are undated bearing just the day of the week, sometimes not even that; luckily Hanns kept them in order and made a note of the month and year): "The Scarlet Woman is a joy! There is, however, one snag, the skirt. We may have to cut it off, in which case, what about this — drapes across as you had them! Only short." That was illustrated by a sketch, and another drawing on the next page showed the "Victorian bobble fringe" he wanted on the skirt. By now he was concerned with practical details: "You might scout around for mesh stockings! Can your father get calico dyed that shade of red for us? If so, I shall get the exact number of yards."

Rehearsals were complicated by the limited availability of some members of the cast and the limited technique of others. For the Scarlet Woman he had Pamela Chrimes, who went to London soon afterwards and was a dancer good enough to be engaged before long as a soloist in the new Sadler's Wells Theatre Ballet. He had cast himself as the Devil, and David Poole (a couple of years older, although also a newcomer to dancing) as the leading soldier. At that time Poole, like John, had to rely on stage presence more than technique, but he had a powerful personality and a quick intelligent appreciation of character which enabled him to give memorable performances in many of John's early ballets. The other women in the cast were students, and Poole told me that the other four soldiers were part-time dancers "who came in the evenings from their offices".

Rehearsals were held in the Club's premises at 136 Bree Street, a former gymnasium acquired and converted only a couple of years

35

before. They had the advantage of providing adequate studio space and being equipped with showers, but other facilities were primitive and the surroundings were not ideal. Below the studio and adjoining the changing rooms and showers (because the building stood on a slope) was a "bottle store" selling alcoholic drinks, and its customers sometimes cluttered the doorstep. Another hazard was that bottles sometimes fell off the shelves because of vibration from above. Adjoining the studio was a funeral parlour with a window opening into the studio, so it was necessary to stop classes and rehearsals whenever a funeral took place.

As well as working on his own his ballet, John had his shaky technique to battle with in daily classes, and there were performances to prepare for. A review by M.S.P. in the *Cape Times* (30 September 1944) of the University's Junior Ballet appearing at the Little Theatre remarked on his "debut in Cape Town ballet, and a very impressive one too" as Pierrot in *St Valentine's Night:* "He is light and deft in movement, and commendably uninhibited as an actor." This was the work which, getting its title not quite right, he had described to Hanns as "wishy washy". In spite of his derogatory comment, it was a successful work by a choreographer much admired in South Africa (Dulcie Howes's ballets were not seen elsewhere). When Hanns wrote an article for the London magazine *Ballet Today* about South African achievements, he described it as having "all the qualities which a good valentine should possess... the girls flit, skip and drift hither and thither in pairs or threes, giggle coyly and point with gloved hands, while the sentimental, romantic Pierrot searches among them for his true love. With such charm and grace does he distribute his roses among them that it is easy to forgive him for having — alas! — one rose too few. This defect is, happily, soon rectified by an exchange of paper hearts." The music was by Mottl.

But *The Soldier's Tale* naturally occupied most of John's energies. Although John Wright had been due to send Hanns a letter about the technical requirements, it was actually the choreographer who wrote again in late September, suggesting simplification to avoid distracting the eye and adding "You must design several feet *around the back cloth,* otherwise what you have designed will be cut off by the back legs and flies". (Dulcie Howes pointed out that he should have written "borders", the theatre term for the cloths which mask the "flies" — platforms above the stage — from public view. The "legs" are the uprights at the side of the stage which similarly conceal the wings.) Early in October, with the exact date of the premiere not yet set, but intended to be some time between 25 November and 10 December, John wrote again to Hanns: "Million sorries for not writing sooner,

36

but I was waiting for (a) Thursday, the official scrutinization of my ballet to see if it definitely would go on, and (b) Friday, the first night of Miss Howes's show. *S. T.* is definitely accepted, and nothing now can stop it." He again promised a letter from John Wright, but instead it was he who again wrote at the end of October, "You obviously haven't read my letter carefully." He provided a sketch showing the exact stage dimensions, then went on with detailed instructions:

1. Draw all the below *carefully to scale*.
2. You must make your *entire* backcloth 42 feet by 25 feet.
3. Now the space A, 32 feet by 20 feet, must be your existing design as this is the size of the proscenium opening.
4. Now you must design an additional five feet all around (shaded portion), this will be seen by persons in the stalls etc., or in the side stalls.
5. So the whole proportion of this old backcloth must be altered, with five feet more designed all round. Have you got this clear?

Now:

1. *The rostrum* is too high, it must be redesigned with the following:
   a. It is to be four feet high.
   b. There is to be *no* lower door but —
   c. A few steps so that she can come back up them to the balcony.
   d. The rails and orange tree must change sides.
   e. The top must measure about six feet by four feet... you can please yourself where you put the steps.
2. *The door* must be at least six feet high.
3. The piece of building on the left (with red tiles and a tree) is bad. What about changing it? It is not as plastic as the other buildings, if you understand me.
   Have you got this clear?

Now:

When the soldiers march across *in the beginning*, do you remember? We were having them simply marching across the proscenium curtain. But now we can have one *painted*. So design one on the same scale as the backcloth. It must (a) try to be a little less Spanish (Jasmine's ballet is Spanish) and (b) give the impression that they are coming to the village. Have you got all this clear?

PLEASE HURRY HURRY *HURRY*.

On 25 October a telegram followed: "Send set at once else *Soldier's*

Tale will be played in black drapes." Even for an experienced choreographer, the suspense could have been hair-raising. Just a month later, on 25 November 1944, *The Soldier's Tale* was successfully given its premiere by the Ballet Club at the Alhambra, Cape Town. There were ten further performances over the next eight days. The programme was a proud occasion for the club, since apart from the opening ballet, *Aurora's Wedding*, all the works given were by South African choreographers. Dulcie Howes had created *Fête galante*, a comedy of manners set to Prokofiev's Classical Symphony; John's playing of the "suave and tenebrous major-domo" in this was praised by Denis Hatfield as a tiny humorous masterpiece. Jasmine Honoré's *Ritual Night* was danced to de Falla's *Love, the Magician*; the setting was designed by John Wright and the costumes by John Cranko. Those two works, like *Soldier's Tale*, were new. The bill was completed by a revival of Alfred Rodrigues's *L'Ile des Sirènes*. John's roles that night included the pas de trois of Florestan and his sisters, the Chinese dance and the cavalier in the pas de six, all in *Aurora's Wedding*.

John's involvement with the designing of Honoré's *Ritual Night* was undertaken out of friendship, keeping their earlier pact to regard each other as brother and sister. Even while he was desperately busy on *Soldier's Tale*, he made time to help her by offering to design the costumes, writing to Hanns that he had told her "you will be here to put finishing touches on to them. There was no time to ask you to do the designing. What I have made are very simple frocks from mattress ticking, which leave a lot of scope for you, anyway you will enjoy playing about with them." These were not John's only ballet designs; the press announcement of a performance given by the Eoan Group in March 1946 mentioned that the programme would include "*The Circus*, to music by Suppé, costumes by John Cranko and choreography by Pamela Chrimes (two Cape Town dancers as present seeking fame and fortune oversea) and *Walpurgis Night* to music by Moussorgsky, costumes by John Cranko and choreography by Jasmine Honoré." John always remained very concerned about the designing of his own ballets but was never specifically credited with responsibility for their designs, preferring to collaborate with an artist to whom he could explain his ideas and from whom he expected further ideas to enhance the final outcome.

That attitude can be seen in his correspondence with Hanns during the making of *The Soldier's Tale*. From the way his instructions became more explicit, it is clear that he was teaching himself stagecraft as he went along, and learning fast. So far as choreography is concerned, Poole's opinion is that John then had "no craft, but invention poured out of him". Poole remarked that the choice of Stravinsky music horrified many people (this was long before the composer had been understood or accepted by general audiences) and the the score "made great difficulty for the cast but none at all for John". Obviously John managed to hide the hard work he had put into unravelling the "hideous complications" he found in it.

Among those who were horrified and given great difficulty by the music were the players of the Cape Town Municipal Orchestra. It was the first time that score had been played in Cape Town, and John Wright told me that the players in rehearsal threw down their instruments in despair. Before the ballet started, an announcement was made in front of the curtains that what the audience would hear was the composer's full intention, and not the orchestra playing incorrectly.

The Soldier's Tale was almost banned at its second performance. A man representing the Cape Town Censor Board arrived at the theatre bearing an order to stop it from being given because Chrimes, as the Scarlet Woman, was "improperly dressed". Her skirt was split to reveal black stockings held up by suspenders. Dulcie Howes was not allowed to take the curtain up until a ludicrous compromise was reached by removing the stockings and suspenders, revealing the pink tights that were worn beneath them. Decency was thus rather quaintly preserved by wearing less. Poole told me that some people were also shocked because John, in his role as the Devil, "disguised himself as a girl in point shoes, a tutu and a blonde wig, with his devil's horns showing through". He actually danced on point, in spite of his uncertain technique. A photograph of him as the Devil (not in female disguise) shows him poised on one foot, the other leg bent so that his whole body is tilted eccentrically. He holds his violin low down, the bow fastidiously poised above it. His almost bare chest and the high, curved horns he wears accentuate his height and his slender build. His expression is quizzical.

Obviously Hanns Ebensten was not an unbiased witness, but he wrote the most vivid account of the ballet:

> Rightly speaking, this is not the Soldier's tale at all but the Devil's, for it is he who controls everyone at all times, playing with them like pawns in his game, a game of wrecking and destroying, of interference and final triumph. But we are thrown a hint that his triumph is hardly long-lived, for when he stands, alone, high above the still forms of the dead below, it is not a look of satisfaction that he throws us, but one of puzzlement at his own work.

Patricia Miller, who was to dance in many of John's later ballets,

39

was then a student in Cape Town. She did not really like *The Soldier's Tale* ("I was all into swans and tutus", she explained) but was impressed by the duet for the soldier and the Scarlet Woman. Ebensten drew special attention to a "dance of lament of the four maidens amongst the dead bodies of the soldiers, who lie forming a great star with their feet as its centre."

The ballet was popular enough to be given again the following summer. Pamela Chrimes had left for England and John wrote that Yvonne Blake "is making an excellent Scarlet Woman, but her ankles are too weak for point shoes, so she's doing it in high heels; it looks quite nice." John thought the ballet was well performed at the revival, but some reviews suggest that the verve had gone out of it. Hatfield's view was that "the wit is too brittle and the inventiveness too superficial to make more than an ephemeral appeal" even though he had been enthusiastic when he first saw it. John never again tried to revive the ballet or rework it, but elements from it reappeared later, for instance in *Jeu de Cartes*, where the Joker is clearly a cousin of his Devil.

Although the new ballet had occupied much of his time and energy, other aspects of life continued. One problem that occupied him was trying to dissuade Hanns from joining the army: "Don't do anything so foolish... it seems a hopelessly idiotic and pointless idea, and I cannot understand *why* you want to do this?" After receiving a reply, he argued

> I hope all these very pretty sentiments about not being strong enough to stand watching other people doing things in the war are just part of a passing phase; or maybe it's these "books of a higher nature"... but I never credited you with being able to talk such utter balls. True, the attraction of becoming "British" is a big one, but as far as I can see it is the *only* one. You will *not* go up north straight away, there is such a thing as training you know, I have heard that the absolute minimum for what you call sitting around is six months. In this time you will be reduced as far as possible to walking cannon fodder and rushed away to some hell hole.

He also quoted a colleague just back from service in Italy who "says don't on any account".

Hanns refused to accept that advice. John later wrote, "I gather from your letters that army life is not a bed of roses? (Who'd want to go to bed with roses anyway, what a mad idea!)" As an admitted homosexual, John himself would have been regarded as medically unfit for conscription into the forces.

John's emotional life was having its ups and downs. While prepar-

ing *Soldier's Tale* he wrote to Hanns describing a party where
> a very uncomfortable thing for me occurred... There were
> quite enough queens to register Casanova impotent, and yet
> every one of them shied away from *me* as if I had the plague.
> It was probably some arrangement of S---- and R----'s, but
> whenever I came into a room where they were, they trickled
> out!

> After a time it got me down, this continued evasion of me,
> it was like a form of torture. I began to wonder if I had halitosis
> or a snotty nose, or green eyes, or a squint — surely I am not
> *so* unattractive! Anyway, at last I got absolutely blind drunk
> through depression, went upstairs to Freda's bedroom and
> cried myself to sleep. Later I was wakened by someone else in
> the room fumbling for the light switch. It was R----. He found
> the switch, turned on the light. When he saw me he smiled and
> said "Why, what's the matter!" not unkindly. I suppose my
> eyes must have been a little red. I said "Nothing." R---- started
> to giggle. "Aren't you missing something?" he said. I just sat.
> "Who are you missing?" "No-one." R---- began to *laugh*. "But
> you look so upset!"

> I was nearly desperate by this time, and in my drunkenness
> I said "Yes, if you want to know I'm in love with Hanns and
> I'm missing him; now please go!" He went.

That incident probably made John's triumph all the sweeter a few
months later, when he gleefully described flirting with a particularly
desirable man, one of the supposed ringleaders of the earlier occasion. His new admirer escorted John home after a party. John
became "rather cool and offhand" now that he was master of the
situation, "bringing all my charms into action, but making it seem
that I was very blasé about the whole thing." He was pressed for a
date and told "before tonight I always thought of you as a child —
but you're not." The Cranko response to that was "(Bitter laugh)
Ha! (And then wistfully, turning on the full power of my innocent
blue eyes) Yes, I'm afraid many people think that." Then, "after a
great deal more chit-chat I let him kiss me a tender goodnight on the
doorstep with the promise to phone when he could and, gathering up
my ermines, swept into the great portal. He phoned several times —
thank god I was out."

More mundane matters also occupied his time. He wrote, for instance, of having bought "*the* yellow wool for a sweater for winter,
I shall also make a black one with one side having very narrow yellow
stripes. The kaffir jersey I shall give to Yvonne Blake, she adores it."
Hanns Ebensten commented, apropos some of these letters, that "If

both John and I sound rather like silly fairies, it is because in the 1940s that is generally how young homosexual men behaved — only later did the male macho style of gays hit the scene. Can you imagine young men today being so preoccupied with fancy clothes — never." Actually, I can vouch that some young heterosexual men of John's age were also obsessed by fancy clothes, and observation today suggests that the interest has not died out. John was capable of laughing at himself in respect of attempts at beautification. He wrote to Hanns about the time when wigs had been needed for Dulcie's ballet *Fête galante*, and one of the part-time dancers in the Ballet Club, a hairdresser by trade, offered to make them, from papier-mâché. Doing that on the victim's head "leaves your hair in one hell of a mess, so after that we all had camomile shampoos from glamorous coiffeuses in white tunics". Then the hairdresser, saying "Now I'll keep the hair out of your eyes", gave John "what he called a 'natural water wave' and stuck me with a *net* and brown cotton wool in my ears under the dryer. I emerged from its jaws a short time later, however, as I couldn't bear the heat — My water wave fell down!"

One thing that made John happy when he went home for Christmas 1944 and the New Year was the presence in Johannesburg of his father's new friend, Phyllis Hirsch. She had been evacuated from wartime Britain to South Africa with her two young daughters; she was married to the violinist Leonard Hirsch, but when she met Herbert Cranko they fell in love. John wrote to Hanns (who was now in the army) "it would be so nice if they could get married." Later they did. John adored the two girls: "It's just like having younger sisters." Another thing that brightened his life was that he changed lodgings on returning to Cape Town, moving to 71 Bree Street, the home of an artist, Freda Lock. Hanns described the house as a Bohemian haven for artists and writers. John loved it and was absolutely at home there.

Before returning to the Cape, he had written "I have been idle so long that I doubt if I shall ever do a single grand battement in my life again — I crack when I move." But it was not long before he was describing projects for further productions. During the fifteen months he remained in South Africa after *The Soldier's Tale* he created three more works and laid plans for others, some of which came to fruition years later. Of his Cape Town productions, only the little party-piece, *Tritsch Tratsch*, was ever directly revived, but musical or choreographic ideas from all the others turned up again, transformed, in later works.

The first new project he mentioned in his letters was for a ballet to be danced to the spoken word. The first reference merely says that

42

"It's all about man before birth, during life and at death — very deep and it never does what you expect it to!" Three months later, in April 1945, he had got further with the idea:

I am planning to do a sort of dance-drama with René Ahrenson in Spotlight. She runs a sort of company for readings and un-costumed actings of unusual plays, and when I told her about *Unisoculous* she said she would put it on. Now I'll tell you about it, terribly roughly of course, because it's very complicated and highbrow. The "music" consists of orchestrated voices, that is, single or groups of high, low, harsh or shrill voices balanced together as in the orchestration of a symphony. The idea of the ballet is to sketch a few facets of a man's life as seen by *him* (hence *Unisoculous* — one eye). Such diversions as Before birth — Birth — Infancy — Awakening — Love — Hate — Inhibi-tions — Growth of prejudice etc., etc. It's all too complicated to write, but I hope this will give you an idea of what it's about.

The work was never made quite as planned, but several aspects of it occur in the ballet he made in Israel many years later, and some in works for Sadler's Wells in the fifties.

Meanwhile another idea had cropped up. On 3 February 1945 he wrote "I have just bought the Moussorgsky records *Pictures at an Exhibition*. I think they will be my next ballet!" By the next letter: "I am planning a large and sumptuous ballet on fisherman and his soul, for which I shall use the Moussorgsky." But that never happened.

Also in February he was discussing ideas for a Botticelli ballet and for a Debussy ballet; these eventually coalesced into one idea, *Primavera*. He met two artists, husband and wife, "awfully sweet, she has a bold yet subtle and exotic sense of colour", and thought of try-ing her for the costumes; he had already got another artist to try and "you never saw such *revue* in all your life". By June he had tried seven different prospective designers without finding one who could give him what he wanted, but was emphatic that he could not work at a distance with Hanns or other Johannesburg artists, "so that's that". But the ballet itself was shaping well "and turns out to be altogether better technically than *Soldier's Tale*".

John was eagerly pursuing other possibilities too. As early as April he wrote that he was going to start "fishing around... all the opera people" to be allowed to produce an opera. "I know this sounds hopelessly conceited of me, but... Olive MacDonald does the choir, soloists look after themselves, all the producer has to do is arrange a sort of ballet of tableaux to the music... which I could do very well." But he was going to have to wait until reaching England before he had the chance to branch into opera production.

43

Then in May came another initiative:

> This is probably the most important letter I have ever written to you. Cecily, Yvonne and I have determined that we are going to tour South Africa — following almost the same route as *Merry Wives* — with either the Ballet Club or, if they won't cooperate, we will form the South African National Ballet. René Ahrenson is being our business manager, and right now she and my father are having discussions prior to contacting ACT re the booking of the tour."

ACT was African Consolidated Theatres, who had been touring Shakespeare's *Merry Wives of Windsor* with a cast headed by Gwen Ffrangcon-Davies; Dulcie Howes had arranged the dances and performed in them. John hoped Hanns would be able to design sets and maybe costumes for the ballet tour; meanwhile he was to start straight away to design posters and programme covers. "I don't have to tell *you* how to design a poster! As long as it's *First Class*... You will be paid when we have some funds — if we ever get any funds, as our aim is to pay *dancers* first. Now then — make it *good*. I await your next letter breathlessly."

Unfortunately, the idea (which many people have held at different times) of a national ballet for South Africa has not come to fruition even now, four decades later, any more than the dream which John cherished when working in Germany of forming a national company there. The German plans persisted in his mind for years, but that particular South African aspiration was transitory, because by his next letter he wrote "Listen and attend a minute. The grand tour which I wrote to you about has been postponed until we can *all* come to Johannesburg for discussions."

However, the three would-be collaborators for the grand tour each revived one of their ballets for three performances by the Ballet Club at City Hall, Cape Town, in July and August; this was when Yvonne Blake danced the Scarlet Woman. The critics complained that there was not "a single new ballet to spice interest". The programme also included the Polovtsian dances from *Prince Igor*, for which a backcloth was needed. John wrote at length to Hanns about colour, shapes and general effect desirable, and asked him to "do a few rough sketches and send them to me to give to Cecily; number them so that I can just send you back a telegram saying 'Do number three', say, unless there is more to be said."

Meanwhile, a crisis had arisen about the University Ballet's plans for a trip later the year to Johannesburg. John wrote to Hanns in June that they had intended to bring a programme of ballets by Jas, myself, Dulcie and Yvonne, with *Igor* produced by Cecily.

44

Now, (a) Yvonne has had a row with Dulcie and won't do her ballet, and (b) as the Ballet Club is producing *Igor* in July, they won't let it out again so soon. So as you will see, this leaves a hole as big as a goat's backside in the programme, and Dulcie wrote to Jas and I that unless one of us would write another ballet, and a longish one at that, the University Ballet wouldn't be able to go to JHB!!! Jas can't, so of course yours truly will have to do it — and YOU *must* do costumes and décor. NB an interpretative ballet, no story, only dancing.

It was to be to Grieg's "Holberg" Suite: "It is all *most* un-Grieg. He has used the old classical forms in the suite so that the music is reminiscent sometimes of Mozart, sometimes of Bach, or Handel, or Gluck. It is for strings alone — try, if you can, to bear it." There followed suggestions of the kind of dresses he would like for the women, and much more specific suggestions about what the men should wear, especially two who would have no dancing and were "old tatty props who stand around holding up girls and sometimes us. They must be well covered as you know how awful their figures are." Later they were dropped from the cast.

John was proposing to divide the corps de ballet into two groups, the taller girls having slower and more statuesque movements than the shorter ones. During the Prelude, all the groups and soloists would be introduced. Then a Sarabande, "very slow and stately", for the two leaders of the taller girls with Poole and himself. The gayer, shorter girls would come on for a general dance to the Gavotte. After that, to the Air, there would be a pas de deux with the taller girls in the background. Next, the Rigaudon, "madly gay", with solo entries for the leaders of the shorter girls with the men; and of course the whole company in the Finale. For the setting, "I thought just a bare cyclorama would be *so* nice! What do you think? We can't spend much on either costumes or sets. Now, dear, get your little brain a-working."

In later letters to Hanns, John mentioned that "we have quite a lot of black tarlatan, so if you *could* use it in your designs, do so", as about £1 had been allowed for each costume and the tarlatan was free. He wanted pink point shoes for the girls, not black, because they "make for romantic mood... they give that airy feeling... Try, if you can, to remember the look of the feet in *Carnaval* where they wear black shoes and *Lac* where they wear pink ones." But eventually, to go with the black tarlatan, they wore black shoes tied with pink ribbons. John insisted that the ballerina's costume must take account of the fact that the pas de deux "is most unfrivolous and very tender — in all the other movements I have used a faint taint of period, but

45

this, being the most lyrical. . . is completely classical." Wigs were out of the question because of the cost, and most of the changes John asked for in the designs were for simplicity in making and comfort in wearing.

For a time he puzzled over the best title. "Not *Holberg Suite*, as Holberg was a Norwegian contemporary of Molière, and the ballet has no bearing on him whatsoever. Someone suggested mere *Opus 3*, what do you think of that? A bit affected, perhaps. But a nice title." Eventually, the ballet was first given by the University Ballet as *Suite, Opus 3*, but for a revival by the Ballet Club he settled on *Suite, "Aus Holbergs Zeit"* ("from Holberg's time"). Poole remembers the finished ballet as being very classical, and also that John took lessons in some of the historical dances on which the music was based, so as to be able to incorporate elements from them in his choreography. John wrote to Hanns during rehearsals that "Lionel and Lillian say it's most difficult pas de deux they've ever had to do."

The designs for *Primavera*, which was in preparation at the same time, were proving a problem. In the summer, a painter named Johannes Meintjies had come to visit 71 Bree Street. John thought him "a most remarkable boy, and certainly the most talented artist I've yet met in S.A. If he can design costumes or not is another question. Anyway he has the right approach and I'm sure *something* will result." Meintjies was equally impressed by John, writing in his diary that this "young ballet dancer and choreographer, who is undoubtedly brilliant, dominated the guests — although he is only seventeen." But their projected collaboration came to nothing, and various other Cape Town artists proved unsuitable, so John began discussing possibilities with Hanns. Eventually he wrote "I am in such a stew over *Primavera* that I have made some sketches myself. These I shall send to you for harsh criticism and *very* helpful suggestions re set." But later in that letter he asked:

> Will you design a set for it? It must (1) reflect the colours of the costumes; (2) be abstract, using plant forms etc; (3) be very symbolical of birth etc., etc. In fact, as I write I realize that the whole mess of *Primavera* must be handed over to you — TAKE OVER THE WHOLE BLOODY THING and get this tremendous weight off my shoulders — change and edit the costumes, but not too much, as they are designed so as not to interfere with the movement of the ballet, as it includes curling up into small balls, rolling, lying etc. Please use *vivid* and numerous colours — the whole thing is rather *erotic* and sexy.

At first, Hanns was clearly taking the original Botticelli concept too literally for John's wishes, and received the comment "Set is

46

quite *wrong*; nothing to do with sea shore or shells *at all*, it must be abstract using plant form... Think of it as Braque would design it — or if you like Bérard." Later John began to worry even about that idea:

> Will Primavera stand out in front of such a cut-out? When she rises in the white garment she must be *terribly dominant*. I think the cut-out must have no plant form then, it should be *earthy* or an old withered tree trunk or some such — because the dancers personify Spring so much that the stage should represent the earth. You see, the dancers must be the décor — *they* must decorate the stage, not the background dominate them... I think Dufy is quite wrong; John Piper is more the type, his peculiar banks and cliffs which have no vegetation on them whatsoever yet look as if they are going to have tiny green shoots peeping out at any minute. The WHOLE feeling is Spring is *about* to burst forth but it hasn't quite done so.

The music of *Primavera* was Debussy's "Danse sacrée et Danse profane", and the ballet incorporated the idea of the goddess being born from a group of girls first seen huddled in near-darkness on the floor. A similar theme was to recur in *Harlequin in April*, one of John's first fully successful ballets in Britain, then again in *Opus 1* and *Song of My People*. John wanted the light misty at first, then becoming brighter, but always radiating from a focal point at the back of the stage; Primavera arising from the floor in white must make a "most phallic" effect. The notes refer to other dancers representing hand-maidens, a bird and winds: rather complex for so short a work.

Suite and *Primavera* were both given at Witwatersrand University, Johannesburg, on 3 to 6 October 1945 (six performances). Lillian Graham and Lionel Luyt danced the leads in *Suite*, but it was remarked that Luyt "no longer has to sustain all the male roles himself, and can share them with useful dancers like John Cranko and David Poole". Delysia Jacobs had the title part in *Primavera*, and Renée Feller also attracted attention as the bird. John's choreography, however, was less enthusiastically received. Fairly typical was the assessment of both works as "picturesque, but at the same time restless, and verging occasionally on the sentimental".

Lionel Luyt told me that it was only when he reached Europe a few years later that he realized how far ahead of his South African contemporaries John had been, doing things which he must have invented for himself because he had not had the chance to see them put into practice by others. In retrospect, for instance, he thought that *Suite* had choreography rather like Balanchine's in the phrasing of sequences and repeats to the music, and in the lines, which were not straight like a corps de ballet of swans or sylphides but went off suddenly at an angle. He said that *The Soldier's Tale*, too, was quite unlike anything else being done in South Africa then. John was full of invention, always making up steps and sequences which he called by odd names: for instance a stamping step he called "Sherman tanks", which he devised for the zephyrs in *Primavera* and used again for the unicorns in *Harlequin in April*.

Although people in the Cape Town ballet world thought highly of his promise, John's talent as a choreographer was not regarded as proved by the time he left South Africa (at only eighteen, why should it have been?), and other young choreographers were at least as highly thought of. Jasmine Honoré's *Ancient Lights*, premiered with *Suite* and *Primavera*, won more praise. It was a ballet about slum dwellers, set surprisingly to Weinberger's Variations on "Under the spreading chestnut tree", in which John had a comic role as a social worker.

Suite was given in Cape Town by the Ballet Club at City Hall for the week of 3 December 1945, with Joan Grantham in the ballerina part. *Primavera* was not seen in Cape Town until the University Ballet's programme at City Hall on 1 March 1946, with Jasmine Honoré in the title part. It had been provided with a new backcloth and costumes by Alexis Preller. Dulcie Howes writes that, as far as she can remember, that was at John's own request. Although Hanns Ebensten's designs were supplanted, he had another commission on that programme, to do new designs for *St Valentine's Night*. *Tritsch Tratsch* was given on the same programme, being hailed with delight for its humour and for the sparkling dancing of Poole and Luyt as "two brisk young sailors, and Renée Feller as the sprightly object of their affections". (Poole's recollection is that John had made the piece earlier, with himself in the role danced by Lionel Luyt, but there is no record of this. Luyt remembers it being set very quickly, in the course of an hour or so). For the first time, one of John's creations received overwhelming and unanimous praise, but he was no longer there to enjoy its success.

Already in July 1945 he had written to Hanns "I want sooooooo badly to get to London. But I really do feel that until my technique develops further I must stay here. I've had this little Dorp in a BIG way." In August, an acquaintance gave him the address of a London representative "who will apparently introduce me to Noël and Oliver and Bobby!" (Coward, Messell and Helpmann). In October 1945 he obtained a passport.

There were many reasons for wanting to go to England. The most important was that it offered far more opportunity professionally. It was to be many years before South Africa could support full-time professional dance companies. Meanwhile, seasons were short and widely spaced, the dancers were limited in ability, and in John's rather impatient view there were no real designers except for Hanns: "I'm *sick* of working with would-be's", he wrote. The strain of trying to do everything himself was taking a toll; after one almost incoherent letter he explained that he had been working from 8 a.m. until midnight, had not eaten and so "was thoroughly depressed and vague".

Also, John often insisted that the treatment of black people in South Africa had been an important factor in his decision. Some of the people who were most closely associated with him at the time find that hard to believe; they remember him as being liberally inclined but not politically minded. There is a vagueness in John's later account of his feelings which makes one wonder how far he was reinterpreting events and attitudes with hindsight. For instance. he told Dr Schäfer of a friend, a fellow student at the University Ballet School, who came from a Coloured family. He and one brother, with pale skins, counted as whites, John said, but their siblings with darker skins were issued with passes as blacks. That cannot be correct, as only those who were actually members of the black races, not Coloureds of mixed race, had to carry passes. On the other hand it may well be true, as John said, that those with pale skins had an easier life and felt guilty about that.

However, it does seem likely that his father's views influenced him even so early. Herbert was more politically conscious than John, and is said to have urged him to leave South Africa because he foresaw trouble in future. Even if John's own feelings were more idealistic than political, it was his feelings about South African treatment of the blacks that prevented him from going back. Patricia Miller remarked that John never really conformed to the way of life in South Africa, and hated to be tied down. She quoted to me an odd and illuminating point, that if he wanted to take a bath when he was with friends, he could not see why they should not all be in the bath together, boys and girls, black and white. That sounds to me like the sort of liberal view which many of John's contemporaries would have expressed at that age, under the influence of reformers like A. S. Neill — a comparison that occurred to me before I discovered that he had been meant to attend Neill's school.

John said (again according to Patricia Miller) that if he left South Africa, he would never return, and he kept to that. He much disliked being described as South African and he later held a British passport.

But he retained feelings of gratitude for the chances he had been given, and he allowed others later to mount several of his works for the University Ballet without expecting any fee.

At the beginning of 1946, John had another reason for fretting; he had to change his lodgings and was living in digs that were "too sordid" to write about. The address on his letter is that of a hall of residence, so the description must have been exaggerated, but it conveys his exasperation. One day in February, on the spur of the moment, he walked into an office of Cook's travel agency and enquired about a berth on a liner to London. Generally they were booked months ahead, but there had been a cancellation on one leaving almost at once. Herbert agreed to pay his passage and give him an allowance until he could find work.

John left without saying goodbye to his mother, but before leaving Cape Town, he wrote to Hanns:

> It's the end of a great chapter in both our lives — we have I'm sure both played a great part, each in the other's. When shall I see you again? God knows — I shall make every effort to write to you of course, but I am such a bad writer and after a while it begins to be very difficult to write the essence of one's personality and atmosphere on paper. So if I do become slack, and I shall try not to, you will, I know, forgive as you always do. And please remember whatever I do and whatever becomes of me, I shall always do my very best to help you. And if on your coming to England I am not the first person you look for, I shall be very hurt indeed! You won't be able to reply to this letter, as when you receive it I shall be on the water. I shall write to you the moment I arrive. I haven't the faintest idea of how to spell auf-wie-der-sein, but that's the word.

HOME COMFORTS

ONCE he had left the modern flat where he lived with his father in Johannesburg, John Cranko always lived in old houses. Not historic buildings, except for his last home at Schloss Solitude, outside Stuttgart, but elderly, ordinary, slightly shabby houses, planned and built in an earlier age, that had acquired a comfortable individuality in occupation by previous occupants, and lent themselves to his own way of living and working.

He was, in a sense, at home anywhere. When he got to Stuttgart, he was to make the bare tables and bleak walls of the theatre canteen seem homely. He looked at his ease there — or almost anywhere else he found himself. It was partly a gift for adaptability, partly a sense of fun or interest that he brought to any situation. He could live happily among poor working people on his holidays, but found immense pleasure in staying in a French house so grand that a servant squeezed the tubes of toothpaste between applications. On a Russian tour when he had a lot of causes for dissatisfaction, snapshots show him still lively: pretending to drop a kopek into the hat Marcia Haydée holds out to him; embracing a Russian colleague, Yuri Grigorovich of the Bolshoi; thoughtfully watching a Russian ballet class. In New York, Tel Aviv, Athens, at a big reception or among friends, taking a curtain call with his dancers, chatting to a stranger, even just waiting for something, he looks easy, interested, at home.

Yet in another sense he had no home, and no country. His attitude to South Africa was epitomized when he went not there but to neighbouring Rhodesia in 1953. He had to supervise dances he had arranged for *Aida*, one of the productions taken by the Covent Garden Opera to the Rhodes centenary celebrations. At the sight of white extras, brought specially for the purpose, blacking up their faces to play Ethiopians in a land full of black faces, his indignation was acute. The one thing that would have persuaded him to accept an invitation for the Stuttgart Ballet to go to South Africa would have been if he could show a really good black dancer working alongside the whites. He took British citizenship, travelled for the rest of his life on a British passport, and disliked being described as a "South African choreographer".

However thoroughly he had pulled up his African roots, however, he never really felt entirely accepted in England. Later, in Stuttgart, he was not just accepted but positively idolized; even so, there were barriers: he complained to Frank Tait, "They don't know the same nursery rhymes as we do!" So there was a restlessness that could help explain his pronenesss to melancholia, and at the same time account for the extraordinary enthusiasm with which, in later life, he identified himself with the people of different parts of the Mediterranean coastline in turn: Greeks, Italians, Jews, Arabs.

After the break between his father and mother, he could not respond to her affection. When she occasionally visited him in London or Stuttgart, she always found him busy, although he would certainly have made time for a new lover, and he did put himself out to entertain his cousin Petrie who, with his wife, turned up unexpectedly in Stuttgart during a travelling holiday. Petrie thought John a little embarrassed to see them, but they were taken to watch rehearsals and John took them in his Mercedes to Alsace-Lorraine to show them museums and other sights, and treat them to a memorable dinner. Yet it never occurred to John, as his mother aged, that she might be in need of any help, until a visitor from Johannesburg, who had known him as a boy, told him that she was hard up, after which he made her an allowance. He also had to be reminded to write to her, which he did (in later years) about every six weeks, just a dutiful account of where he had been, what he had done, with little of his usual animation.

Cut off from her, with his father and stepmother both dying while he was still a young man, John several times tried to live with a man he loved, but it always ended in disappointment. Sex was no problem; love was. There were always plenty of boys; they might arrive on a Friday and be gone by Monday, but he wanted an enduring relationship too. When he thought one might be possible, he was immensely sentimental, would give up everything for a lover; yet it was his own exigence that made it difficult for anyone to live up to him, to match his quick apprehension, his wide range of interests, the fervour with which he experienced everything. "Can't you *see*?", he would ask; "don't you *feel* . . . can't you *hear*?", as he rushed from one place or book or topic to another, expecting others to have the same reactions, so that Frank Tait, a cultured and intelligent man, described how he "hurried out of breath to seem less far behind". No wonder that John, in his later Stuttgart years living with Dieter Gräfe and Reid Anderson, would say enviously, "It's easy for you — why can't I find somebody?"

All the same, he did find eventually a settled domesticity with them. He had a curious mixture of enthusiasm and impracticability in his approach to some everyday things, as for instance studying a most complicated recipe from one of his cookery books (they included Mrs Beeton and Elizabeth David), then going out to buy not only the ingredients but equipment too. On one such occasion, he bought a mixer and a special dish in order to make an elaborate terrine. It turned out to be so big that he invited people specially to help eat it, and then it proved so salty that they could manage only a little of it. Cooking became a kind of therapy which he greatly enjoyed, but the results could be bizarre: "things in pastry" were a favourite (the things might be tins of beans and of peppers), and sometimes so awful that Dieter and Reid would wait in the car until John had fallen asleep, to avoid having to eat them.

Yet he loved food. One of the reasons he travelled often from Stuttgart to France was to enjoy meals at Strasbourg or Riquewihr or Illhäusern. On journeys, he would study both the red and the green Michelin guides, in search of gastronomy and culture, and sit in the back seat issuing careful instructions to the driver that "in about a quarter of a mile you come to a place to turn right".

Just as he ate with relish in the three-star Auberge de l'Ill or a Greek working-man's café, so he could be both careless and dandified about his clothes. Sometimes he would sleep in them and wear them unchanged the next day, but at other times he took hours to choose what he would wear, then positively preened. His taste was individual: he had a pink suit and matching overcoat, both of thick wool, that cost him 3000 Marks (the fee for a three-act ballet); they were worn with an orange tie. At the Met in New York, he took curtain calls wearing a beaded gold kaftan. When Queen Elizabeth, on a state visit to Germany in May 1965, arrived in Stuttgart for a formal lunch, John took care over his clothes but either forgot or did not think it necessary to find a pair of socks less obtrusive than the bright reds or blues he favoured at that time. The eccentric appearance he presented, together with his having forgotten his invitation card, resulted in his being refused entrance until somebody arrived who could satisfactorily identify and vouch for him.

Others had to look after him: friends sometimes; a Spanish couple he employed at others. He expressed his thanks obliquely, like saying "Some magic fairy came in my room while I was asleep, and put a pile of clean shirts on the dresser". He was liable to forget to buy birthday or Christmas presents (one year when he resolved to mark Christmas properly, he bought everyone gift vouchers because he could not decide what to get), but would make a gift out of the blue for no other reason than that it was a nice day. He wanted to share his joy — or his misery.

Books were what he bought most assiduously. He bought them
literally by the armful, and read as many as three in a day, picked
up at random from the piles he had brought home; yet afterwards he
could tell of what he had read, so beautifully, according to Reid, that
the book itself would be a disappointment by comparison. Once he
stood, a cooking pan in one hand, with tears in his eyes over the
sadness of Byron's life. He would read anything, but there were
certain books he returned to, that especially influenced his thought:
Dr Schäfer, the Stuttgart theatre director, was astonished to find a
man from the ballet who was actually familiar with *The Golden Bough*,
and Robert Graves's *The White Goddess* was even more important in
his work.

Other things, John would see and ask, "Can I afford to buy that?"
— as when he fell in love with two leather suitcases he saw in a
Munich shop window. He never expressed any special wish to own
a Mercedes until he could afford one: then he had to have it, and it
had to be bright red. Even so, he did ask, "Wouldn't it be nice to
have a Rolls Royce — have you noticed, nobody here has one?"

The most precious possession he had was time. Life in South
Africa, once he started dancing, was one long rush, and his early
days in London too, but when he stopped dancing he was in an
unusual position. Most choreographers either have other responsibilities (as a company director, for instance) or are themselves tied
to the strict daily schedule of a performer. John, required to mount
his ballets but nothing else, had time to visit art galleries or schools
in search of new ideas or designers, to listen to music, to read. That
period of his life also freed him for his experiments in other kinds of
theatre which, although he never reverted to them after taking on his
Stuttgart responsibilities, enriched his subsequent work.

He went back to the ballet, he said, after a period of doubt,
because he walked into a studio and saw a young woman putting her
feet into the rosin box to stop her shoes from slipping: the familiar
action, a mixture of habit and discipline and grace, made him realize
where his heart belonged. All the other experience that he devoured
was put to the one obsessing activity.

LONDON

Scene One
MAKING A NAME

Scene Two
ACHIEVEMENT

Scene Three
WHEEL OF FORTUNE

_____MAKING A NAME_____

LONDON, when John Cranko arrived, was suffering the after-effects of an exhausting war, and it was to be several years before the restrictions and shortages were overcome. But he wrote to Hanns "Don't worry about conditions here: although they can be grim, I've known them a lot grimmer in S.A." He declared that "being new in London is a full time job" and described the town rhapsodically as

> wonderful, friendly yet austere, huge yet intimate and minute, kindly and terrifying all at the same time. When you've been in London five minutes you never want to leave... Now to descend to earth... I am at the Sadler's Wells School until my father arrives in April. I don't know if I shall join the company yet, I may do, I may go to Paris, I may die, my face may even turn blue. The classes are not large and I find myself not too bad and rated as "senior" by the Sadler's Wells gods. Most of the boys' mental age is about eleven. They are the last people on earth one could imagine to be dancers. However, some are very good.

His scathing attitude to most of his fellow pupils is only partly accounted for by a difference in age. At eighteen, he was physically much more mature than most English ballet students, because at that time they left school and began dancing professionally at sixteen or even younger. While his fellow students were still schoolboys, John was leading a raffish private life, and described how a friend from South Africa had taken him to "some Queer pubs which are too fantastic and revolting to be true. Lewd songs are sung over the microphone... Leicester Square on a Sunday night has to be seen to be believed, and half the police are queer too!" His voracious and informed interest in the arts, not only ballet but plays, books, music, painting, also set him apart from most of the other students. He described plays and revues he had seen, but most of what he wrote to Hanns was about the ballet.

The first work he went to see was *The Sleeping Beauty*, "which you would hate, with sumptuous settings and dresses by Messel which you would adore." This had just opened the Sadler's Wells Ballet's first season at Covent Garden, to rapturous acclaim, but a month or two later John had decided that the costumes, "although very gorgeous and great fun to wear are, in my opinion, far too ordinary for a ballet, they are more like costumes for a historical play... The dancing is of a superbly high standard and Margot Fonteyn and Moira Shearer as alternate Auroras are wonderful." I am not sure that we would think the dancing, except by some of the principals, quite so wonderful by today's standards, but we saw it with different eyes then, and John would have for comparison his memories of the Cape Town Ballet Club's brave but handicapped attempt at the last act of the ballet, *Aurora's Wedding*.

His comments on the work of the Sadler's Wells house choreographers are interesting in their percipient mixture of eager praise and sharp criticisms. Some ballets by them soon joined *Beauty* in the Covent Garden programmes, others were given by a newly formed second company at the Wells. John at once decided that

> Fred Ashton is a mature choreographic genius, things of his like César Franck's *Variations*, *Nocturne* and *Dante Sonata* just cannot be written about, and have to be seen over and over agian...
> De Valois too is wonderful at reconstructing a period. You remember our idea about Handel? Well, she's done it in *Gods go a'begging*, using the same Watteau that we liked so much with the columns and the landscape in the background. In *Rake's Progress* she reconstructs Hogarth... in *Promenade* she gets an atmosphere of Directoire France.

He found *The Rake's Progress* "perspicacious, witty in spite of its stark drama, and thorough as regards research into the period", but he added that "I'm afraid it's not half what it's cracked up to be." John wrote scathingly of Robert Helpmann, after seeing his *Miracle in the Gorbals*, as "a pseudo-intellectual who has discovered (after Hollywood) that there exists such a thing as mob psychology" and later added that "his ballets, although all extremely intelligently constructed, and all marvellous theatre, I always find acrobatic and dull from the dancing point of view... He is a very fine actor, but only with his face — his body is quite inexpressive, when he turns his back on the audience he loses all meaning."

As implied by his reference to wearing Messel's costumes, John had begun by May, while still working at the Sadler's Wells School, to appear in the corps de ballet at Covent Garden, although only in *The Sleeping Beauty* which needed a large cast. "It is really great fun and I enjoy every minute of it." By that time he was sharing a flat at 46 Belsize Square, Hampstead, with Pamela Chrimes, and was making "a gorgeous carpet". Chrimes, who preceded him from Cape Town to London even before the war ended, had studied at the Sadler's Wells School, then joined the Sadler's Wells Opera-Ballet, the new company started at Sadler's Wells Theatre when the original

Sadler's Wells Ballet moved to Covent Garden. Most of the other dancers in the company were straight from school, some of them taking leading parts while only about fifteen. However, their leading woman for the first two seasons, June Brae, was a contemporary of Margot Fonteyn, returning to the stage after a break during the war. She was joined for a short time by another dancer back from war service, Alan Carter. John wrote to Hanns at the end of May that Tamara Karsavina, a former star of the Diaghilev Ballet, was planning to use Brae and Carter in a ballet "for some small society... and it's then to be repeated when Alan Carter is away on tour — and she's trying *me* out! Can you imagine the excitement!" But that came to nothing. Karsavina duly mounted *Valse Fantaisie* for the RAD Production Club, but it was another of the Sadler's Wells dancers, Eric Hyrst, who partnered Brae in it.

All the same, John did soon find himself dancing with June Brae, as one of her partners in *Assembly Ball*, a ballet by Andrée Howard to Bizet's Symphony in C, when he too joined Sadler's Wells Opera-Ballet. He got into the company because one of its few experienced male dancers, George Gerhardt, was leaving. In one of the new ballets, Celia Franca's *Khadra*, which was inspired by Persian miniatures, Gerhardt had to catch Anne Heaton, playing his wife, from a platform at shoulder height, raise her above his head and lower her gently. The sequence was made to measure for Gerhardt who, in Heaton's phrase, was "built like a tank". He also had to lift Sheilah O'Reilly, in the title part, in a "lotus position" above his head. The young men at Sadler's Wells had neither the strength nor the training for that sort of feat. But in South Africa, because male dancers were scarce, every available man willing to go on stage and hold up one of the women had to be encouraged and enabled to do so; consequently, even the most rudimentary beginners were taught partnering. With that background, John went to Peggy van Praagh, ballet mistress of the young company, and asked whether he could have the vacant post provided that he could manage those lifts. She agreed. John trained frantically hard with press-ups to increase his strength and, as Pamela Chrimes described it, "used me as a dumb-bell until he could cope". The first time he tried it, with elastic supports round his wrists, Anne Heaton was terrified and wondered whether she would live to tell the tale, but it worked. So he obtained the job, unfortunately at the cost of giving himself a hernia for which he needed hospital treatment.

The reason he wanted desperately to get into the company was that Ninette de Valois, to whom he had already spoken about his choreographic ambitions, had told him that experience of working

61

with other choreographers and dancing their ballets was essential to learn his craft. Peggy van Praagh told me that, even so early, de Valois had said to her "I think he'll make a choreographer", but she was already trying out several other aspirants, so could not give him immediate chances. Also she was greatly occupied with the other company at Covent Garden, and it was van Praagh to whom John turned for help. Her home was on the other side of Belsize Square, and he would often drop in at night to tell her about his latest ideas, just as he had done earlier with Dulcie Howes and was to continue doing with one friend or another all his life. Van Praagh became a close friend of the Cranko family, Herbert and Phyllis as well as John; she proved a valuable ally, not only for her position within the company but also because she had a flair for bringing out the best qualities of young dancers and choreographers, and guiding them in their careers.

There were quite a few South Africans within the Opera-Ballet during John's time there. Besides Pamela Chrimes, Nadia Nerina had been one of the company's early members; John had known her briefly in Johannesburg when they were both schoolchildren, and they met again in Cape Town just before she left for Britain in October 1945. David Poole, who arrived in London in January 1947, was accepted for the company in May, but later that year Chrimes went back to South Africa and Nerina to Covent Garden. Hanns, although not in the company, was one of John's group once he arrived in Britain about the same time, and another of the dancers, Peter Darrell (who also became, in time, a choreographer and ballet director) was closely involved with them, although he was English. He described the coterie around John as "a kind of Chelsea-Bloomsbury Group" and said that they were in and out of each other's flats all the time. Some of the other dancers made life difficult for them at first, resenting the physical advantages the South Africans had enjoyed, growing up far away from the hardships of wartime Britain. On the other hand, Maryon Lane, one of two further South African girls (the other being Patricia Miller) who joined in August 1947, thinks the chief cause of ill-will had been the obnoxious behaviour of one person, and says she herself never suffered from resentment but was accepted by the company where everyone seemed like family.

When Poole arrived, he and John sometimes spoke to each other in Afrikaans. Jane Shore, a dancer in the company at that time, remembers it only with amusement: "We were always simply dying to know what rude words they were using." But it only increased the suspicion with which they were regarded by some of the boys, and there were those who were upset by the homosexuality which John and some of his friends made no attempt to hide.

Not all the other dancers were in sympathy with the intellectual attitudes of John and his friends, either, but he needed all the intellectual stimulation he could get because, although his work as a dancer was meant to help him develop as a choreographer, the repertory was far from ideal for that purpose. The only role created on him by an experienced choreographer was that of a Negro pugilist in Andrée Howard's *Mardi Gras*, and that ballet, although striking in its strange, suggestive drama, was such an idiosyncratic, atmospheric piece that he was unlikely to learn much from it about form or structure. The other new works given that season were by apprentice choreographers. John's roles were mostly, in Hanns Ebensten's teasing phrase, "A Man": in Anthony Burke's *The Vagabonds*, Celia Franca's *Bailemos*, de Valois's *The Haunted Ballroom* (where he was actually "A Ghost"), Howard's *La Fête étrange*, and the tumblers' dance by de Valois in the opera *Snow Maiden*. The Spanish dance in *The Nutcracker* and the Yodelling Song in Ashton's *Façade* gave him slightly more chance to make an individual impression, but his only leading part was in Fokine's *Carnaval*, where he played Pierrot, not very memorably, sharing the role with Poole, whose interpretation was universally admired.

More important for John was the chance to do choreography. His first opportunity at the Wells was to stage the dances in Humperdinck's opera *Hansel and Gretel* mounted at Christmas 1946. That is not the sort of thing that is going to make anyone's reputation. His contribution was professional, but not more than that, within the limited scope available. The angels promenaded in neat and pleasing lines, three witches cavorted wildly for a brief moment, and some of the singers were given a few simple but effective steps. I did not see the production until the following Christmas, when it contained an amusing touch which I imagine John must have added that year, after Leonide Massine had revived *The Three-cornered Hat* at Covent Garden: Hansel and Gretel danced a few steps with a bunch of grapes, a good-humoured quotation from the dance of the miller and his wife in Massine's ballet.

His first real ballet for the company was also slight. This was *Adieu*, which John described as "a sadly romantic story of a nymph, whose lover is called away to war". As well as the two principal characters, there were a warrior, to do the calling away, and two attendants. The music was by Scarlatti ("Les Adieux") and the designs were by Hugh Stevenson, who was also responsible for giving John the chance to make the ballet. They had met when John danced in the creation of

63

Mardi Gras, which Stevenson both wrote and designed. He was helping with the "Vic – Wells" charity costume ball in January 1947 and
Adieu was given as part of the entertainment there. De Valois saw it
and accepted it for the repertory. Its public premiere was at the
Theatre Royal, Brighton, on 19 May 1947, first night of a tour which
also brought the company a change of name, to Sadler's Wells
Theatre Ballet.

The setting for *Adieu* consisted of a couple of pillars and a couch
that was all too obviously a crude wooden structure draped with
material, giving the clear impression that the ballet had been
mounted on the cheap. The dresses, by contrast, were ornate to a
fault. The nymph wore an encumbering baroque skirt and a headdress with tall feathers. Her lover had a romanesque skirted tunic
and a short cloak. Although John was generally a quick worker,
Anne Heaton remembers him as taking a long time over this work
and seeming nervous about it. The result was not without promise,
but distant memory suggests that the piece was as artificial as the
clothes, a minor and mildly amusing exercise in an old-fashioned
style. Although given a total of fifty-four times on two tours, which
was not bad for an apprentice work mounted as a try-out, the nearest
Adieu got to central London was the open-air theatre at Finsbury
Park, where they danced that summer.

It must have been discouraging that *Adieu* was not thought worthy
to be given at Sadler's Wells, and that the more handsome setting
which Stevenson had designed for it was not used at that time. But
within a month of its first public performance, John had another
premiere, admittedly in the modest circumstances of an experimental
matinée, presented by the Royal Academy of Dancing Production
Club at the New Theatre on Sunday 15 June. For this, he used
Debussy's piano suite, "Morceaux enfantins", as the inspiration of
dances whimsically reflecting both memories and fantasies of
childhood. The cast was drawn from the Sadler's Wells School, with
Stella Claire as the heroine, a wooden doll, and Poole as a golliwog
(complete with cakewalk, of course). There were a little husband and
little wife, who had a duet during which she manipulated a parasol
to comic effect, and the other characters were three tinsel fairies and
a monkey. The dolls became amusing, and at times touching,
symbols of childhood moods, and although the treatment was at
times sentimental it also had a genuine gaiety. The ballet's most
notable virtue, widely remarked upon in the reviews, was the
sensitivity with which John had matched movement to music. The
work was successful enough to be repeated at the Club's next perfor-

64

mance, given at Sadler's Wells in November, this time with Nadia Nerina as the wooden doll.

Hanns Ebensten designed the scenery and costumes for the original production of *Morceaux enfantins*; his backcloth imaginatively showed a page from a child's copybook with rows of carefully copied letters. During the early months of 1947, he and John had shared lodgings in Upper Berkeley Street, just north of Marble Arch. In the week before the premiere, John, out on tour with the company, sent several telegrams there, asking Hanns about tickets for the performance ("two plus one if possible"), about where he would stay, where they would meet and, on the day before the performance, "Please buy gift for dressmaker".

His work was encouragingly received, but about that time his emotional life was thrown into turmoil because his closest friend in the company began an affair with another member of their circle. The postcard he wrote to Hanns at the end of the tour reveals John plunged into deepest gloom: "My dear — The past weeks have been like an unforgettable nightmare. I don't know what to do with myself. It all seemed so sure — and it's all so utterly, utterly useless. We arrive 6 o'clock Sunday evening. Couldn't you fix something with Neville? If I had his address I would write myself. Perhaps we three could go and eat at the Cross Keys in Chelsea."

Long afterwards, in fact only a year or so before his death, at a party after the London premiere of his ballet *Poème de l'Extase*, John sat up until about four in the morning, in a mood of black melancholy, talking to his friend Peter Rosenwald about the misery of a homosexual life. The theme of his unhappiness was that "I can't have continuity, and I need continuity for my work". It is true that the homosexual world is less inclined than heterosexual society to long-lasting and exclusive sexual relationships, partly because it is not subject to the pressure for such relationships imposed by family economics. That was even more true when John was young, because a discriminatory law forced most homosexuals to keep their preferences secret. Even so, many succeeded in establishing a relationship similar to a heterosexual marriage, and Hanns Ebensten believes that "had he not been a homosexual, John would have had the same occasional hours of despair and misery, and maybe had a succession of failing marriages and affairs. Like many homosexual men, he had a longing for a fine, close, loving relationship with some men, and a frantic exciting rough-trade sexual fling with others."

John's problems seem to have arisen mainly from his own nature, the other side of the very qualities that brought him success. All his life he had an urge to know and experience as much and as deeply as possible. Hence, on the one hand, his wide knowledge of books, paintings, music, his interest in the specialist knowledge of people he met from other walks of life, his responsiveness to many artistic influences, and his concern for people. On the other hand, that attitude complicated his relationships. He had a desire for strong and lasting friendship, but he judged his friends severely, expecting them to be as eager as he was to know, see and feel everything. He also had a real enjoyment of brief, casual relationships, sexual or otherwise; one of his gay friends remarked to me that even with a passing infatuation, a pick-up, John never tried to impress people with who he was, never used the glamour of his position to dazzle them, but was interested most in finding out who they were, what kind of person. To look at large numbers of photographs of him, most of them unposed, is revealing: his eyes are always concentrating on someone or something, never bored or inattentively gazing.

All that accentuated the swings of mood in a man capable of intense enjoyment but subject also to persistent melancholy. Both moods were apparent during that summer of 1947. He ended the tour so upset and disorganized that he had no plans for the summer holiday. Hearing that Peggy van Praagh was going to the south of France with a friend and had a spare seat in her car, he asked if he might come too. So he found himself unexpectedly spending his holiday in the little port of Cassis. That quickly brightened his spirits, and he wrote to Hanns:

> I can't begin to write it all down, it's so lovely. One sees at a glance all the blue period of Picasso — the wild horses of Chirico — the extraordinary landscapes of Dali — the Italian primitives — Botticelli.
>
> Colour intensifies, the sun dries out all the sogginess of the soul. The air glitters like diamonds and the night air is like warm honey. The men are so lovely, enormous and gentle, brown as amber — enormous black eyes and stiff bristly black hair which spurts off their foreheads like solidified jet and glitters blue in the sunshine. Their clothes — culottes in white, green, blue of the most vivid shades, cork-soled sandals through which one sees their gleaming brown toes — such men inhabited Olympus, truly.

He spent most of his time watching the fishermen at work, and wrote with enthusiasm about having made friends with a family of "three brothers, each surpassing the other in beauty" and the Spanish wife of one of them, "yellow skin like a magnolia and hair black as moonshine. No wonder great art has been inspired from here for countless centuries — all is beauty and colour, harmony and affability are everywhere. At night we sit in the cafés on the front, people come and go, there is an excited bustle... Tonight we are going fishing. God bless us every one!"

Several photographs from that holiday went into the huge scrapbook which John compiled at that period. It is a curious miscellany, where photographs of his early ballets are mixed in with family snapshots, pictures of his friends, souvenirs of journeys, Christmas and other greetings, a book of clothing coupons from the days of rationing, costume drawings and various illustrations cut from magazines, including a feature on Roland Petit's ballet *Carmen* and examples of the "new look" in women's clothes when long skirts came back to fashion for the first time since the war; he proposed a ballet about that, but it was rejected. The jumble of different contents suggests a double motive in keeping the book: to remind him of past happiness and to provide ideas for the future. The collection provides insights into his enthusiasms: he got both Margot Fonteyn and Alexandra Danilova to sign photographs of themselves for him, for instance. It also provides examples of his sense of humour. Down the edge of one page, adjoining a big picture of Markova and Dolin in *Giselle*, is a series of pictures showing John clowning with a length of gauze, as if burlesquing one of the Wilis in that ballet. Characteristically, a photograph showing a back view of himself sitting gawkily in his bathing drawers beside the Mediterranean at Cassis is captioned "An English Tourist". (Note, incidentally, that already he was thinking of himself as English, not South African).

On the way back from that holiday in Provence, the party stopped in Paris, which John was also seeing for the first time. There, too, he was overwhelmed by what he saw; so much so that he went back with Hanns for a hectic fortnight at the end of September.

By then, John had something to celebrate. *Tritsch Tratsch* had been mounted for Sadler's Wells Theatre Ballet (the first performance was at a matinée on 20 September 1947) and was an immediate success. So much so that, although it had not been mentioned at all in the advance publicity, it was given no fewer than 87 times that season and remained in the programmes for the next six seasons, by which time the company had danced it more often than any other work in their repertory except *Les Sylphides* and two of Ashton's ballets, *Façade* and *Les Rendezvous*.

Tritsch Tratsch lasts only about three minutes but in that time it does not waste a second. The three characters are portrayed with vivid detail and lively humour: two sailors who flirt with a girl but find her more than a match for either of them. Many casts followed

Elaine Fifield, Michael Boulton and Poole into the work and all delighted audiences. The costumes for the Sadler's Wells production were designed, at de Valois's insistence, by Hedley Briggs, an old associate of hers, but they seem not to have differed materially from the ones by Hanns Ebensten which were used for the original Cape Town production. Could de Valois have thought that it would be too much to risk giving chances to two hardly known South Africans in one production? More likely, she did not share the admiration others felt for Hanns's work. Although it was eventually pushed out of the company's programmes by the success of *Pineapple Poll*, another comedy in which John developed further the idea of sailors getting their come-uppance, *Tritsch Tratsch* has never lost its popularity as a number suitable for galas and concert programmes.

During John's brief stay in Paris, his father remarried; John's mother had married again in June 1946, becoming Mrs Aubrey Martin. Herbert Cranko and his bride, Phyllis, were already living together at 6 Montpelier Walk, Knightsbridge. They would have married sooner but had to wait for her divorce; Pamela Chrimes told me that it took some time to obtain the evidence of adultery which was then necessary. They adopted the time-honoured device of spending the night together at an hotel, but Herbert, nervous that something might go wrong, overtipped the chambermaid, who then through misplaced gratitude would not give the required evidence against him. Later, an appointment was arranged for a private detective to call at Montpelier Walk. That was before John had moved in with them; he and Chrimes happened to call there that morning on some business errand before the detective had arrived, and the door was opened by Herbert in his dressing gown, begging them to hurry away again in case their presence spoilt the evidence.

About that time, Herbert became managing director of a new airline, Universal Airways, with headquarters in Johannesburg, flying a regular weekly service from there to Israel. The founder was a man who had become interested in aviation during the thirties, spent the war in the South African Air Force and, on returning to civilian life, foresaw the opportunities that could be won with cheaply acquired and converted military aircraft. He had the expertise and financial backing; Herbert was recruited to provide the business sense and organization. Herbert's work involved travelling to various parts of Africa, Europe and the Middle East, and although theoretically based in Johannesburg, he told an interviewer that he had never spent more than six weeks continuously in his office there. London was the family's real home, and the time John spent there with his father, his stepmother and her two daughters was a happy

68

period for him. Clover Roope, who later became a dancer, remembers going there to take lessons from a governess she shared with John's stepsisters, and described how absolutely devoted she and they were to this young man with "a fantastic nose and fantastic eyes and this rather long, lanky figure, who was not really a dancer and not really yet a choreographer, but gave the sense already that here was somebody important."

With the beginning of the 1947–8 season, John was transferred to the Sadler's Wells Ballet at Covent Garden to give him more chances to work as a dancer with experienced choreographers. He took small parts in ballets by Ashton (a courtier at the ball in the premiere of *Cinderella*, one of the revellers in the cave scene of *Apparitions*) and de Valois (*Checkmate*, *Don Quixote* and *Job*), walked on as a pall-bearer in Helpmann's *Hamlet*, and appeared in the classics, where his most prominent parts were a mazurka dancer in *Swan Lake* and a marquess in the hunting scene of *The Sleeping Beauty*. It was Massine's ballets which suited him best, especially *Mam'zelle Angot*, in which he took several parts at different times; the sardonic humour he showed as the bootmaker in the market scene still lingers in my memory. He also occasionally appeared at Sadler's Wells, and even learned and danced a leading role there, as the Reveller in White in *Mardi Gras*, when its creator, Leo Kersley, was ill in December 1949. He continued performing only until July 1950, then gave up completely and seems — unlike many choreographers — never to have been tempted to dance publicly again.

At Covent Garden, John was joined by Nerina and Heaton from the group of dancers he had worked with at Sadler's Wells, and he quickly made new friends, including Ray Powell and, especially, Henry Legerton, an Australian who had also just joined the company after dancing for Massine in a play with ballets, based on the novel *A Bullet in the Ballet*. John was not universally popular with his new colleagues any more than he had been at the Wells; his ambition aroused suspicion, scorn, envy or fear in some, and his sense of fun (including a rather observant line in mimicry) left barbs in some of its victims. All the same, his scrapbook shows him obviously happy with his cronies.

John's only choreographic activities at Covent Garden that first season were a couple of tiny opera-ballets, in *Rigoletto* and *The Mastersingers* which made no great impression. At Sadler's Wells, he mounted *Morceaux enfantins* for the Theatre Ballet and, having no new ballet to work on, spent time preparing the new cast for its public premiere on 6 April 1948. It was given this time under the English title of the music, *Children's Corner*, and de Valois insisted on the

69

ballet's being redesigned. Jan le Witt, best known then as a designer and illustrator (he later gave up graphic design for painting), provided a semi-surrealistic backcloth and not particular helpful costumes. The ballet was quite well liked, and offered the most substantial evidence of John's ability since his arrival in Britain two years earlier, but without causing any great stir.

From his point of view, opportunities must have seemed slow to come, but de Valois gave him at least one chance every year from the time of his joining the company: *Adieu* and *Tritsch Tratsch* in 1947, *Children's Corner* in 1948 and, for the following year, his most ambitious production to date, *Sea Change*. As she was also trying out several other would-be choreographers and having new ballets made for Sadler's Wells by Ashton and Howard too, she could hardly have done more for someone who was regarded as promising (by some people as highly promising) but unproven.

Besides, the promise John had shown now attracted his first outside commissions. One brought his first, none too successful, attempt at staging dances and ensembles in a revue, *Calypso*, produced by Hedley Briggs at the Playhouse. The other was a ballet at the request of Alan Carter who (having left Sadler's Wells) formed and directed the St James's Ballet, a company of only thirteen dancers sponsored by the Arts Council of Great Britain to tour small towns with no proper theatre. John's ballet for them was given in their first programme, presented at Chatham on 20 September 1948. *The School for Nightingales* was danced to music by Couperin and set (in the period when he lived) in a singing academy where "the arrival of a visitor suggests that singing is not the only lesson to be learned". John explained in a programme note that he had tried "to get the robustness of the early eighteenth century as well as the extremely mannered movements of the period" and, although I saw it once only, memory suggests that he succeeded to good effect. The cast list shows his sense of literary style, with a maestro named Scintillo, his wife and protegée Philomele, and "Jacques, a distraction" as the chief characters. John told me that he himself never saw the work performed on stage, being busy elsewhere by the time it went on. The designs were by Hanns Ebensten, his last collaboration with John, because he gave up his ambitions to make a career in stage design after he had visited the homes of two other ballet designers, both highly regarded and much in demand, but both living in very modest circumstances. He decided that he was never likely to do even as well as they and that he had better look for another career, which eventually he found successfully in the world of travel.

The School for Nightingales marked not only the end of one collab-

70

oration but the beginning of another, since the cast included, among the "young ladies of the Academy", a dancer using the stage name of Anne de Mohan. She was also the company's assistant ballet mistress and later became, under her real name of Anne Woolliams, John's ballet mistress in Stuttgart. She remembers him, from those early days, attending class at Vera Volkova's studio. Volkova was the best ballet teacher in London. John used to enter very simply, did his class "not very well but with complete concentration, and between exercises, when others would talk, adjust their clothes, or wipe the sweat from their faces, he stood perfectly still and watched closely as the next group went through the exercises; Margot Fonteyn would do that too."

John worked hard and played hard. For his summer holiday he went with Henry Legerton to Positano, seeing Italy for the first time, and sent a card to Hanns: "We have lounged like lizards. Life is very cheap and food excellent. Vermouth is threepence and brandy six-pence! Treasures abound, one keeps itching to buy, but then thinks better of it. Life is smarter and more pre-war than anywhere I have yet seen." Then in September, when the Sadler's Wells Ballet danced in Paris (opening the day after the premiere of *School for Nightingales*), he added to his scrapbook, besides snapshots of Legerton, Powell and himself in the obvious tourist spots, a picture of two puppets; he also pasted a picture of Marie Antoinette in the middle of a page other-wise devoted entirely to gargoyles from Nôtre-Dame.

The new season again brought some work on opera-ballet, with a new production of *Die Fledermaus* at Sadler's Wells on 10 January 1949 giving a bigger opportunity than he had yet enjoyed in that genre. So far, everything he had produced in London had been light-hearted, but his next creation, *Sea Change*, was a complete contrast in mood. It was also on a bigger scale and, for the first time, he was to collaborate with a distinguished painter for the designs. It was Ninette de Valois who put him in touch with John Piper, whose work he had already known and admired before leaving Cape Town, although only from reproductions, just as much as his musical knowledge came from recordings. But Myfanwy Piper, John Piper's wife, remarked how penetrating and imaginative John Cranko's taste and judgement already were, in spite of limited opportunities in South Africa, and that since his arrival in England he "never stopped looking, listening and absorbing". She described by implication the Pipers' first impression of him when she wrote that

> those who met him ... were exhilarated by his ardour, his generosity and his receptiveness. He knew how to extract ideas and information from people without ever making them feel

sucked of vitality — because he never failed to give back as much as he took. For someone who needs, as a choreographer needs, the imaginative cooperation of artists and musicians, as well as the enthusiastic obedience of dancers, that is a great gift.

The first inspiration for *Sea Change* came from the attraction which the sea and the fishermen's lives exercised on the choreographer during his holiday at Cassis in 1947. He wrote that "all the activity on the beach had a great fascination for me — the nets hanging out to dry, people mending them, various types standing round watching, all the usual incidents that happen in a fishing village. Certain movements such as boys kicking a football gave me ideas for the choreography." But I cannot help wondering whether the dark mood of the ballet was at least partly influenced by Britten's opera *Peter Grimes*, which also included episodes of fishermen mending their nets. Having to use existing music, John considered several possible scores, all of which were rejected as unsuitable for one reason or another. Among the rejected choices was Sibelius's *Tapiola*, and, at that stage in planning, the story was to have been of

a rather simple girl who hangs about on the outskirts of a village... She finds a fisherman who has been washed up on the shore. She revives him and looks after him until he gets strong. During this time he becomes all the world to her, and he is grateful but unaware of her affection. When he is completely recovered, he sees some other villagers and returns to the world he knew, leaving the girl to her solitary existence.

When he rather reluctantly accepted the suggestion of another Sibelius score, *En Saga*, he found that "the music suggested rather a different story". It eventually showed fishermen preparing and setting out on a peaceful evening for a night's work; while they are at sea, a storm blows up. The women wait anxiously and when the boat returns one of its crew has been lost, causing inconsolable grief to his young wife. It was a simpler and better story.

The music finally chosen helped greatly in creating a sombre mood, but John did not find it interesting or easy to work with. He closely questioned Charles Lisner, who had come from Australia to join the Sadler's Wells Ballet, about a ballet which Laurel Martyn had made for the Victorian Ballet Guild using that score: her subject matter, general treatment and what Lisner thought of the ballet. John repaid his debt of gratitude two or three years later, when Lisner was wondering whether to return to Australia and try to start his own company. He showed that he understood Lisner's thoughts and encouraged him in his dream; Lisner wrote to me that "John was excited about my plans... my enthusiasm stimulated him and his own infectious enthusiasm affected me in turn."

John had always a group of dancers within the company whom he particularly liked to work with, and the cast of *Sea Change* included two of them: Poole as the skipper and Jane Shore as an old woman. John was always prepared to take suggestions from his chosen dancers and also from Peggy van Praagh, who told me that her function was most often to suggest that he was attempting too much and ought to take something out. One day during rehearsal of *Sea Change*, she remembers, when things were getting too complicated, she simply told him to stop and leave it altogether until the next day.

The cast of *Sea Change* included, among the fisherfolk, a dancer new to the company who became closely associated with John in later years, Peter Wright. John gave the leading part, of the woman whose husband is drowned, to a young dancer he had not previously created for, although he had partnered her in *Khadra*, Sheilah O'Reilly. She was beginning to attract attention in dramatic roles but had never been given such an opportunity for anguished emotion, and she rose to it whole-heartedly. The ballet had some rough edges to its structure and the groupings, like the emotions, were sometimes a little too obviously contrived, but it marked a step forward for its choreographer in its attempt to achieve dramatic seriousness and depth. He took the trouble to work on it further when it was given again the following season, eliminating the somewhat superfluous role of a pastor, for instance, and putting the women into soft shoes instead of point shoes so that the movement looked more natural.

Piper's designs were admired for their sombre beauty. He had previously designed only two ballets, working with Ashton on *The Quest* and with de Valois on a revision of her ballet inspired by Blake's drawings, *Job*. In fact *Sea Change* was a better example of his art than either of those. Most of his earlier stage designs had been for opera, and the latest of them, *Simon Boccanegra*, had been the big hit of the preceding season. That, together with his high reputation as a painter, made it possible for John to feel much less responsibility on his own shoulders than in former collaborations. He became close friends with the Pipers and gained great benefits from their taste, experience and enthusiasm.

John could hardly have found a better influence. John Piper had seen the Diaghilev Ballet in his twenties, had gone as often as possible because "the excitement — the tinge of exultation — in the dancing married to modern music and modern art, worked in my blood and bones." From that experience, he derived an ideal of stage unity stemming from a close collaboration "regardless as far as possible of individual prestige and personality", which was reinforced by working in the Group Theatre of the thirties with Auden, Isherwood, Spender, Britten and others. Offstage, too, the Pipers became like second parents to John, and he picked up from their example many influences on his daily life as well as art. They affected his taste in food, for instance, his liking for antiques — even, one friend thought, the way he walked. Years later, he described to friends in Stuttgart, with whom he was sharing a house, what he thought a kitchen should look like. When they visited the Pipers' home they recognized the source of John's description in every detail.

Shortly before the first performance of *Sea Change*, unhappiness struck John's domestic life. His stepmother Phyllis died of cancer in a nursing home in Guildford on 29 June. She and Herbert had enjoyed only a few years of happiness together. The blow was almost as great for John, who had begun to enjoy a family background after years of being on his own or part of a split family. Just a few weeks before her death he had written fondly to her on a postcard from Florence (where the Sadler's Wells Ballet went for the Maggio Musicale festival) that she "would love it so. So much to see it's quite overwhelming. Florence quite unspoilt and Florentines charming. Prices on the whole good... We open tonight, expect wonderful reception judging by other performances." Herbert was there too and wrote the same day that "It's heavenly here — the air is wonderful and one never feels tired..."

The intention had been to give the premiere of *Sea Change* at Sadler's Wells to open the Theatre Ballet's new season there, but it was thought that by then John would already have left for New York to take part in the Sadler's Wells Ballet's first American tour, so the decision was made to present the ballet first on 18 July 1949 at the Gaiety Theatre, Dublin, where the company concluded its summer tour. John went over with them and, an indefatigable sightseer as ever, found time to visit Trinity College as well as being photographed looking proud and happy beside the poster outside the theatre. In fact, too, he was still in London when *Sea Change* was first given there on 28 September; the other company did not leave until five days after that.

At the Sadler's Wells Ballet's historic debut in the Metropolitan Opera House on 9 October 1949, with Fonteyn dancing *The Sleeping Beauty*, John played his customary small role as one of the four marquesses in the hunting scene (Kenneth MacMillan was another of them). It was characteristic that he stuck into his scrapbook not only the programme of that performance and the rave review from *Dance*

News, but also such memorabilia as publicity photographs and sketches about the clothes and accessories which all the women in the company were given as ambassadors of British fashion, and, significantly, the handsome illustrated brochure of Balanchine's School of American Ballet. He was an exception among the British dancers in wanting to find our as much as he could about American ballet teachers.

Before the American tour, John had already prepared his next new production, and he came back in time to supervise the final rehearsals before its premiere at Sadler's Wells on 20 December. This was one of his enduring pieces, *Beauty and the Beast*. Although it has a cast of only two, it is a complete short story-ballet, not just a showpiece duet. He had seen Cocteau's film on the subject several times, was full of admiration for it and wanted to achieve a similar kind of fantasy. But what he produced was by no means an imitation of Cocteau. John kept his plot very simple and concentrated on expressing the emotions of the two characters at every moment. At the same time he was equally concerned that the dancing itself should be interesting. Poole was again his choice for the male role, with another of the young South African dancers, Patricia Miller, as Beauty. He told her "I'm going to do a ballet for you and I will make you or I'll break you. I'm going to give you all the things you can't do." That drastic formula meant, for instance, that the ballet turned out to be full of controlled balances on one leg, which until then she had just not been able to sustain. Somehow John forced or persuaded her to achieve what she had found impossible before and, more important, he also won from her a performance of quietly expressive lyricism.

Some people complained that the realistic sobbing of the Beast, slumped on the ground at the ballet's opening and again when Beauty hurls the rose back at him, was out of place in a ballet, but it conveyed the point without needing any artifical mime — something he always tried to get away from, wanting anyone to be able to understand his work without needing to learn the conventions first. In fact, the choreographer's growing skill was manifest in the way he combined different elements, from that sobbing at one extreme to the rapturous final duet at the other (in which influences from Balanchine and Ashton could be seen), into one fluent whole, and fitted it all so smoothly to the music he chose, Ravel's "Mother Goose" Suite with one section omitted. The designer was Margaret Kaye, who had just had an exhibition of collages made with fabric, and she used a similar technique to try to provide the mixture of fantasy and realism needed to match the ballet. That succeeded only partially in the setting, but the costumes were attractive. The Beast wore a tunic with a special inside breast pocket in which (with back turned to the audience) he could hide his mask and gloves when transformed to human form by Beauty's kiss, and that ingenious idea must have been John's own. *Beauty and the Beast* proved highly popular and was given with many casts during later seasons; it has also been revived for several other companies, with various designers. John was happier with this work than any of his others, and Myfanwy Piper recorded that it was the first of his own ballets which John seriously believed in.

The success of *Beauty and the Beast* was fortunately timed. New York City Ballet was hoping to have its first London season in the summer of 1950 and Lincoln Kirstein, its director, wanted to commission a work from a young British choreographer. He asked Ashton, who was an old friend and had just created *Illuminations* for the company, to suggest who would be most suitable. Ashton nominated John as the most promising newcomer. Balanchine, City Ballet's artistic director, came to Britain to mount his *Ballet Imperial* for Sadler's Wells Ballet, was able to see *Beauty and the Beast*, and approved the choice. Unfortunately, the commission did not work out well.

John was invited to have dinner with Balanchine, and to his surprise the latter proposed to him the theme, music and designer to be used. He was so overwhelmed and flattered that he could not argue, but when he started working on the ballet he found that the music (an orchestrated version of Schubert's four-handed piano pieces) "said nothing to me". All the same, he did not dare tell Balanchine "it's not working", he thought he must try. In that unhappy mood he went to Paris to meet the designer Balanchine had stipulated, Dorothea Tanning, who followed the surrealist manner she had previously applied to one of Balanchine's own ballets, *Night Shadow*. When John saw the costume designs, he was horrified, finding them quite impracticable for dancing. In spite of that, he got on well with Tanning, whom he found a "nice woman", and with the man who shared her studio, always painting away while John was there. They had some good meals together, and when John left, the man gave him an inscribed copy of the lithograph being used as poster for his exhibition. Back at his hotel, packing for his return to London, John wondered how to fit this large acquisition into his luggage, could not think of a way, decided that he did not want a souvenir of the trip anyway because of his gloom about the impending ballet, so tore it up and threw it in the wastepaper basket. It was only later that he realized he had destroyed a Max Ernst.

Eventually, John summoned up courage to ask permission to use

76

different music: Ravel's two-handed piano concerto in G. Presumably he was happier working with that, but few people found it an apt choice for the subject of the ballet, about a witch who destroys her lover.

Kirstein wanted to see the ballet in preparation before confirming the commission, so John began working on it with dancers of Sadler's Wells Theatre Ballet, including Miller as the heroine. She was represented as a nice girl temporarily turned into a witch by strange creatures (including, in Tanning's designs, men described as Owl Heads and Bald Heads) who interrupt a rendezvous with her lover in a mysterious castle. Balanchine, Kirstein and Tanning went down to Bournemouth at the end of June to watch a run-through by the company, which was on tour. The critic Richard Buckle accompanied them and described how they sat in the stalls of the empty theatre afterwards while Balanchine told them "what he liked and did not like about it and how it could be improved". The tenor of his advice was that every step must be given its full measure of beauty and significance; he wanted John to guard against falling back on clichés between moments of happy invention. This must have been the only time John ever had his work discussed in detail by a choreographer of Balanchine's gifts and experience, and although Buckle described him as "looking somewhat quelled" his nature was such as to profit from it. But that was not enough to save *The Witch*.

The leading parts were given to two of City Ballet's most interesting dancers, Melissa Hayden and Francisco Moncion. There were a lot of complicated lifts, and Hayden found some moments of the opening duet highly erotic; the witches and other apparitions were given some ghoulishly eccentric movements. The ballet was not originally announced for the London season, but the company was persuaded to stay for an extra week and *The Witch* was premiered on 18 August, the night before the last. It was the first real ballet of John's to be seen at Covent Garden, since his dances for operas had so far all been on a small scale, and it was far from being a success. John was relieved when the executors of Ravel's estate announced their objection to the use of that concert music for a ballet, so that no further performances could be given and, in consequence, the ballet was never shown in New York. Also, it was no longer possible to take it into the Sadler's Wells repertory, as had been intended. Although the ballet flopped, simply to have been invited to work with a major American company was already a valuable recognition of John's gifts.

There was better recognition still to come, adding professional achievement to a period of happiness in his private life. Towards the

77

end of 1949 he had met a young psychiatrist from Australia, Frank Tait. They soon became close friends and decided to buy a house together at 19 Alderney Street, between Victoria Station and the River Thames: a mixed but lively and convenient neighbourhood. This remained John's London address for the rest of his life. They moved in during September 1950 and just about that time Ninette de Valois announced that she was appointing John resident choreographer of Sadler's Wells Theatre Ballet for the following season. The time of proving himself was over; John Cranko now held an official and important post in the Sadler's Wells organization, only four and a half years after arriving in Britain as a student at the Sadler's Wells school. He was just twenty-three.

ACHIEVEMENT

THE season of 1950–1 was crucially important to Sadler's Wells Theatre Ballet for two reasons. The Festival of Britain was to be held in the summer of 1951 in an attempt to prove to the world, and not least to Britons themselves, that the era of economic hardship was over and the country was full of life again. A brilliant theatrical season in London was high on the list of attractions and Sadler's Wells was expected to make an important contribution to that. Then, early in the following season and consequently relying largely on the same repertory, the Theatre Ballet was to make its first full-scale overseas tour. It had only once before played outside Great Britain, on a visit to Belfast and Dublin in 1949. Now, following two immensely successful tours of North America by the Sadler's Wells Ballet from Covent Garden, the younger company was to spend six months visiting sixty-seven towns in Canada and the United States. It was a young company in two senses: having been formed only five years earlier, and also because it was now for the first time relying for its stars entirely on dancers who had begun their careers more or less within that period.

John was not the man to be worried by that. He had always preferred working with a small group whom he found sympathetic to his ideas and (except with New York City Ballet, where he had to do what he was told) since arriving in London he had only once cast any of the older dancers in his ballets, when he used Hans Züllig for the small role of the pastor in *Sea Change*. He wrote of the dancers at his disposal for this season that they were "the pick of carefully trained and nurtured talent... the best possible material for the apprentice choreographer... Dancing holds a bright and provocative future for them, a future not in any way dulled by overwork, frustration or the thousand bitternesses which so often overtake the 'old stagers'. Perhaps it never will; their enthusiasm runs so strongly for each new work they undertake." Describing the season as "one of my happiest working years", he explained that

> the two most essential factors in the creation of a ballet are teamwork and a mutual belief. Because ballet has no working notation it exists only when it is performed, and it may further be said that the decor and music only have their true existence when seen and heard in conjunction with the choreography for

79

which they were designed. Consequently the three creators of a ballet are entirely dependent on the human beings who interpret their style and ideas: the slightest lack of understanding from wardrobe-mistress, coryphée, or instrumentalist, and some important fragment of the production can be lost.

In Sadler's Wells Theatre Ballet, those difficulties were "understood by everybody. Personalities and personal ideas are respected, but the final goal is always unity of approach and 'theatre'. Ideas are discussed, grow and flower, or are discarded, and by this process each production naturally emerges as a whole."

At that period, John took his dancers far more into his confidence than he did later. Patricia Miller reported that, when making *The Lady and the Fool* in 1954, John started by telling them the story; and Maryon Lane, writing about the early days at Sadler's Wells, described how "whenever he was creating a new ballet, he would call us all together, and the company would huddle around him while he explained his ideas. His exuberance was infectious; he vibrated enthusiasm, love for whatever he was creating, and excitement. We would have done anything to please him. Technically, the entire company danced the almost impossible feats (for that time), but how John pushed the standard of technique up." By the time he created *The Angels*, in 1957, Clover Roope says that "he did *not* explain his ideas in detail unless asked, but could explain them in fascinating detail if asked", and the dancers then still found that "he could captivate you entirely and make you want to serve his ideas". A few years further on, during his Stuttgart days, he was to claim that "I am very secretive when I create... I tell the dancers what to do, but not why. If it is not right, I change it, but I never give them a reason." He did continue to discuss ideas and projects with his colleagues, and to prefer dancers used to his demands, but no longer found it a benefit to give his cast the why and wherefore of their roles.

That 1950–1 season began in mid-September with a week at the Opera House, Manchester, during which a work that Balanchine had offered the company in exchange for *The Witch* was premiered. His *Trumpet Concerto* was set to Haydn's music, so insecurely played that the ballet would have had little chance of succeeding anyway. Besides, British audiences at the time (and most British critics even more so) tended to be unenthusiastic about Balanchine's plotless ballets. On top of that, even Balanchine presumably had some reservations about this example of the genre, as he never revived it for his own company, although with hindsight it is possible to see its light-hearted, semi-military manoeuvres, for a cast dressed in a stage adaptation of uniforms, as containing the seed that blossomed in two notably popular ballets he made years later, *Stars and Stripes* and *Union Jack*.

Because of its limited success, *Trumpet Concerto* was soon withdrawn. As a result, the alarm when *The Witch* also had to be cancelled was even greater than would otherwise have been the case. It had been announced for its Sadler's Wells premiere on 12 December. To take its place, John began work on a ballet of quite a different kind, which he completed so quickly that the premiere date had to be postponed only one week, until 19 December.

He at least had learned a lot from New York City Ballet's visit to London, from the opportunity to see their repertory as well as the experience of mounting a ballet for them. In technique, he began to show far more skill and confidence in the way he handled a corps de ballet (or, in this instance, a small supporting group), making their entries more animated and interesting. In general approach, he was emboldened by Balanchine's emphasis on plotless classic ballets to pursue his own characteristic variant of that style. What he achieved in *Pastorale* was a kind of theatrical sleight of hand, by which the dancers were ostensibly playing specific characters but in fact there was no real plot. Audiences accepted the ballet as if it were a dramatic work, but the interest actually lay in the relation of movement to music and the suggestion of mood through the dancing. When he revived the ballet in Stuttgart ten years later, he dropped the characters' names and retitled the ballet *Divertimento*.

The music was by Mozart (Divertimento No. 2 in D, K.131); John had thought of using Scarlatti but there was no time to have it orchestrated. The ballet was danced in the setting which Hugh Stevenson had designed for *Adieu*, properly made this time rather than the former semi-improvised adaptation. The ostensible theme was of different aspects of love as treated in Elizabethan poetry, and John sent Frank Tait to search in the library for suitable names to give the characters. For "Love Triumphant" in the first movement John used one of his favourites, Patricia Miller, and an interesting young dancer, Pirmin Trecu, as a radiantly happy pair of rustic lovers, Phillida and Corydon. The slow movement, "Love in Sadness", was the first role John made for Svetlana Beriosova, just turned eighteen but already a real ballerina in the making. She had joined the Theatre Ballet that summer after the dissolution of her former company, Metropolitan Ballet. She had a great gift of simplicity which he used touchingly in an episode where, as Lamilia, she was courted by two admirers but rejected both until finally turning to the older of them, Melanthus (Poole) out of pity. Damon, the younger suitor, was played by the company's exceptionally gifted young leading man, David Blair; in the next section he found consolation with the gay and virginal Diaphenia, Elaine Fifield. The management of the company was pushing Fifield as a future star and asked John to feature her in this ballet. He agreed, and set her solo first, but then made at least equally good parts for Miller and Beriosova. For some reason he did not really like working with Fifield, perhaps partly because she was always slightly stubborn and prickly, but you would never for a moment have guessed his reluctance from the roles he created for her in this ballet and in his next one. Although happiest when working with sympathetic colleagues, he was professional enough to be able to find the best qualities of others too. Fifield's role in *Pastorale* made good use of her cool reserved manner; her solos included swift darting leaps and unsupported pirouettes to show off her strong clean technique. In the ballet as a whole the choreography ranged outside the familiar hackneyed steps; for instance, he used many small quick jumps as well as the more obvious big ones in achieving an impression of lightness, and he was already (in *The Witch* as well as here) introducing many sequences in which the women were carried high in the air by their partners, something that became almost a signature in his duets. David Blair's role emphasized his exuberant personality and bravura technique; he was then twenty years old and rapidly coming to prominence as a virtuoso.

One very minor consequence of the rush to prepare *Pastorale* was that John had to postpone until January 1951 a visit, announced for the previous term, to the Oxford University Ballet Club which Clive Barnes and I were running then. We were all three of an age and trying to build careers for ourselves in different parts of the ballet world. I must have met John a year or two earlier although, in contrast to the many people who told me how vividly they remembered their first meeting with him, I cannot recall exactly how, where or when. The talk John gave at Oxford was one of the earliest examples of the public analysis and exposition of his art at which he became adept. His subject had originally been announced as "How I make a ballet", but he widened it to cover choreography in general. He included a certain amount of philosophical background which, according to my diary, I found less than totally convincing, but the main substance of his presentation was a practical demonstration and discussion which showed him able to explain fluently his ideas on

82

making a ballet. He brought two dancers with him to demonstrate different types of movement, and himself gave acutely observed imitations of various unconscious gestures, ways of standing and the like which revealed character and thoughts.

By that time, John was well advanced with the next of the three ballets he created at Sadler's Wells that season. *Pineapple Poll* was his real breakthrough which proved his talent not just to the ballet audience (*Beauty and the Beast* and *Pastorale* had already done that) but to a wider public. The idea of *Poll* came from Charles Mackerras, who was then an assistant conductor and répétiteur for Sadler's Wells Opera. He had noticed that two outstandingly successful ballets, *Gaîté Parisienne* and *Le Beau Danube*, both had scores which were arrangements of melodies selected from the works of, respectively, Offenbach and Johann Strauss. Why should not a similar arrangement of music by Sullivan be equally popular, he wondered. He asked Peggy van Praagh to suggest a young choreographer to work with, and she told him that John was the most brilliant. The two men got on well at once; Mackerras thinks that being both young "colonials" (he came from Australia) helped towards that, and Frank Tait, also Australian, made a similar remark about his first meeting with John. I suppose, too, that John's early liking for the Gilbert and Sullivan operas must have helped predispose him to the idea. They began working with enthusiasm.

Mackerras (Sir Charles, as he now is) thinks that it was he who had the idea of looking in Gilbert's *Bab Ballads* for a suitable plot, and John who found the one they used, *The Bumboat Woman's Story*, although he says it might have been the other way round. In any event, John greatly elaborated the simple plot of the original comic poem, introducing new characters and episodes. The heroine, Pineapple Poll, who disguises herself as a sailor for love of handsome Captain Belaye, was turned into a younger and more attractive woman than is implied in the poem, and given an admirer of her own, Jasper, for a happy ending. Another newly invented character was Mrs Dimple, aunt and chaperone of Belaye's fiancée Blanche, a marvellous comic character combining outrageous behaviour with an entirely proper manner.

Lady Mackerras remembers John coming to their home to work out the details with her husband and trying out the suitability of the various pieces of music by improvising to them in the sitting-room of their flat while her husband played the piano. If necessary, John would ask Mackerras to change a piece for something longer or shorter, faster or slower. When the score was settled, John recorded it all on a "wire recorder", a predecessor of tape recorders, which he had brought back with him from America; he used that to work from because he could not read music.

It was John Piper's idea to ask Osbert Lancaster to provide the decor. Cranko enthusiastically agreed. He used to look eagerly every morning for Lancaster's pocket cartoon on the front page of the *Daily Express* and thought that the artist's sense of style and humour (manifest also in his satirical books about architectural history) would suit the project. Lancaster was delighted to be asked to design for the stage, and his brightly coloured settings, full of comic detail, proved ideal. He also suggested the idea of transforming Mrs Dimple into Britannia during the finale by draping a flag around her and handing her a trident; her open umbrella served to represent the shield. That joke was not so well understood abroad as in Britain; the impresario Sol Hurok, who was to present the company in America, failed to get the point until Lancaster showed him the back of a penny (and now it would have to be a pound note, since the image no longer appears on coins). Lancaster's settings and the influence of Gilbert and Sullivan gave *Pineapple Poll* a very English flavour, even though neither Cranko nor Mackerras was English. That is doubtless why it has never been quite so popular in other countries, but in England it was and has remained a great hit. When the *Ballet Annual* in 1953 invited its readers to write in saying which new ballet since the end of the war in 1945 had impressed them most, *poll* headed the list, followed by Ashton's *Symphonic Variations* and Roland Petit's *Carmen*.

The premiere of *Pineapple Poll* on 13 March 1951 provided, for the first time ever, a complete evening of Cranko ballets; the others were *Sea Change*, *Beauty and the Beast* and *Pastorale*, offering quite an impressive range of moods and styles. Some of the first notices of *Poll* seem slightly cautious, probably for fear that, however funny the ballet appeared at first sight, the jokes might wear thin on repetition. That fear soon vanished. Inventions like the disconsolate way the love-sick maidens make their entry, one after the other, repeating the same steps, or the trio for Belaye, Blanche and the garrulous, forgetful Mrs Dimple, constantly dropping her scarf or umbrella, still seem funny after more than thirty years and innumerable performances, thanks to the perfect timing of the comedy and its aptness to the music and the characters. Also, the ballet offers roles in which dancer after dancer has enjoyed success, because the plot cleverly mingles a sweet pathos with its knockabout comedy, and presents even its most farcial elements with stylish flair. When Belaye is picked up and moved aside by his angry crew, for instance, it exactly parallels the way he has earlier removed the importunate woman from his own path; repetition and contrast underlie many of the visual jokes.

The ballet provided good parts for the women; even the "sweethearts, wives etc." (as John neatly defined the supporting ensemble) were individually characterized and they had the chance to join Fifield, the brilliant and rumbustious first Poll, dancing fouettés in the finale. But part of the ballet's strength was that it put even more emphasis on the male dancing, from Jasper's sad or whimsical solos to the vigour of the sailors' dances in the long exuberant finale. Above all, the role of Belaye, created for Blair, provided an exhilarating mixture of humour and virtuoso display, especially in the two hornpipes with their fast, intricate footwork in an idiosyncratic style. When Sadler's Wells Theatre Ballet made its North American tour, the quality of the male dancing was particularly remarked, and that was largely thanks to John's influence, through the chances he gave them and the forthright though subtle way in which he encouraged them to perform.

His next creation, premiered only eight weeks after *Poll* on 8 May 1951, continued that tendency. In plot and in much of its choreography it was a reworking of one of his Cape Town creations, *Primavera*, but part of the change it underwent is indicated by the fact that in this new version the ballet was named after a hero instead of a heroine: *Harlequin in April*. A further transformation came with the introduction of a strong comic element into what had been an entirely serious work. The idea of a "clown-like Chaplinesque person" was suggested by the composer, Richard Arnell, "since John felt at that time that the ballet needed another dimension. The characterization of course was entirely his own, and very poignant I believe it to have been."

It was the first time John had music specially written for one of his ballets, thanks to one of three special commissions awarded by the Arts Council of Great Britain as a contribution to the 1951 Festival of Britain. (The others, Constant Lambert's *Tiresias* and Peter Racine Fricker's *Canterbury Prologue*, had little or no success). John provided Arnell with a detailed synopsis running to more than 1400 words (equal to three and half pages of this book) and then discussed all timings with him.

The programme for *Harlequin in April* carried a quotation from T. S. Eliot's *The Waste Land*, the well-known first lines:

> April is the cruellest month, breeding
> Lilacs out of the dead land, mixing
> Memory and desire, stirring
> Dull roots with spring rain...

There was also (unusual for John's ballets) a detailed programme note which, by trying to give some of the ballet's images an explicit meaning, may have confused some spectators instead of helping them. It is easy to make *Harlequin* sound very much a "literary" ballet, but it was really literary only in the sense that its structure was like that of a poem which conveys its meaning through metaphors and images rather than with the logic of prose. The actual images in the ballet were entirely visual and theatrical. Patricia Miller, remarking that the ballet was paradoxically very simple and very complex at the same time, told me that John said to her, after explaining his ideas, "Just you watch what people will read into it!"

Harlequin, the central character, represented human aspiration. At the beginning of the ballet he was "reborn with the plants in April", a blind, half-naked figure rising up out of a mass of bodies huddled low on the stage, their stretching arms or legs suggesting plant growth. Pierrot, the ordinary human muddler who nevertheless wants to be like Harlequin the idealist, brought him his tunic and bat. Gaining magical strength from them, Harlequin tried in vain to turn one of the plants into human form by removing her mask, but she sank back exhausted. In a second scene, Harlequin found his desired lover in the person of Columbine but was soon separated from her by unicorns, the traditional guardians of chastity. Chasing after her, he found instead only a kind of scarecrow dressed as her, that fell apart when he tried to embrace it. Sad and disillusioned, he sank back into sleep with the flowers, but the expectation that he would be born again after winter was raised by the final tableau, in which Pierrot tried to put on Harlequin's doublet.

One of the ballet's virtues was that the comic and romantic elements were fully integrated, not kept in separate compartments: for instance, Pierrot brought on a watering can and sprinkled the plants with it to bring about their spring awakening. Pierrot was mainly a comic figure, whose attempts at art all failed. He was given a prologue in which he tried to sing but without producing any sound when he opened his mouth, and an interlude in which he tried to play a violin that he could not master. But, particularly as performed by Stanley Holden, then just beginning to reveal his marvellous gifts as a balletic clown, he was touching too. Miller was the first Columbine, and Blair alternated with Trecu as Harlequin. The two duets were especially beautiful, the first with the man taking the initiative, exploring and brutal; the second with the two dancers equal in playfulness and triumph. But in a way the ballet's most striking choreographic passages were for the corps be ballet. Two passages especially haunt the memory. One is of the plants trying to rescue the one of their number whom Harlequin has left injured; individually they have no strength, but by helping each other creep forward they gradually succeed through collective strength. The other striking passage was for the unicorns, two at first, who are joined by their magical duplications to overwhelm Harlequin. Thrusting forward from the sides of the stage, they were not at all the gentle creatures that these mythical beasts are usually shown as in art and literature, but fierce beings, snorting and stamping their angry threats.

Lionel Luyt, who had danced in *Primavera*, happened to arrive in London while *Harlequin in April* was in preparation. John took him to a rehearsal and he recognized much of the choreography from *Primavera*, including steps which he had danced as a zephyr, now given to the unicorns. Yet the original concept had been completely absorbed into the larger theme of man's eternal aspirations for love, achievement and glory (at least, that was how it seemed to me, even bearing in mind John's warning about "what people will read into it").

Trying to tell Hanns Ebensten what he wanted from the *Primavera* designs, John had written that John Piper was "more the type" to take as a model, and now he had Piper to design the ballet. But the suggestion of spring about to burst forth, which he had wanted before, came only in the costume for the plants. The more theatrical treatment this time, with three characters borrowed from the commedia dell'arte, was enhanced by setting the ballet in the framework of a burnt-out theatre; Piper's set design was inspired by the ruins of the Theatre Royal, Hanley, which caught fire while the company was playing there in June 1949, while *Sea Change* was being prepared.

Three new works in less than six months was not bad going, but John had another task at Covent Garden before his season's work was ended. On 31 July 1951, also for the Festival of Britain, Purcell's *Fairy Queen* was revived. Based on Shakespeare's play *A Midsummer Night's Dream*, this was an adaptation using singers, dancers and actors. In 1946, a production with choreography by Ashton had provided an introduction for the newly formed Covent Garden Opera, jointly with the Sadler's Wells Ballet, before it undertook its first real opera performance. Ashton had a large cast of experienced dancers headed by Margot Fonteyn. The specially assembled ballet group at John's disposal were mainly inexperienced, some of them only advanced students, although he had Sally Gilmour (formerly leading dancer of Ballet Rambert) and Donald Britton from Sadler's Wells as soloists. Not surprisingly, his dances showed more discretion than boldness, carefully avoiding too close a comparison with what Ashton had done. But by giving the young dancers mainly simple group dances, with imaginative use of arms and of floor patterns, John found his own solution to the problem of providing the sort of decorative entries that the plot structure dictated. A quasi-Elizabethan dance for four men dressed as monkeys had vigour and humour, and he made good solos in the masque of the seasons for Gilmour, Britton and a newcomer named Johaar Mosaval, who was later to be particularly associated with some of John's ballets. Altogether, John held his own quite respectably in comparison with memories of what Ashton had done in this work (and that at a time when Ashton himself was coming in for fierce criticism of his own new ballets).

During the season, between the premieres of *Poll* and *Harlequin*, Herbert Cranko had moved to Israel. Universal Airways had been absorbed into El Al, the national airline of the newly independent state of Israel, and Herbert was given the post of assistant to the Managing Director, Louis Pinkus, who was an old legal colleague from their days in South Africa. His duties seem to have included travelling around building good will, without any very onerous burdens. He went to live for a while in Tel Aviv, taking one of his stepdaughters, Ysabel, with him. She had recently left school and "was to be travelling secretary and controller of the tedious travel documents; opponent at the cribbage contests we soon found the best killer of the tedium of the multitude of air journeys involved; housekeeper, chauffeuse, hostess, and pupil in a unique school of international contacts which I thought might be (and in fact was) to a great extent as good a substitute for conventional teenage university life as our circumstances made possible." There were, not surprisingly, some who were willing to put a less reputable interpretation on the fact of this respectable-looking gentleman travelling and living abroad with a much younger woman who, with her smart clothes, was "a little glamorous amongst the hard-working, aggressively tough 'Sabras' of her age in Israel," but I know of nothing to support that view. Herbert's papers do give a slight hint that he rather enjoyed letting people think the worst.

After his hectic year, John had only one major commission for the whole of the following season, but that was to be his first creation for the larger Sadler's Wells Ballet at Covent Garden. Naturally they wanted a comedy to follow up the success of *Poll*, and anyway the lack of understanding which *Harlequin* met from some people made him shy away from a serious theme at that moment — he was not yet secure enough as an artist to resist pressures. Advance publicity soon began hinting at some surprises. Under the heading "Covent Garden Will Be Taken for a Ride", the *Evening News* reported that "two Rolls

Drawing of John Cranko by Dorothee Zippel

Herbert Cranko

Grace Cranko

LEFT
Riding in South
Africa

LEFT
John as a schoolboy

John with puppet witch

RIGHT
John in *Norskyana* with the Cape Town
University Ballet

John in London

LEFT John in Cape Town 1944

LEFT John at Alderney Street

Hanns Ebensten and John Cranko
in Hyde Park, about 1947

Tritsch Tratsch: Michael Boulton, David Poole and Elaine Fifield

Sea Change: cartoon by Ronald Searle for *Punch*

Pineapple Poll: the finale with David Blair as Captain Beloye

ABOVE Henley: the company in *Dancing* with Kenneth Macmillan centre

Pastorale: Svetlana Beriosova with David Poole (kneeling) and David Blair

OVERLEAF Rehearsing The Lady and the Fool at Sadler's Wells:
Patricia Miller with Peter Wright, David Gill and David Poole

Harlequin in April: David Blair as Harlequin, with plants

Royces (vintage 1920), studded with 'jewels' and upholstered in leopard-skin, will be wheeled on to the stage... London's sedate opera house will resound to jungle rhythm, cakewalk and band music, and dancers will wear the shapeless fashions of 1920. The ballet will have a surprise ending to the story of a young social climber who jilts a eries of suitors and finally marries an African king." If that conveys the idea that John and his collaborators were letting their fancy run away with them, it proved only too true. Yet *Bonne-Bouche* (sensibly, John soon abandoned his original title *Epithalamion*) had many merits, and the sheer overwhelming exuberance of it all was one of them. The story which John devised for this "cautionary tale", as the programme defined the ballet, was of a sweet young thing egged on by her socially climbing mother to reject a loving, handsome, but poor young suitor, first for a rich gentleman who promptly died of a heart attack, next for an officer whose past arrived to confront him with his offspring, finally for a black king who turned out to be a cannibal. The faithful, rejected lover returned from weary travels, having made his fortune, in time to mourn not exactly her ashes but a bowl of soup. The complicated plot was told entirely in movement, without any need of programme notes.

The dancing was interesting, amusing and varied, its highlights including a solo in which the poor suitor, played by Brian Shaw, tried to commit suicide, and comic dances for two other male dancers, Alexander Grant as the black king and Peter Clegg as his witch doctor. Two women who at this time spent much of their professional lives appearing as second cast in Fonteyn's roles, Pamela May and Pauline Clayden, were given a chance to create the parts of the mother and daughter, which they carried off with stylish humour. The large cast also included a band of religious revivalists, hilariously burlesquing the Salvation Army. John invented for them the gently comic title of the League of Light, long before some less humorous campaigners took that name in all seriousness.

Bonne-Bouche had a score specially written by Arthur Oldham, who had previously composed two works for Ballet Rambert. He found some good comic touches to match John's, especially in the jungle scene where the League of Light all died gruesome deaths, but composer and choreographer both gave so free a hand to their enthusiasm for every inspiration that the total effect of the ballet was uneven. That, and a deliberate ignoring of the kind of good taste expected at the Royal Opera House, resulted in its lasting only a couple of seasons in the repertory, but during that time it was popular, which was rather important at a time when many of the new productions at Covent Garden had been rather coolly received. The designs were perhaps the best which Lancaster ever did: a handsome Kensington square for the first and last scenes, and a Rousseauesque jungle for the middle scene.

Lancaster, Piper and Cranko were all involved with an ambitious venture that summer, but first John had another opera-ballet commission, for a production of Tchaikovsky's *Eugene Onegin* at Sadler's Wells on 22 May 1952. A peasant dance he devised for the first act was particularly enjoyable: not even trying to be authentic, but full of crisp vigour. In the second act, his dances kept the birthday party going in lively manner, though the grander ball in act three was perhaps a little stilted. His liking for this opera led to one of his most successful ballets, although thirteen years passed before he achieved it.

That summer's venture with his artistic friends was also to have a big effect on John's future career. Piper, who lives near Henley-on-Thames, had become keen to restore the fortunes of the Kenton Theatre there, which had fallen into neglect. Having redecorated the building, he asked John to get together a group of dancers and stage a programme for them. Three of the dancers came from Sadler's Wells Theatre Ballet: Peter Wright, who was about to leave, Yvonne Cartier, who had just joined, and Kenneth MacMillan, who had just transferred back to the Wells from the company at Covent Garden. Geoffrey Webb, a dancer with Festival Ballet, was the third man. The other women were Sonya Hana, who made her career mostly in musicals, and Margaret Scott, who had been prevented from dancing for about a year by a bad back. John suggested that coming to Henley would be a good way for her to slip quietly back on stage; he did not realize that the names of Piper, Lancaster and himself would bring many people from London to supplement the local audience the friends were aiming for.

The two-week season, timed for the dancers' summer holidays, ran from July until 2 August 1952. The company stayed at Henley in a big empty house, using furniture lent by local residents. Domestic chores were shared among them. Margaret Scott told me that she and MacMillan were in charge of the Aga cooker and were terrified by the noises it made. They ate sometimes at the house, sometimes at the Pipers' home; there were afternoon picnics in the long grass of the garden, and after rehearsals they entertained themselves with musical evenings, singing Mozart.

The whole project was undertaken with very little money. The dancers helped to make their own costumes, aided and supervised by Svetlana Beriosova's mother, who was a skilled theatrical costumier.

John went round the dressing rooms at Covent Garden with a bag, asking if anyone had any ballet shoes to spare. Piper searched a scrapheap behind the theatre to find objects which he used for some of the decors. He and Lancaster worked the curtains during performances; on the first night, reporters came looking for the distinguished painter and found him backstage in dungarees. Lancaster's young daughter Cara came from London to act as a dresser for the dancers: her mother was a little concerned about her but father assured her that it would be all right. All took turns in the box office.

For the programme, John created two substantial ballets and three shorter pieces, supplementing them with *Tritsch Tratsch*, *Beauty and the Beast* (which was given new designs by Piper) and the comic trio for Belaye, Blanche and Mrs Dimple from *Poll*. The most admired of the new works was *Dancing*, which ended the programme. It was set in an attic, filled with junk which Piper had assembled and had enlivened with skilful lighting and a few splashes of colour. The curtain rose on MacMillan, wandering morosely about the room and whistling. Finding a gramophone record, he put it on an antique player with a giant horn and began to dance. The music of the next record he found summoned up Hana, and other discs brought on the rest of the cast for solos, duets, trios and a finale which sustained their exhilarating mood right through, until the end when MacMillan, alone again, departed whistling.

There were suggestions that *Dancing* ought to be preserved in a permanent repertory, but there would have been difficulties, since it was conceived to be danced to recordings by the jazz composer and pianist George Shearing. For a season in a tiny theatre at Henley, that was fine, but the Musicians' Union would not have taken kindly to the same procedure at Sadler's Wells. Also, the time and place helped, by their informality, to enhance the receptiveness of spectators for such a light, frothy work: during the interval they were able to walk in the sunny street outside the theatre and admire the old houses of the pretty riverside town. The atmosphere was so informal that one night John's dachschund, Clytie, wandered on stage during *Beauty and the Beast*. She sniffed around a little, then waddled down the steps into the auditorium, along the aisle and settled on a lady's lap.

Even if *Dancing* did not endure, its effect lasted. Myfanwy Piper, remarking that its "freedom and absurd gaiety... startled many ballet enthusiasts", commented also that it was "the beginning of what has become to be Cranko's ideal: variations; formal, abstract, brilliant, but linked by story of human interest." It was a pattern that would recur in many of John's ballets. Mrs Piper's description of the role John made for MacMillan is also significant: "lonely, imaginative, a natural clown, puzzled by the appearance and disappearance of the dancers, and longing to be one of them." That has a familiar ring to it, and reminds us that John had already divined within MacMillan the role of the outsider who was to become a characteristic of MacMillan's own ballets when he took to choreography.

During the Henley season, John was nudging MacMillan into trying his hand at choreography. Two years younger than John, MacMillan had attracted attention in important roles but was unhappy all the same about his progress as a dancer. He had tried designing for ballet (the decors of some of Peter Darrell's earliest ballets were by MacMillan under a pseudonym), but was miserable because he felt he was not getting anywhere, and was not really sure what he wanted to do. John told the other five dancers "Kenneth is going through a very difficult time; you must all be nice to him. He's at a turning point, and I think he might become a choreographer." To push him into this, when the new works were in preparation, John would start a phrase of movement and ask Kenneth to finish it.

But if this summer season proved important in Kenneth's career, it was no less so in John's own, since the relaxed, informal way it was organized, as an effort among friends with himself as leader, not a remote dictator, was the only precedent he had to go on when he found himself, nine years later, running his own company in Stuttgart. He had found that it worked, and that it suited him. It had the approbation of Piper. What more natural than that he should slip into a similar attitude to meet the problems of his new job? It was to prove the secret of his success, making the efforts and the larks of that summer far more significant than anyone could have foreseen or remotely imagined at the time.

The other ambitious production for Henley was *The Forgotten Room*, a romantic work set to Schubert's Fantasia in F major, played on two pianos. Lancaster's design showed a room in gothic revival style, where a young woman found a book which absorbed her so completely that she began to live its events and was wooed and carried off by the imagined embodiment of its hero. At the end her sister or friend, returning to collect her, found her dead in a chair. Made for Margaret Scott and Peter Wright, this work may have left an idea in its choreographer's mind which affected the way he staged Tatiana's letter-writing scene in *Onegin*, again with an imagined lover appearing, although with less alarming result.

John Lanchbery, who was then conductor for Sadler's Wells

Theatre Ballet, arranged some traditional Spanish music for a duet, *Paso Doble*, gently burlesquing typical Spanish dancers, and he wrote music for *L'Après-midi d'Emily Wigginbotham*, in which a respectable visitor to a museum (Margaret Scott) began behaving very oddly under the influence of the slyly smiling mask of a faun, devised by Piper. The other new work for the programme was *Umbrellas*, a mildly amusing revue-type dance, also with music by Lanchbery.

In contrast to the light-hearted mood of *Bonne-Bouche* and most of the Henley productions, John's next ballet was so serious in intent and crammed with ideas that it proved beyond most people's comprehension and lasted for only eleven performances, before being ignominiously abandoned. This was *Reflection*. The first idea for it came to him at a dinner party to which he and Frank Tait had invited some of the latter's medical colleagues from the Maudsley Hospital. Talk turned to their speciality, psychiatry, and John remarked that narcissism was "the most balletic psychoanalytic complex". He developed the idea of showing Narcissus as an egomaniac who tries to mould his girl friend, Echo, to his own likeness. When he succeeds, he wants to escape from her, but cannot. That fairly simple theme was complicated by suggesting that Echo is his "Negative" and by introducing also an aggressive child (explained as symbolizing the hero's warlike self), a tender child (female), two lovers and a group of adolescents.

As he often did, John found himself some interesting and rewarding collaborators for the work. John Gardner, the composer, was a répétiteur for the Covent Garden Opera. He had written a symphony and other pieces, but it was his first ballet score, achieving a sense of drama in its brittle rhythms with lyrical sections between. Keith New, also inexperienced in ballet, was the designer: his backcloth, a sky with menacing clouds above a grey landscape, made a strong impact. The side panels of two huge figures, painted to resemble stained glass, were intended to clarify the symbolism, but they did not succeed in this. Poole established the self-centred hero as an imposing presence, and the cast as a whole danced as though they at least knew what they meant, but the ballet failed to communicate its point to audiences, either at the Edinburgh Festival, where it had its premiere on 21 August 1952, or in London. John learned something, however, from his attempts to twist classical ballet technique to express something new: elements from the choreography, the daring acrobatic falls over the shoulders of the ensemble, turned up again later in *Opus 1*. He also revealed an aspect of Donald Britton's quality as a dancer (as the aggressive child) which was to find full scope in some of MacMillan's early ballets.

His remaining commitments during 1952 afforded no great scope to make up for the flop of *Reflection*. For Sadler's Wells Opera's new production of *Samson and Delilah* on 20 October he provided two ballet sequences, including an original duet in which Esteban Cerda lifted Sonya Hana in "oriental" poses and carried her in patterns arranged for two-dimensional effect; a neat solution to the problem of the limited space available for dancing in most operas.

Just before Christmas, on 20 December, an adaptation of Lewis Carroll's *Through the Looking Glass* was presented at the Kenton Theatre, Henley. It must have worked well enough there for someone to have the idea of reviving it the following Christmas for a run at Brighton followed by a London showing at the Princes Theatre. That was where I saw it and found that, except for Kenneth Rowell's settings, whatever merits the production might have had at Henley were lost in the bigger theatre. It was as if, after a successful charade, friends in a fit of giggles had blown the original funny idea up until it burst. John's dances, for Margaret Scott (replaced in the revival by Anne Lascelles) and Joyce Graeme, were a flower dance for two daisies, a mime sequence for the Walrus and the Carpenter, and a danced duel for the Lion and the Unicorn; all of them best forgotten.

The Henley premiere of *Alice* was sandwiched between two other Cranko occasions. The night before, the University of Cape Town Ballet had for the first time danced *Sea Change* and *Beauty and the Beast*, both staged by Poole. John allowed the company to have the works without any payment, in gratitude for the help he had received in his early days, but he refused then or at any other time to visit South Africa himself. The night after *Alice*, a dance by John entitled *Her First Party*, for Anya Linden, then a very young dancer with the Sadler's Wells Ballet at Covent Garden, and Donald Britton, was included in the BBC Television series "Ballet for Beginners".

The turn of the year brought an upward turn in John's fortunes. One event that gave him pleasure was the debut of the Sadler's Wells Choreographers' Group, organized by David Poole to give chances to new choreographers. Their first programme, at the Wells on Sunday 1 February 1953, began with a London showing for *Umbrellas*, which made little effect out of its original context and deprived of Piper's setting. The hit of the evening was MacMillan's first ballet, *Somnambulism*, which at once made clear his immense promise. It could well be that the idea of setting it to Stan Kenton recordings may have owed something to what John had done with Shearing's music in *Dancing*; and Margaret Scott pointed out to me that (whether consciously or not) MacMillan had borrowed a trick from John of having a body fall out from the wings when a dancer on stage

94

caught hold of an outstretched hand. But MacMillan turned whatever influences he followed into a style that was entirely personal to him, using jazzy movement to build a sense of threat. John was tremendously excited by MacMillan's success. He had taken Margaret Scott to the performance, and afterwards told her that he must go backstage for a moment before driving her home. He was so carried away that he forgot to return for her. She guessed what had happened and took the bus home, where John rang her at about three in the morning to apologize.

John's next ballet was for Covent Garden. He again took a theme from psychiatry, but a much simpler one than *Reflection* and treated in a more romantic way. *The Shadow* showed a young man attracted to a beautiful and virginal young woman, but kept away from her by a dark menacing figure. When, at the end, he summoned the courage to attack the threatening shadow that always came between them, it proved to have no substance: his fears had been nothing but illusion. Once again John used a cleverly devised costume to reinforce his dramatic climax. Bryan Ashbridge, playing the Shadow, wore a long black cloak and a plumed hat. He made his entrance always from the same dark corner. At the end of the ballet, the cloak and hat, suspended from a wire, came on stage at that same point, so that the young man could throw them aside and reveal that they had no wearer.

The youth was played by Philip Chatfield, a tall, handsome young man who made a good foil for Beriosova's shy grace as his romantic love. To contrast with their lyrical duets, the choreography introduced a flirtatious girl whose solos put all emphasis on speed and brilliance: she showed a frankly amorous interest in the hero in spite of being provided already with no fewer than three lovers, who threw her, one to another, with a daring that would not have disgraced a team of apache dancers. Nerina was to have danced that role but she was ill, and the relatively inexperienced Rosemary Lindsay replaced her with notable success.

The weakness of *The Shadow* lay in the choice of music, which was not altogether John's fault. He had wanted to use Bartók's Music for Strings, Percussion and Celeste, but allowed himself to be persuaded that the music was unsuitable because its quiet opening would be lost at Covent Garden. Instead, he turned to Dohnányi's Suite in F sharp minor: music that imposed an irrelevantly folksy flavour on the production and perhaps caused Piper's setting to evoke a pretty but unspecific milieu, a sort of romantic no-man's-land. Even so, the work was popular and the choreography, in a manner successfully combining the best qualities of *Pastorale* and *Reflection*, revealed a new freedom in the bold handling of the corps de ballet as well as exciting dances for the principals.

The Shadow was first given on 3 March 1953, and for the remainder of the 1952–3 season John had other tasks to keep him busy. There were dances to arrange for a production of Sutermeister's opera *Romeo and Juliet* at Sadler's Wells in April, and then for a production of Sean O'Casey's play *Purple Dust* at Blackpool on 11 May: the director was Sam Wanamaker, Malcolm Arnold had writtten the music, and the designs were by the cartoonist Gerard Hoffnung. Altogether more important was the premiere at Covent Garden of *Gloriana*, Benjamin Britten's new opera which was to be attended by Queen Elizabeth as one of her official engagements during the week of her coronation.

Even before he arrived in London, John had coveted the chance to work with Britten (as he had also with Piper), and *Gloriana* provided the occasion. It was in fact Piper who introduced John to the composer and thus helped to bring it about.

There was a good deal of ill-feeling between the opera and ballet companies at Covent Garden over the fact that an opera had been chosen for the coronation gala (and David Webster, general administrator of the Opera House, made clear his belief that the kind of audience present on such an occasion would not appreciate the work). Consequently, there was some foot-dragging by the ballet company over the arrangements: first, in agreeing that John should stage the dances, and even after that it took repeated requests on his part (accompanied, finally, by the director, Basil Coleman, for an interview that lasted almost an hour) before de Valois agreed to allow Beriosova to dance in the ballet. Webster's forecast about the unsuitability of a long and serious opera about the first Queen Elizabeth for an audience containing a high proportion of people who would not normally attend Covent Garden proved only too well justified. Most of them probably enjoyed the dances as much as anything else in the opera. These included an attractive morris dance, led by Johaar Mosaval, and a court ball during which the Queen was shown performing the energetic La Volta, a popular dance of the period in which the ladies jumped high with the help of their partners. There was also an elaborate masque, presented as an act of homage to the Queen on a visit to Norwich, and representing the marriage of Time and Concord. This ornate spectacle probably gave some idea of the spirit of the Elizabethan masques, and thus of the artistic and social background of the drama, but it held up the action and was understandably omitted when the opera was given again the next season.

The main importance of *Gloriana* for John was that it led to further opportunities. One of them was an invitation to direct a revival of Britten's first opera, *Peter Grimes*, the following season. John described his contribution later in terms of "patching up" the production, which had originally been directed in 1947 by Tyrone Guthrie and had been out of the repertory for three or four years. Looking back on his experiences as an opera director much later, after he had fallen out with Britten, he made it sound a depressing experience:

> Opera direction, essentially, is the art of making singers look not quite so bad as they really are. There are exceptions, of course, singers who can move and act, but basically the act of singing is so ugly. And directing is difficult. If you work with a dancer and you say kneel down, he kneels down; but with a singer it may take a week to get it right. I never found a solution. I simply became aware of the dilemma. Either you send your singers to movement school and teach them how to walk and gesture, or you put them stationary on stage and let them sing... In a funny way, *Peter Grimes* is an effective opera to produce, because the movement is supposed to be clumsy and ugly.

Since he was never given to undue reverence for established conventions, it is likely that the seed of those thoughts was in John's mind even at the time, but at least then there were compensations, not least the fact that Britten took to John himself, and to his work, with great enthusiasm. One early consequence was an invitation to present a programme at the 1953 Aldeburgh Festival, based on the one he had given with Piper the previous year in Henley. It was to have come afterwards to the Royal Court Theatre in London, but that fell through because John had to go off to Southern Rhodesia, where the Government had organized a big exhibition for the Cecil Rhodes centenary celebrations.

A big theatre had been built in the centre of the exhibition site on the outskirts of Bulawayo. It looked like an aircraft hanger but had a superb stage, excellent dressing rooms, splendid orchestra pit and fine auditorium. The Hallé Orchestra, Sadler's Wells Theatre Ballet, a company of actors including Gielgud, and the Covent Garden Opera were all invited from England. There were complaints about the extreme cold of the south African winter, and of discomfort caused by the altitude, but the warm hospitality offered and the interesting places to be seen made up for that and for the tiresome length of the journey, which even by air could take up to three days before jet aircraft had been introduced.

John's mother determined to fly up from Johannesburg to see him in Bulawayo. It was more than seven years since they had met, and she remained very fond of him without any encouragement on his side. Because the town was so full, she had great difficulty in obtaining accommodation, but managed through her own efforts to secure a furnished room from an acquaintance. Once there, she says, she found her two weeks' stay very happy, because she was able to see John during the day (they visited the exhibition together) and was found a seat for the performances in the evenings.

Another collaboration with Charles Mackerras was John's main production for the new season in London. The Sadler's Wells directors hoped to repeat the popular success of *Poll*, and John had a story prepared about a great beauty who turned down rich, dashing and powerful suitors for the love of a clown. He and Mackerras started looking for suitable music to adapt. They thought of Minkus, who had written many popular ballets for Petipa in the nineteenth century, but decided that they could not find enough good music by him. Donizetti was another composer they considered, but Andrée Howard had settled on music from his operas for her ballet *Veneziana* at Covent Garden. Finally they picked Verdi, partly because it occurred to Mackerras that his music was just coming out of copyright, as had happened also to Sullivan's about the time they made *Poll*. Mackerras took passages from a dozen or more of Verdi's operas, mostly early ones which had never been played in Britain (they were all produced later, and perhaps the ballet played a part in reminding people of treasures unexplored). As with *Poll*, the music proved attractive in itself, always apt to the plot, and excellently arranged with a scintillating orchestration.

In spite of that, *The Lady and the Fool* proved initially disappointing. Partly that was because John had entrusted the designs to a painter untried in the theatre, Richard Beer: many of the costumes were attractive, and the sketchy style of painting he adopted for the scenery worked well in the street-scene curtain against which the prologue and epilogue were played, but made an unsatisfactory compromise for the main scene, neither realism nor fantasy but a muddy no-man's-land between those choices.

Even more important, in the original production the choreography was as lacking in focus as the decor. The dances for the corps de ballet were sadly conventional, and remained so even when the ballet was drastically revised the following season. For the soloists, there were many good and original inventions, including one which was striking enough to be given occasionally out of context as a display piece at galas: an adagio in which three suitors each in turn removed a mask worn by the heroine, only to disclose another mask beneath. In the ballet, she took off her last mask when left alone, and danced a solo expressing her sorrow at being admired only for her glamour, not herself. That episode was observed by one of the clowns, who had crept back into the otherwise empty room because of his heartfelt admiration for her kindness as well as her beauty. He then overcame her fears and won her love in a duet of rich emotional and dramatic impact, achieved through unusual passages of partnering which nicely balanced strength and hesitation on his part, longing and alarm on hers. The ballet's other highlight was the dance of the two clowns, both attracted by a single rose lying in the centre of the stage. Each of them wanted it for himself, and their attempts to secure possession grew from friendly rivalry into an angry obsession and eventually a fight. But the winner, coming to his senses, realized that friendship was worth more than transient possessions, revived his defeated comrade and shared the now fallen petals with him.

True love was the ballet's theme: the love between the clowns, Moondog and Bootface, and the love between Moondog and the heroine, La Capricciosa. The fact that it was all expressed in the course of an artifical and sentimental story did not make it any the less heartfelt; realism was never John's genre. Peggy van Praagh remarked to me that she thought John always identified himself with the "little man" who occurs in many of his ballets, but Frank Tait, who knew him better than anyone else at the time he made *The Lady and the Fool*, said that he thought something of John himself was to be found in all three of the leading characters: the capricious heroine, tired of social life and convention, and both the clowns, the romantic one and his tenacious, sad but hopeful partner.

Unfortunately the central theme got overlaid by the incidentals. There was a subplot involving a society hostess, Signora Scintillarda, her two lovers and their wives: not very interesting in itself, and distracting, especially as the two lovers were given showily brilliant solos, so that they overshadowed the dramatic impact of La Capricciosa's admirers, who had only acting and partnering roles. Perhaps John's fertile imagination ran away with him again, as in the case of *Bonne-Bouche*, and caused him to develop his idea too elaborately; or it could be that he completed the ballet in too much of a hurry. It had been intended for premiere at Sadler's Wells towards the end of 1953, but had to be put off for various reasons including the fact that John had fallen ill. In consequence, the work was first given on tour at the New Theatre, Oxford on 25 February 1954, and shown at the Wells on 31 March during a one-week visit which Sadler's Wells Theatre Ballet paid to its home theatre before setting out on a visit to South Africa.

Happily, John had the chance the following year (June 1955) to rework *The Lady and the Fool* for Covent Garden. Signora Scintillarda and her lovers vanished altogether, but curiously enough the two wives, vainly chasing after their errant spouses, remained in the ballet, although now transformed into a couple of husband-hunters in the other sense of that phrase. The men's solos, revised to fit other dancers and a different dramatic context, were given to two of La Capricciosa's suitors, David Blair as the disgracefully rich (and amusingly mannered) Signor Midas, and Desmond Doyle as the gallant Capitano Adoncino. A solo was added for the third suitor, the world-weary Prince of Arragonza, but although John Field managed to make it look stylish and funny, some of his successors in the role allowed it to seem effete and eventually it was dropped from the ballet. Those changes allowed attention to focus far more clearly on the main action; they also made the characters much more interesting and permitted the comedy to be better developed. An improved, though still less than fully satisfactory decor by Richard Beer also helped, as did the larger and stronger orchestra available in the opera house, and the wider choice of first-rate male dancers. Blair, in particular, had one of his best roles in this ballet, one that showed his virtuoso technique at full stretch, allowed his flair for comedy to run riot, and displayed his ebullient personality at its most scintillating. His solo included, among other bravura steps, one baffingly ingenious trick which John had devised, whereby he leapt into the air with his legs thrown out sideways, and appeared to start turning only when he was at the height of the jump. Yet he made something equally effective of a throwaway gesture such as the insouciant flick of his moustache at the very end of the solo. John's sense of fun was in notably rich form, achieving some sure-fire laughs by such simple but ingenious devices as having Capitano Adoncino dance in with a crisply military series of cabrioles while a servant chased after him to take his hat and cloak, or having the gallant captain and Signor Midas shake hands while both performing entrechats.

In most respects the cast at Covent Garden was stronger than at Sadler's Wells. The exception was in the leading parts. John had made the parts of the clowns for Kenneth MacMillan, who was a good Moondog, and Johaar Mosaval, who was a superb Bootface, and it took time for the other dancers to work into those roles. He had cast Patricia Miller as La Capricciosa, and at Covent Garden would have liked to use Fonteyn but was asked to give the role to Beryl Grey, a very tall dancer for whom he had to adjust the choreography, omitting many of the smaller steps, because of her different physique. All the same, *The Lady and the Fool* enjoyed a far greater success in its new form and won a lasting place in the repertory; it is the later version which has subsequently been given at Sadler's Wells too. When the company (by then the Royal Ballet) went to perform in Russia, this was one of their most popular productions there.

It seemed like a good time for John, especially as it was about the time of the first version of *Lady* that the results of the *Ballet Annual* poll were published, voting *Pineapple Poll* top among readers' choices for the best new ballet since the war. But success brought its own difficulties impeding further progress. The policies and circumstances of the Sadler's Wells companies made it impracticable to show more than a limited number of his ballets, and every popular piece he produced made it harder to fit in other works by him.

The Sadler's Wells Ballet at Covent Garden devoted approximately half its total performing time to the classics. The greater part of what remained was given over, rightly, to the ballets of Frederick Ashton (the "mature choreographic genius" as John had called him). That left few enough performances to be shared out among all the other choreographers represented in the repertory: at that time, three other house choreographers (Cranko, Howard, de Valois) and four outsiders (Balanchine, Fokine, Massine and Petit). During the 1953–4 season, John's ballets occupied a higher share of the programmes than any other living choreographer except Ashton, but that still amounted to only twenty performances of *The Shadow* and twelve of *Bonne-Bouche*: not exactly the equivalent of a long run.

With Sadler's Wells Theatre Ballet, although no longer listed as resident choreographer (he held that title for one season only), John's ballets occupied a much higher share of the programmes, something like a quarter, all told. This company had fewer classics in its repertory, and fewer Ashton ballets. But, as at Covent Garden, works by about seven or eight modern choreographers were shown each season, including newcomers to whom Ninette de Valois was conscientiously giving chances to try their hands. So although John was given a reasonable showing of five or six of his works in any one season, heavy public demand for any one work, such as *Pineapple Poll*, meant that others could be shown comparatively seldom.

One consequence of this was that *The Lady and the Fool* (admittedly in its two successive versions) was the only ballet which John had the chance to create for either of the Sadler's Wells companies during a period of almost four years between *The Shadow* in March 1953 and *The Prince of the Pagodas* in January 1957. According to his own account, he was asked to start planning *Pagodas* somewhere about the time the original version of *Lady* was presented, and it might be thought something of an honour for a young choreographer (he was still only twenty-six) to be commissioned to make a three-act ballet for Covent Garden, something which until then only Ashton had attempted. But someone as eager, ambitious and brimful of ideas as John could not be expected to look at it in that light. So he had to make opportunities for himself elsewhere.

Luckily, invitations to mount ballets elsewhere were beginning to come in, largely thanks to the fame of *Poll*. One of the first was from the Borovansky Ballet in Australia to mount *Poll* for them. Thus it happened that he went off to work in another new continent at just about the time Sadler's Wells Theatre Ballet visited South Africa with three of his ballets (*Pineapple Poll, The Lady and the Fool, Beauty and the Beast*) in their programmes, giving John's former colleagues there a chance to assess his development since leaving Cape Town.

The Australian production of *Poll* was given during a long season by the Borovansky company in Melbourne, and proved a popular addition to a repertory that derived heavily (in its creations as well is its revivals) from Edouard Borovansky's origins in the Ballets Russes. The slogan "Ballet of world standard" which hung outside Her Majesty's Theatre, Melbourne that season was something of an exaggeration, but he did have some dancers who had achieved success overseas, among them Kathleen Gorham and Peggy Sager, both of whom danced as Poll, and Paul Grinwis, who played Captain Belaye. By all accounts, Tom Merrifield's performance as Jasper was notably successful, although he soon afterwards abandoned dancing for sculpture.

On the first night, John caused a sensation (and scandalized the management) by the curtain speech he made. Obviously he had heard comments from people in the company about the standard of press reviews in Australia at that time, and it seems not impossible also that he had been slightly carried away by having a drink to steady his nerves beforehand, since what he said might represent what many dancers think, but actually to be so outspoken in public was unheard of. His reported words were:

> Ladies and gentlemen, before you leave the theatre tonight I want to say something to you. You will probably read in the newspapers in a day or two how this ballet was danced. I understand that one of the critics here this evening is a fellow

who writes up the sports page, and that the other one does three sorts of things, none of which is related one to the other, and that none of them know anything at all about ballet. But this is my ballet, and I've choreographed it, and I've been out front and watched the performance, and I'd like to say that it was better than any performance of *Pineapple Poll* I have ever seen, and this company is really rather marvellous. Now, you gentlemen, just go away and write what you like, but these people here have got to know the truth.

There was something of the *enfant terrible* about such an incident, but in other ways John was becoming part of the ballet establishment. In February 1954 the *Gazette* of the Royal Academy of Dancing had reported a special meeting of the RAD Production Club to present its grandly named New Project concerning the Theory and Practice of Ballet Production. The Production Club had been formed in 1932 for a mixture of purposes, among which were to discover and encourage new talent. Its most important activity was organizing occasional performances when advanced students had an opportunity to perform before an audience. Some of the works given were the first attempts of would-be choreographers, a valuable experience for aspirants, but few of them went on to a professional career in that line. John himself, having been given the chance to make *Children's Corner*, was one of the exceptions; another was Robert Helpmann, who had staged his first ballet, *La Valse*, for the Production Club in 1939. The Club occasionally arranged classes or lectures, too, on ballet or other arts connected with production, and now for the first time it decided to experiment with a course in ballet production. That was a controversial idea: most people would have said that choreography cannot be taught, but John agreed to try out some classes of his own devising. Other members of the panel for the course were authorities on music, historical dance styles and Dalcroze eurhythmics as well as ballet.

A demonstration by John and the pupils at the end of the first year's course showed how movement can be worked out and developed on simple geometric principles. He had arranged a *Ballet Suite* to illustrate the year's study, but although he took music from the rococo period, which had been the special subject of study in the other sections of the course, he made no attempt to relate the steps to that period. The pressure of time explained that omission, and one might even wonder whether that particular period was really a good choice in the first instance. The Production Club's pioneering courses have been followed, many years later, by choreographic

103

courses, at the Royal Ballet School and elsewhere, more specifically related to the practical elements of composition such as John had attempted.

Also during 1954, John worked for the first time with Ballet Rambert. For this smaller company, with a reputation based on original creations by almost all the leading British choreographers, he was able to choose a serious theme. Marie Rambert had been particularly impressed by *Harlequin in April*, with its poetic imagery, and happily accepted John's suggestion that he should make a ballet based on Britten's Variations on a Theme of Frank Bridge, the strong rhythms and brilliant writing of which have attracted many choreographers, before and since. The ballet had its premiere at Sadler's Wells (where Rambert customarily gave a short London season each summer) on 21 June 1954.

The music dictated an episodic form for *Variations on a Theme*. A young man encountered an innocent child but was led away from her by the attractions of a charlatan, met strange adventures, gazed upon the sadness of death and the anonymity of a confused life, finding peace eventually only when the child returned to lead him into simplicity again. Many emotional themes ran through the ballet, some of them related to earlier works: the hero, for instance, cut himself off from ordinary human feelings as completely as Narcissus had done in *Reflection*. There were some gruesome touches in the ballet, notably a solo, to the bourrée, for a woman with scissors, with implications of castration, but there were passages of delicate invention also, such as the waltz for a woman with her shadow. The lament, danced by four women around the body of an unmoving man, combined both elements, using images from religious paintings to develop its mood of tender but desolate mourning. Kenneth Rowell's designs contrasted brilliantly gay colours for some of the apparitions with sombre tones for the hero and his background. Many reviewers claimed to have difficulty in understanding the ballet's implications, but audiences were appreciative, and the ballet was admired by Rambert herself and the more serious critics. When Ballet Rambert went the following year to Aix-les-Bains for a festival, and also to dance in Italy, *Variations on a Theme* was the most admired of their modern works.

Unfortunately, it was to be John's last new work for any British ballet company for two and a half years. However the 1954–5 season at Covent Garden did include, as well as the revised *Lady and the Fool*, an opera-ballet much more substantial than most. This was in Michael Tippett's first opera, *The Midsummer Marriage*, where some of the most interesting music and quite a lot of the plot's significance were in the Ritual Dances. There was a snag. Three of the dances occurred in act two. Subtitled Earth in Autumn, Waters in Winter and Air in Spring, they each showed a huntress attacking her male prey: a hound after a hare, otter pursuing fish and hawk swooping on a smaller bird. Two fine dramatic dancers, Julia Farron and Pirmin Trecu, were available for those roles, and although the theme restricted the choreographic scope, there was some memorable invention. The fourth dance sequence, Fire in Summer, was set in the third act and quite different in its treatment (musical, dramatic and choreographic), thus depriving the dances of the opportunity they might otherwise have had to establish themselves in their own right.

Straight after *Midsummer Marriage*, John was off to Paris to create a ballet commissioned for the Opéra. At a press conference in February for John to explain his work it was revealed that Maurice Lehmann, the administrator of the theatre, had specifically commissioned a gay ballet — wanting to emulate the success of *Pineapple Poll*, which had led to the invitation. Once more the music was to be taken from light opera, in this case one work, Offenbach's *La Belle Hélène*. John was presented with an already prepared synopsis in four scenes and was also obliged to use certain leading dancers, a way of working that did not appeal to him. He did manage to select some relatively junior dancers for certain roles, and in his own estimation he scored a small triumph over the rigid conventions of the company by addressing the dancers in rehearsal by their first names instead of the customary Monsieur, Madame or Mademoiselle so-and-so.

The ballet, premiered on 6 April 1955, was admired for its pace and burlesque invention, and particularly for the way in which John revealed an unexpected side of Yvette Chauviré, the favourite French ballerina, hitherto famous for her tragic performances but cast for once as a coquettish Helen. Although not an unqualified success, the ballet gave pleasure to audiences, while critics put the blame for some unevenness primarily on the management which had circumscribed John's artistic freedom.

While in Paris, John characteristically scoured the Marché aux Puces for unusual discoveries, and found there Indian curtains of beads to take home, long before they became fashionable. But he was not happy. A friend with a house in the fourteenth arrondissement had offered to put him up, and at the metro station there one day he suddenly remarked to Frank Tait, "I hate it here. *They*" (pointing to the passing crowds) "all know where they are going to."

Most people by then would have thought that John did too, at least in the metaphorical sense. The magazine *Dance and Dancers*, naming him its personality of the month on the strength of being the first British choreographer ever to be invited to create a ballet at the Paris Opéra, summed up his career as

> the golden boy of British ballet... born with a choreographic silver spoon in his mouth. The going has been easy. Sometimes he has probably felt himself stifled with the atmosphere surrounding a national ballet, he has almost certainly at times felt doubts about the direction his talents were taking, and he has not had the opportunity to create as many ballets as a young choreographer of his fertile imagination would perhaps have wished, but he has never starved either physically or artistically. His struggles have been as much with himself as with his opportunities. He has studied, absorbed and worked. His natural gifts have been polished and matured, and now, a leader among the world's younger generation of choreographers, he is bracing himself for the final test of the full-length Britten ballet.
>
> The three Fates who control our destinies, Talent, Industry and Luck, have all been kind to him. His gifts are mercurial, and the height to which they rise is probably going to depend on the climate in which they find themselves.

Nobody then could have foreseen just how mercurial his gifts were going to prove themselves within a few months, nor how much the climate was going to change for him over the next few years.

One thing was sure. However much he might be the "golden boy", he never behaved like one of the jeunesse dorée. On holiday that summer, the evening before John's twenty-eighth birthday in August 1955, Hanns Ebensten "had an unexpected and amusing meeting with John in the raffish Zanzi Bar, in Cannes, in France. As when he was a schoolboy, John wore rather grubby khaki shorts and a khaki army shirt; and the overdressed young men in that bar thought he was destitute. I much enjoyed the situation." So, we may guess, did John.

____WHEEL OF FORTUNE____

DURING the next five years, John's life was subject to wilder fluctuations of fortune than at any other time. He wrote a run-away theatrical hit, and devised the first three-act ballet ever to have music, choreography and design all by British artists. He was hounded for his homosexuality, bereaved of his father, and saw some of his productions become ignominious flops — not only those which he knew to be bad, but, what was worse, others which were good but unappreciated. He became a friend of royalty — and that complicated his problems. Up and down went Fortune's wheel, until it must have felt more like a treadmill. No wonder that, when the chance came to go off and make a fresh start, he grabbed at it.

This period in his life began with the revue *Cranks*; or, strictly speaking, with two short ballets which presaged some aspects of *Cranks*. The London Ballet Circle, a club of enthusiasts, decided to give two evenings of ballet at the small Fortune Theatre on 30 September and 1 October 1955. The programme consisted of a ballet revived from Pavlova's repertory, *The Magic Flute*, and four specially created works, one each by Peter Darrell and Rupert Doone, two by John. His *Dances without Steps*, performed in plain leotards by a cast mainly of students, was described as "five disconnected sketches for ballets to come", but could equally well have been regarded as a miniature danced revue. To music by Afredo Casella ("Puppenzatti"), he developed five studies of movement, some of which looked back as well as forward, recalling earlier works (*Harlequin in April, Reflection, Variations on a Theme*) that were part of his repeated, and subsequently continuing, quest for a non-literary poetic symbolism achieved directly through danced images; at least one other presaged a work he presented a couple of years later, *The Angels*. John's other creation for the programme was *Corps, Cous, Coudes et Coeur*. The heavily alliterative and anatomical title ("Bodies, necks, elbows and heart") was in keeping with the burlesque spirit of these dances set in Stravinsky's Eight Easy Pieces, but the ballet contained some daringly difficult passages for its French leading dancer, Hélène Constantine (she had been engaged for Pavlova's role in *Magic Flute*), with Gilbert Vernon and Peter Wright as her stalwart partners. This work even had the benefit of scenery and costumes designed by Desmond Heeley.

107

It was understandable that Doone, a former dancer and director of the Group Theatre, and Darrell, busily trying to build a reputation, should be willing to take part in a production under modest auspices, but for a professional choreographer of established fame to do so was surprising. However, as Clive Barnes pointed out in a review for *Ballet Annual*, John's contributions were "exercises in experiment. Given a group of dancers, Cranko obviously decided to play a game with them, himself and the audience... not to increase his reputation but to enlarge his experience." It shows his way of responding to circumstances: original, unconventional, quick to see and seize opportunity.

Cranks, which had its premiere less than three months later, on 19 December 1955, also began in modest circumstances, in the New Watergate Theatre Club, which used a tiny auditorium in Buckingham Street, off the Strand near Charing Cross. The idea of what could be achieved by a few performers in an informal setting had come to John in Paris, while preparing *La Belle Hélène*, when he had gone to watch cabarets in little cellar theatres, such as La Fontaine des Quatres Saisons, or groups like Les Frères Jacques. Back in London, he went to watch a revue for which he had staged a dance number, found it all horrible and said as much to the producer during the interval. Asked if he thought he could do better, he replied, "It could hardly be worse." "Try it then", the other suggested, and he did.

What he devised was simplicity itself. There would be no big-name stars, no large cast divided into comics, singers and dancers, no elaborate settings, no sketches, almost no dialogue; in fact, virtually none of the ingredients considered essential in sophisticated revue at that time. Instead, there would be a cast of four who all sang and danced a series of musical numbers given without any pause. In a way, there was a touch of bravado in having John Piper as designer for a show given with minimal decor. As at Henley, however, Piper devised an assemblage of objects (chairs, tables and the like) which the cast were able to arrange themselves for the different numbers, as if playing charades. There were splashes of colour which, with the aid of subtle lighting by Michael Northen, helped change the look of the permanent setting between items. The three men wore shirts and jeans from Vince Man's Shop (a trendy boutique before such places became widespread); the one woman was dressed in a black leotard and fishnet tights.

John wrote the words, occasionally in a mood of straightforward sentiment, more often with a neat twist of parody, sometimes with an exuberant burst of wild humour. The best, and I think probably

the longest, of the songs, *Metamorphosis*, is worth printing in full as
an example of this. It is not great literature, but its use of a manner
and metre modelled on Edith Sitwell is stylish and inventive:

> I had a dream the other night
> that all our care was turned to bliss
> that all the wrong was turned to right
> by magic metamorphosis.
>
> In attic rooms the dusty brooms
> are sprouting blooms of golden leaves.
> The Mayfair tarts ride round in carts
> with ruby hearts pinned on their sleeves.
>
> In Billingsgate they've diamond bait;
> they catch the skate with precious stones.
> Every housemaid who once was staid
> plays serenades on saxophones.
>
> But in Asprey's and Cartier's
> the pearls are dead, the silver's lead,
> while in coalmines the dross now shines
> with sapphire bright and diamond light.
>
> And every clown, like Mr Brown,
> now wears a crown in Camden Town.
> The Odeon's in Babylon
> and all the flicks have crossed the Styx.
>
> Virgins in Slough rose-garlands now
> wear on their brow though they are plain.
> Along Whitehall the guardsmen sprawl
> in waterfalls of pink champagne.
>
> And every man who drives a van
> has hooves like Pan and shaggy shanks.
> The crowd exclaims at phoenix flames
> upon the Thames, which bursts its banks.
>
> And you can hire a car of fire,
> get Phoebus' car for your mama.
> The public schools are run by fools,
> the silly dunce is king for once.

109

In Wormwood Scrubs they put nightclubs,
the prison bars become guitars,
the iron locks are cuckoo clocks,
and the police are turned to geese.

Old maiden aunts get up their chants
for all their wants just for this once.
In oyster bars they're serving stars;
no need for 'R's in any month.

Angels in mink begin to wink
from too much drink out of the sink.
The Blackpool Tower bursts into flower,
the blossoms shower in red and pink.

In Barclays Bank the cheques are blank,
no-one purloins the filthy coin,
and all their cash is turned to ash;
the jamboree is without fee.

Sweet Philomel sings a rondel
which sounds a knell for every hell.
No need to slave until the grave,
no word for grief, no word for thief.

All Balham hes and Peckham shes
do as they please and laugh with glee,
and in Torquay the sepia sea
is flowing free with eau de vie.

All debauchees will all agree
the recipe for jeux d'esprit
is always free. The Sadducee,
the Pharisee has ceased to be.

The prime motive of that song was pure fun, but a recurring theme
ran through much of the revue, that of personal identity (and you
could see *Metamorphosis*, if you wanted to look for underlying meanings, as being about identity transformed). The opening number of
Cranks consisted simply of the performers, musicians included, speaking or singing their own names in rhythmic patterns. Then they went
straight into a number called *Adrift* during which they asked

Are we poets or peasants?
Nice Christmas presents?

110

> Dancers or singers?
> Bankers? Bellringers?
> Do we belong to clubs?
> Get drunk in pubs?
> What is it that we're about?
> Where do we go when the lights go out?

Later in that number they suggested various possible identities for themselves:

> Am I Marilyn Monroe?
> Jean Cocteau?
> Marlon Brando
> or just dumb crambo?
> John Gielgud?
> Wee Georgie Wood?
> Robin Hood
> or misunderstood?
> La Traviata?
> Frank Sinatra?
> A knight of the garter
> or mere errata?

Crazy lists of names multiplied in other songs, such as *Arthur, son of Martha*, which in its first stanza listed all his brothers, sisters, aunts, uncles and cousins; in the second, all the places he visited, and in the third, commemorating his death, a hilarious collection of euphemisms for that deplored state. The identity theme never became too obtrusive; I do not remember that it was mentioned in any of the reviews, and I became aware of it myself only when playing repeatedly a recording of most of the numbers from the show. Subliminally, however, it must have helped to give *Cranks* the sense of unity in diversity that was one of its strengths: the fact that its separate parts, although varied in mood, did not strike audiences as just a random assemblage.

Once again John found himself an apt new collaborator, this time in the person of John Addison, whose music was consistently entertaining and, in one or two numbers, struck a vein of vivid imagination. The original cast included Gilbert Vernon, a dancer who had just left the Covent Garden company, and a black actor, Gordon Heath, who had sung in a Paris night club. The main experience of the other two performers, Marcia Ashton and Anthony Newley, was in singing. There were only two musicians in the first production, Anthony Bowles at the harpsichord and piano, Jack Hayward at the harp (harpsichord and harp, a definitely arty combination, but used by the composer with a light touch).

111

Cranks became a great hit, first with a small cult audience who heard of it by word of mouth, then with a wider public whose interest was at least partly aroused by reports that Princess Margaret had been to see it. She liked it enough to go three times (a fact dutifully trotted out in newspaper gossip columns on every possible occasion) and adopted its amusing young author as a friend. Following its run at the tiny Watergate, *Cranks* transferred on 1 March 1956 to the larger St Martin's Theatre, where it was given a more elaborate but still informal setting of screens and other structures, and two wind parts were added to the score. Annie Ross, then almost unknown, replaced Marcia Ashton, and Hugh Bryant took over from Gordon Heath. That theatre was available for a limited period only; according to John, managements would not believe that a long run was likely. Demand from the public remained brisk, so the revue transferred on 28 May to the Duchess Theatre, and from there on 9 July to the Lyric, Hammersmith. It also went on tour in Britain, but audiences further away from central London did not take so kindly to its sophisticated manner. For a midweek matinée at the huge Streatham Hill Theatre — hardly a suitable auditorium anyway for an intimate revue — the total audience comprised a half-dozen or so old age pensioners, admitted at reduced prices, and some actors from the resident company at the nearby Wimbledon Theatre, who received complimentary tickets. At the interval, the pensioners departed, leaving the actors in their free seats as the only spectators in the vast expanse of stalls.

Even if the London suburbs were not bowled over by *Cranks*, the fame of the show and its author spread widely. It won an award as best musical of the year. HMV recorded a long-playing disc, and extracts from the stage production were shown on BBC television. Invitations arrived to mount versions of it abroad; the languages into which it was translated ranged from Danish to Spanish. It was a bitter disappointment to John, however, that *Cranks* failed to repeat its London success when it opened, with the same cast, on Broadway on 26 November. Some people liked it very much; an enthusiastic notice in *The Saturday Review*, for instance, described it percipiently as "not the usual revue which merely strings together assorted songs and skits, but rather a concerted effort to explore human phobias and manias in much the same way as does the good modern painter, writer, and dancer." But the crucial overnight reviews in the New York papers were mixed, and the most influential of them, by Brooks Atkinson in the *New York Times*, damned it with faint praise, writing that Cranko "has a satirical manner that never comes to grips with the subject or finishes the theme, and, as a matter of fact, eliminates the theatre. It is so sophisticated that it manages to dispense with its own medium. All the players are talented and attractive."

It was just as well that John had *Cranks* to keep him occupied most of 1956, since it became necessary to postpone the big ballet he was working on for Covent Garden, when illness delayed Benjamin Britten's completion of the score he was writing for it. When John was asked early in 1954 to submit a scenario for a three-act ballet he responded by developing an idea that had been in his mind for some time, namely what he described as a "mythological fairy-tale". His intention was "to make a series of images from traditional fairy stories, linked by a thread of plot which was as important or unimportant as the audience chose to make it." The images would give opportunities for the dances he wanted to make, and thus "provide a vehicle for creative choreography rather than 'classical' pastiche, which would still have the immediate box-office appeal required." Like most people, he had been told many fairy stories when young, and when he grew up his appetite for reading a wide range of books led him to read some of the classic fairy tales with increased understanding and appreciation. For *The Prince of the Pagodas* he devised his own original story, but drew on memories of many well-known tales in the hope that people would leave the theatre saying "I'm sure I've heard that story *somewhere* before."

As usual, John insisted that his ballet should be intelligible without the need for a synopsis in the programme, but the list of scenes and characters did provide some hints for anyone still needing help in spite of the evocative familiarity of many of the narrative elements. The ballets concerned the two daughters of an aged emperor.

Kings arriving from the four corners of the earth to court the heiress, Belle Epine, are repulsed by her malicious nature and turn to her sweeter sister, Belle Rose. To soothe Belle Epine's anger at that, her doting father lends her his crown; she keeps it, thus gaining the kingdom. Belle Rose, once more neglected, sees a vision of a prince and is visited by four messengers in the shape of frogs, bringing a trunk which mysteriously opens of its own accord to reveal a jade flower. When she accepts it, the frogs fly off with her, through realms of sky, water and fire to the kingdom of the pagodas. She is courted by the prince but, through magic, can see him only in the guise of a green salamander, and runs away. Arriving home, she finds her father in a cage and all the courtiers ill-treated by their new ruler. She too is imprisoned but the salamander arrives and rescues them. In gratitude, she promises to marry him, and now he can resume his real form; all are happy except Belle Epine.

The mixture of *King Lear, Beauty and the Beast* and several other sources proved something of a muddle, but the only serious faults of the plot were that Belle Rose was too passive a character, and her father was treated too conventionally in the first act to be able to take on the tragic quality expected in the last. Those defects could have been put right, and the ballet had virtues to outweigh them.

Chief among those was its score, much the most ambitious ever written for a British ballet until then, and probably still the best. According to an account he wrote at the time, John was well advanced with his ideas about the ballet's content and style before he consulted Britten on the question of music. The first draft of the scenario was made, and John explained his ideas to John Piper, who

> understood and was excited about them. We decided in favour of relating the pagodas to the strange edifices of Steinberg and Paul Klee, and against making a pastiche of eighteenth-century chinoiserie... The scenery was to move, too, and become a part of the dance... Piper began his first drawings and, with Desmond Heeley designing the costumes, soon our ideas became real. The decor was under way, but what about the music? No composer available to me seemed to have the kind of imagination the ballet demanded. One evening I asked Britten if he had any ideas about composers, little dreaming that he would become excited enough with *Pagodas* to undertake it himself.

So John did not exactly go out to commission a score from Britain's leading composer, but he was the cause of its being written. And, as other choreographers have found (Balanchine, for instance, described a similar experience when he worked with Stravinsky on *Orpheus*), John's ideas were changed a good deal by the music. First, "the whole ballet was rediscussed, and Britten suggested various themes on which he would make variations short enough to provide the episodic dances, but which would give the work as a whole a sense of continuity."

Then they worked out together

> a sort of "shooting script" of the whole ballet, almost as if we were planning a silent film. For example:
>
> *Belle Rose enters sadly and looks off-stage to see if she is alone (short introductory bars).*
>
> *She dances her loneliness. (One minute.)*
>
> *She sees a vision of a prince dressed in green. (Slow music, to allow for smoke to spread, then quickening when she sees prince, whole time not more than four minutes.)*
>
> *The prince vanishes. (Some sort of crash, but very rapid.)*

Then Britten started to compose. As the music grew, the ballet sprang to life and, carefully as Britten had followed my script, his imagery was so strong that the entire choreography had to be revisualized... When the piano reduction of the first act was ready, I began rehearsals with the ballet company. I was nervous of misunderstanding the music: by this I mean that a piano skeleton is very different from a full orchestration, and very often when one hears the final effect one is horrified at the difference in quality between what one had imagined and the actual sound. In this case I was lucky, because Britten's descriptions of his musical intentions were so clear.

Although the music played so important a part in the work's final shape, and although many of Britten's earlier scores had been used for ballets, this was the first time the composer had written a score specially for a ballet, and he did what he described as "a lot of homework" in preparation for it. He made some research into oriental music — Japanese and Balinese — for exotic colour, and also, for better understanding of ballet's needs and possibilities, he bought and studied a complete edition of Tchaikovsky's music. That was very much to the point, since John's intention was that the choreography should take Tchaikovsky's great collaborator, Petipa, as its starting point, although

there were to be differences. Firstly, no "deaf and dumb" mime passages. Relationships of dancers to each other or to objects, or the quality of their movement, were to convey all the meaning. The classical dance was to be quite freely interspersed with acrobatics or popular dance steps as long as these were used poetically, and not merely as stunts to steal a cheap gasp from the audience; the moon would be like a white trapezist swinging in a crescent through the air, the fishes would tumble and somersault through the waves.

By the "deaf and dumb" school of mime, John meant the stereotyped conventional gestures with accepted meanings such as "mother", "but" or "I shall die" which were used in nineteenth-century ballet on the assumption that audiences, like dancers, would have the key to them. He explained that he rejected that in favour of a more kinaesthetic expression of the dancer's feelings; for instance, the way a small child wrinkles his nose in anticipation of something delicious, the way a pompous man will rock to and fro on heels and toes, or the comic dilemma of a fat woman running bumpily, arms clutching her body, to catch a bus. These kinds of movements, allied to self-explanatory relationships with people or objects, convey a situation to an audience. Actually, almost every modern choreographer adopted a similar approach; Cranko was unusual only in the lucidity with which he could explain his methods, and in the choice of older contemporaries he took for his models. On the one hand there was Balanchine, greatly influential in America and in continental Europe, but not so much followed in Britain. John's assessment was that he had "created a visual equation of musical patterns, deliberately suppressing all meaning", and his example had enriched the younger man's ballets ever since the experience of working with New York City Ballet six years earlier. More recently, John had been one of the few enthusiasts attending Martha Graham's first London season in 1954. He told an interviewer that she had

> invented a whole new system of establishing relationship of dancers (a) to each other; (b) to a prop or object; (c) to a convention in space. Sometimes she achieves an effect of violent agitation by fairly static poses, and, conversely, a feeling of tranquillity through very full, flowing movement. In my opinion, the task of the modern choreographer is to bring about a wedding of these two methods, Balanchine's and Martha Graham's.

By the time *Pagodas* reached the stage, a further big influence on Cranko's work had arrived in the form of the Bolshoi Ballet's first season at Covent Garden in October 1956. Their practice of having the women lifted and carried high above their partners' heads encouraged him to extend the inclination he had already shown to try something similar; he also echoed something of the broad, powerful effect the Russians aimed for in much of the male solo dancing. That was seen especially in the solo he made for a young soloist, Gary Burne, as King of the South in the first act of *Pagodas*, and for Burne among others in a classical pas de six in the last act. Many of the roles were given to young dancers, including Beriosova and Blair in the leads, both only twenty-four, and two girls still in their teens, Merle Park and Doreen Wells, who were later to become ballerinas. All these and several others were given dances which made more severe demands on technique than was customary in British ballet at the time, and even the supporting ensembles were pushed fairly hard. Cranko was beginning to do for Covent Garden what he had already done at the Wells: extend the general expectation of technique and, in particular, develop male dancing to become the equal of the women's.

He also brought in a theatricality generally lacking at the Royal Opera House. Even the moving decor, pagodas that regrouped themselves on the stage and opened out coloured fans like Victorian fireguards, played a part in that; so did the magically opening box

116

from which a mechanical hand appeared with the flower. The flying effects made a particularly strong impression.

Unfortunately there was one respect in which John had not been sufficiently influenced by the Bolshoi visit, or by Martha Graham: both of those expected an emotional commitment in the performers which neither the plot nor the dances of *Pagodas* brought out. Also, the style in which Cranko and Piper had conceived the designs, "sharply defined shapes in contrasted colours which . . . would make our feeling of space", did not find favour. The palace scene especially, with an orange background seen through the openings in harsh blue walls, came in for scathing comment.

All the same, *Pagodas* was a great achievement for a choreographer not yet turned thirty. Only the far more experienced Ashton in two works at Covent Garden, and Nicholas Beriozoff in *Esmeralda* for Festival Ballet, had previously attempted to create three-act ballets for major British companies. *Esmeralda* had proved something of a disaster, and Ashton in *Cinderella* and *Sylvia* had the benefit of starting with plots and music which had already proved their worth in productions elsewhere. John and his collaborators, starting from scratch, created a work that was in some respects exceptionally fine, and never less than good entertainment. It needed some second thoughts for complete success, but nothing more than would have been applied without hesitation if it had been a musical in the commercial theatre. Unfortunately Covent Garden schedules (committed far in advance to accommodate two resident companies, opera and ballet, with their quotas of new productions, revivals and guest stars) proved too inflexible. There were a few changes in the choreography the following season, but that was all. Ninette de Valois thought highly of the work, both musically and choreographically, and recognized the need for some revision, but did not manage to bring it about. And so *Pagodas* was allowed to disappear. It had a respectable quota of twenty-three performances at home during 1957, and ten more on an American tour, but there were only five performances at Covent Garden in 1958, and three in each of the next two years. Probably a lack of enthusiasm for the work in New York, and the troubles John ran into during that period, helped diminish any chance there might have been for polishing the work, and then John's departure for Germany ruled out the possibility. After 1960, *Pagodas* vanished entirely from the London stage, except for a couple of excerpts given at galas. De Valois described the circumstances of its loss as one of the major tragedies of the English ballet scene.

Even on the first night, there was something unexpected and sad about the almost apologetic tone of John's little speech of thanks for

117

the applause, explaining that the ballet had been made chiefly for the younger dancers. That should have been cause for pride, not apology. With both *Cranks* and *Pagodas* behind him to clinch the success of many earlier works, he was featured in *The Sunday Times* as the subject of their weekly Portrait Gallery with the summing up that "certainly he has arrived". But arrival did not mean staying still; he was already planning to do the choreography for a musical, based on Max Beerbohm's classic comedy *Zuleika Dobson*, and after that to write a musical himself in collaboration with John Addison, followed probably by another revue. Meanwhile there had already been an invitation, even before the premiere of *Pagodas*, to stage it also for the ballet company of Teatro alla Scala, Milan. It went on there in May, with Beriosova, Blair and Julia Farron (the first Belle Epine) as guests, and Britten, as at Covent Garden, conducting his own score for the premiere. However, the ballet did not stay in the repertory of La Scala; its importance was that it led to an invitation to return a year later and stage another work.

That further work was *Romeo and Juliet*, which was to prove as important in his career as *Pagodas*. Between them, these two ballets unlocked the door to the most successful time of John's life, his Stuttgart period. But there were to be further ups and downs before that happened, including a time of much discontent and distress.

Having produced his first three-act ballet at Covent Garden did not bring fresh chances there. Rather the opposite; in fact, it was to be almost three years before he had the chance to make another new work for the resident company, and that in turn proved to be almost the end of his creative connection with them. There were also two commissions to come from what had been the Sadler's Wells Theatre Ballet, which during 1957 was taken under the management of Covent Garden because the Sadler's Wells governors wanted to concentrate all their resources on opera. To confuse the issue, that company and the former Sadler's Wells Ballet were both renamed the Royal Ballet under the terms of a charter granted in October 1956, but in spite of the shared nomenclature they remained, at least for a time, clearly distinguishable and separate bodies.

The first of the two remaining creations for the touring company was first given on 26 December 1957, the opening of their first short London season at Covent Garden. It was an almost unmitigated disaster. Called *The Angels*, it used a theme that was attacked at the time as too literary, although with hindsight it can be seen as holding as much potential as *Harlequin in April*. A group of people with contrasted temperaments (categorized in the cast list as startled, morbid, strident, terrified, lyrical and vigorous) were seen

118

surrounded by a chorus of angels; finally one of the human characters was picked out for immortality by being hoisted aloft as a star. Almost nothing about the work was liked. Richard Arnell, the composer of *Harlequin in April*, wrote a score for *The Angels* which was dismissed as heavy, old-fashioned and unimaginative. Desmond Heeley's decor of ladders, reaching the full height of the stage, was thought too much like the design of scaffolding he had recently made for a ballet by Kenneth MacMillan, *Solitaire*. There was a resemblance, but the *Solitaire* setting was a painted backcloth, whereas *The Angels* had real ladders with dancers climbing up and down them, sometimes opening their arms to spread enormous wings (that brought criticism, too, for resembling an effect in *Pagodas*). Looking now at photographs of *The Angels*, it looks rather handsome, but at the time there was an almost unanimous opinion that it was a total flop. The choreography was dismissed out of hand, even though one or two dancers were admired in it, notably Donald Britton as the chosen mortal and Clover Roope, hitherto entirely unknown, as the lyrical one. Note, incidentally, that it was vigour rather than any more obviously poetic quality that brought immortality; I am reminded of that *Sunday Times* portrait of Cranko which referred to "the charmed luck that often attends those of driving energy and talent". This time the luck had deserted him, and although *The Angels* undoubtedly was a bitter disappointment, the harshness of its critical reception perhaps arose partly from the disappointment of high hopes.

The bitterness for John must have been increased by the fact that he had taken a theme close to his heart; that he had again tried to give chances to a young cast and to bring a strongly theatrical element into ballet. For the dancers, too, it was an unhappy experience: the first time they had appeared at Covent Garden, and under the proud title of the Royal Ballet, too — as Clover Roope remembered it, "there was this cavernous space, all this red plush, and at the end, boos. We felt so ashamed, because we felt somehow we had failed him and his ideas, failed to make them clear." But the trouble was not any inadequacy on the part of the dancers. The real problem was that, with layer upon layer of meaning, which he could discuss in fascinating detail if asked, John did not find a way of making it intelligible to his audience.

There was worse to come. Only a few weeks later, on 13 February 1958, John's musical *Keep Your Hair On* opened at the Apollo Theatre in Shaftesbury Avenue. Fourteen performances later, it closed. Great hopes had been built on it to give a new look to British musical shows by using native resources instead of importing ideas from Broadway, by developing the comic tradition of Chaplin, Grock and Mack Sennett, and by implying a serious theme in a contemporary setting beneath the comedy. The idea was to show an idealistic but muddle-headed young man, totally bemused by the world and incapable of decision. The plot embodying that theme, however, proved more mundane. The indecisiveness revealed itself in always finding some excuse in political activities to defer fixing a date for his intended marriage. Mabel, his betrothed, consequently took up with a shy foreigner who lacked a work permit (a private joke, because the role was written for Erik Mork, a Danish actor who had been in the successful Copenhagen run of *Cranks*; John had become very fond of him and through this part was able to secure a work permit for him to prolong a stay in England — unfortunately not for long, as things turned out). After further changes of intention on both sides, Mabel ended up with the foreigner who, to everyone's astonishment, turned out to be a king in disguise.

The reviewer in *The Times* asked what there was to choose between this "and all the other stories that have gradually brought our native musical comedy into contempt?" He thought the lyrics had an occasional witty line, praised the energy of the actors, the good intentions of the author and the lively, often expressive movement, but was apparently so little impressed by the music that he did not even mention it. The scenery was dismissed as "amusing" — with quotation marks around the word to emphasize the irony intended.

That scenery was designed by a young man then known as a photographer but not yet as a designer, Anthony Armstrong-Jones (later Lord Snowdon). Years later, he recorded his gratitude that John had been "prepared to experiment and give opportunities to unknowns." His setting used giant photographs to provide quick-changing, non-realistic backgrounds; an original process, which he later described as "a combination of huge, grainy semi-abstract blow-ups and extremely complicated mechanical and electrical gadgets. All very self-indulgent, and nothing worked on the first night." But that was only one of the reasons why the gallery jeered and booed, and reviewers condemned the show.

Interviewed about the flop, John declared himself ready to fight back:

> From now on, I intend to go my own way, even at the risk of appealing only to a minority public. When I am working on a new ballet or show, I have certain feelings of what I want to do and, so far as I am concerned, they don't work out if I try to sugar the pill. Once an author tries to please the public (known

rather frighteningly in the theatre as Them), he ends up by not
pleasing anyone.

Unfortunately, in the heat of the moment when the show closed,
John also made some bitter remarks to another journalist, which
were given prominence in the *News Chronicle* (a newspaper generally
well respected). He was reported as having said "I hate ballet. In this
country, it's run like a civil service. It's a hundred years out of date.
They expect you to sit on your behind at the Wells for £14 a week
and turn out masterpieces every year. But I'll have to go back to it
— for a while, I suppose."

That caused hard feelings, and when an interviewer from one of
the specialist magazines, *The Dancing Times*, quoted him in similar
terms, John wrote to the editor complaining that his real meaning
had been misrepresented. He explained that

the very nature of ballet companies is such that there is not
enough work to keep a choreographer fully employed, and I
have therefore turned to other forms of theatre between ballets.

A large ballet company is, of necessity, a complicated and ex-
pensive hierarchy, depending largely on old ballets (i.e.
established classics) to maintain a classical standard, and
because they are good box-office. The number of new productions is therefore limited to about three or four a year, and if
a choreographer gets one of these three or four ballets to do, it
is all he can hope for in that year. For this one ballet, the
Sadler's Wells is able to pay very liberally, but looked at in
terms of a weekly salary it is very low. Added to this, it is very
difficult for a choreographer to sit on his bottom for a year and
then produce a masterpiece. He must find some means of
experimenting in order that, when his turn comes to
choreograph a ballet, he has a certain amount of experimenting
behind him which he can consolidate.

As you will see, this is a plain statement of fact applying to
almost any ballet company in the world, and in no way an
attack on the Sadler's Wells — in fact I have often discussed
this dilemma with Dame Ninette de Valois, and she very keenly
appreciates the problems, as she is herself a choreographer.

Being able to explain rationally the cause of his difficulties did not,
unfortunately, make them any easier to bear, and the angry way he
first expressed it revealed his true feeling.

John had another cause for being upset: Herbert had returned to
London during the summer of 1957. Now aged 62, he busied himself
with the stories and manuscripts already mentioned, and involved

himself also in setting up a limited company, Oknarc Ltd, to receive John's royalties, with consequent tax advantages. One of the notebooks contains a list of necessary purchases ("1 filing cabinet... rubber stamp pad... letterheads" and so on) for this. But Herbert was dying, and knew it. Characteristically he made a joke about it when he ran into John Wright, the puppeteer, in South Africa before coming back to London. He said that the doctors told him he might live longer "if I give up smoking, drinking and women. I'm trying to cut down on the cigarettes." During his last illness, he occupied himself also with writing the notebooks and typescripts mentioned earlier. He died in 1958, on 6 September, of heart failure.

Luckily, although the Royal Ballet was making no use of his services for the moment, John had other work to occupy and distract him. For the Aldeburgh Festival, which Britten directed in the village where he lived, he was to stage a double bill of Monteverdi's *Ballo delle Ingrate*, which demanded a rather formal style, and Poulenc's *Les Mamelles de Tirésias*, which gave him scope for comic invention: the climax of the opera is when the two balloons which have the title roles come adrift and float up, out of sight. Premiered on 13 June 1958, the production was reasonably well liked, even though the composer's illness meant that a late replacement had to be found for his intended participation, with Britten, accompanying the work on two pianos.

The next month saw a far more important occasion for John's career when the Ballet of La Scala, Milan, in a joint venture with Teatro le Fenice, Venice (which provided the orchestra), presented a new production by him of Prokofiev's *Romeo and Juliet* in a new open-air amphitheatre, Teatro Verde, on the island of S. Giorgio, Venice. Surrounded by trees, the huge stage allowed plenty of space for dancing but little opportunity for theatrical effects. The setting by Nicola Benois (son of the famous Alexander Benois, and resident designer at La Scala) was magnificent but allowed only slight modifications from one scene to another. So everything depended on the expressive quality of the dancing and gestures.

At that time Ashton, in a production for the Royal Danish Ballet, and Serge Lifar, in an abbreviated version at the Paris Opéra, were the only Western choreographers who had tackled the Prokofiev score, and almost everybody's concept of it was dominated by the Bolshoi Ballet's production, widely disseminated on film and also the great hit of the company's London season. John took some ideas from Lavrovsky's Bolshoi version, especially in the tragic intensity he tried to give to Lady Capulet's wild grief at Tybalt's death. That role had been played for the Bolshoi by a former ballerina, Elena

Iliushenko, who had stayed on after retirement age to play such older parts. Like most people, John had been bowled over by her performance, and he had the idea of asking another famous dancer, long retired, to take the part in his production. This was Lubov Tchernicheva, by then almost sixty-eight, formerly Diaghilev's ballet mistress, who made her name mostly in mimed parts during the thirties. Working with her awoke the interest which John showed all through his Stuttgart days in making roles for older dancers. At the other extreme, he chose the twenty-one-year-old Carla Fracci as his first Juliet (the more experienced Vera Colombo also took the role). A dark-haired beauty who had only just been promoted to be principal dancer, Fracci had a lyrical quality and a warmth that communicated directly to audiences.

Although made for the open-air theatre, the ballet was given five months later at La Scala, but did not survive beyond that season. The main benefit of the experience was that when John came to mount the ballet for his Stuttgart company four years later, he could build upon this earlier attempt instead of starting from scratch.

Less than a month after *Romeo*, his next premiere was due on 25 August, on the opening programme of a new company formed to present a dozen creations by the same number of choreographers during the Edinburgh Festival. Two old friends from Sadler's Wells were in charge: Peggy van Praagh as dance director and Charles Mackerras as music director. The latter had settled upon a large chamber ensemble of fifteen players, and all the scores had to be chosen accordingly. John's first idea was to make a ballet to Schoenberg's *Pierrot Lunaire*, a landmark of modern music, but the composer's estate would not allow that. The alternative he chose was completely different: the smart, bright, frivolous sextet for wind instruments and piano by Poulenc. To this, he invented a slight theme of a husband bored with his wife, who flirts indiscreetly at a party and sends the other guests off in a mad whirl of gossip. (Some people thought the theme superficial, but John's own social life was never marked by discretion and was soon to demonstrate the more serious effects of gossip). Each choreographer was allowed to invite one or more guest stars to take part in the season; John brought Fracci to play the wife, and gave the other leading roles to two dancers from Denmark who were appearing also in a ballet by John Taras on the next programme, Henning Kronstam as the husband and Kirsten Simone as the sweet young thing. *Secrets* had a simple, colourful setting and handsome dresses by John Piper, and although nobody ever thought it an important enough work to revive, it pleased the festival audiences.

All the same, John was intensely miserable at this time. His father's death, the apparent stagnation of his career with the Royal Ballet, the failure of *Keep Your Hair On*, and his own lack of any stable emotional relationship combined to make him want to get out of Britain. There were times when it could seem that John, believing himself not accepted, was almost consciously trying to provoke a situation where he would have to go. John Taras, who had been one of the other choreographers for the Edinburgh venture, was ballet master of the International Ballet of the Marquis de Cuevas, and through him John was invited to make a ballet for that company. They had a London season during September, and when that was finished, John went on tour with them in France. Taras tried to cheer him up and drove him from one engagement to the next, but was not able to do as John would have liked and obtain a permanent connection with the company for him. The new work, *Cat's Cradle*, was given on the first night, 28 October 1958, of the company's Paris season at the Théâtre des Champs-Elysées. With music by John Addison and designs by Desmond Heeley, it was another of John's episodic, revue-like ballets, with both comic and mysterious passages. Some of the dancers were much impressed by it, but it did not make a great impact on the Parisian public.

After that burst of activity (three new ballets, one of them in three acts, within about three months) came a fallow period professionally. He was as full of ideas as ever but unable to do much about realizing them. His only productions during the next seven months were revivals, this time at Covent Garden, of *Harlequin in April* and (for a single performance at a gala) of *Tritsch Tratsch*, followed by a polka for a television programme. However, his name was soon front-page news again in a most unpleasant way.

The story first appeared in the London evening papers on 8 April 1959. The account in the *Evening Standard*, under the headline "John Cranko fined", read:

> John Cranko, the 31-year-old choreographer who achieved fame with his revue *Cranks*, was fined £10 at Marlborough Street today when he admitted persistently importuning men for an immoral purpose. P.C. John Duncan who arrested him in Britten Street, Chelsea, early this morning after 20 minutes' observation, said that Cranko had been drinking but was not drunk. Cranko, a single man whose address was given as Alderney Street, Westminster, told the magistrate that he would not offend again. He said that before his arrest he had been drinking a mixture, mostly of wine and whisky. Mr

124

Wilson warned him: "If you do anything of this sort again, you
will most certainly land in prison."

The account in the *Evening News* was so similar that it was clear both
papers must have taken the story from a news agency report. The
daily papers next morning carried similar reports, in some instances
much shortened, and with one exception they relegated the story to
an inside page. The *Daily Express*, however, put it on the front page
under the heading "Trouble all the way, says Cranko". To the bare
facts printed elsewhere they added the detail that the police constable
had been in plain clothes when he made the arrest at about midnight.
They had also sent a reporter to interview John, and described how
"bachelor Cranko, in cabbage gréen sweater, talked in his flat in
Alderney Street, Pimlico, a setting almost as weird as the birdcage
and chicken-wire scenery of *Cranks* which Princess Margaret saw
three times". Under a cross-head "His need", they quoted John's explanation of the circumstances: "I needed cheering up and some
friends asked me round. They made it as jolly an evening as they
could. But when you are depressed nothing cheers you up. So many
troubles. I'm still getting over a broken love affair. Bills, bills, bills.
And April is tax month."

Apart from the insinuating description of his clothes and bachelor
quarters, that report was not unsympathetic, but to put it so prominently on the front page of a national paper might have seemed excessive. The explanation was to be found inside the paper, on page
eight, which carried a long article by John Deane Potter under the
heading "Isn't it about time someone said this... plainly and
frankly?" It began:

> I read with dismay the news yesterday that a 31 year old South
> African called John Cranko was fined £10 at Marlborough
> Street police court. It was not the fine, it was the man and the
> offence. Because he pleaded guilty to a crime which has become
> known as the West End vice.

The phrase, actually, was not one that was ever heard or read outside
the *Express*, but John had been caught in the crossfire of a political
controversy. In September 1957, a Home Office committee with Sir
John Wolfenden as its chairman had reported recommending
changes in the laws relating to homosexuality and prostitution. A
Street Offences Bill giving effect to its proposals on prostitution was
introduced the following year and passed into law in the summer of
1959, but many politicians were afraid of coming under suspicion or
disfavour if seen to be supporting the report's recommendation that
homosexual behaviour between consenting adults in private should

125

no longer be a criminal offence. It took nearly ten years before that reached the stature book, and the *Express* was campaigning strongly against reform.

The report had mentioned a widely held belief that homosexuality was peculiar to particular professions or classes, or to the intelligentsia. It contradicted that opinion and said that homosexuals were found among people of all callings and classes. Opponents of reform disputed that (and the secrecy forced upon most homosexuals at that time by a harsh criminal law helped to hide the facts). Consequently, the *Express* article went on:

> Cranko is the latest on the list of famous stage names who have been found guilty of this squalid behaviour. He is a talented man of the theatre. He was the co-author of the spectacularly successful revue *Cranks*.
>
> The private lives of people, whether they are a brilliant ballet designer and author like Cranko or an ordinary office worker on the 6.15 should, according to the Wolfenden report, be their own business. But this question is public business. It has become a sour common-place in the West End theatre that unless you are a member of an unpleasant freemasonry your chances of success are often lessened. For the theatre is far too full of people belonging to a secret brotherhood.
>
> Most of them are not tortured misfits. They do not want psychiatric treatment or cures. They live complacently in their own remote world with its shrill enthusiasms. *But they are evil...*

The article went on at length about the personal and the professional power of these "evil" men, corrupting innocents who wanted to get on, and foisting a false set of values on the public. It insisted that "these are dangerous men... they should be driven from their positions of theatrical power".

There was a reply the next day from the playwright John Osborne, making no mention of John Cranko and dealing only with the general argument. The same was true of a selection of letters printed some days later. But the damage had been done.

As the *Express* mentioned, Cranko was not the first prominent man to be convicted of a homosexual offence, and he was not to be the last. But the Royal Ballet is part of the Establishment, ruled by various boards of governors or directors all of immense respectability. They were doubtless aware of other homosexual men at Covent Garden in more exalted and powerful positions, but discretion was important; scandal had to be avoided. In John's case, the scandal was made more embarrassing by the fact that references to him in gossip columns thereafter tended to mention his bachelor state and his colourful dress (always a suspicious sign in those days). They also kept on identifying him as the author of *Cranks*, to which was added, as automatically as any reflex action, a reference to Princess Margaret's admiration for that work.

Neither then nor later did Princess Margaret turn against him. She not only admired his work but liked his company (even in his times of depression he could still be a highly entertaining companion). He on his side was naturally flattered by her friendship, enjoyed the good food and the fun at her supper parties. But there were undoubtedly some people at the Palace who thought him an unsuitable person to be included in her social circle and were relieved when he left England.

No immediate effect on his opportunities for work resulted from the court case and the unfavourable publicity. He was already preparing a ballet for Covent Garden, to be given later that year, and had also agreed to create a second work for Ballet Rambert. Given in their London season on 1 June, this was *La Reja*, an atmospheric evocation of Goya's Spain to music by Scarlatti. Mysteriously cloaked and masked figures watched the dances in a handsome setting by Carl Toms, another designer discovered by John for ballet. About the same time, John mentioned publicly that he was planning a successor to *Cranks*.

For a concert tour in their native land, Rhodesia, that summer by Royal Ballet soloists Merle Park and Gary Burne, John set a pas de deux, *Pièce d'occasion*, to music by Delibes. At the beginning of the new season, in September, he added solos and a coda, and the same couple danced it on tour with the Royal Ballet, although its first British performance was given by Carla Fracci and John Gilpin in a Festival Ballet gala at the Royal Festival Hall: the only time John worked with that company.

His most important premiere of the autumn, however, was *Antigone*. The programme credits described the plot as having been freely adapted from Sophocles, but in fact John had worked mainly from a play by the French dramatist Racine, *La Thébaïde, ou Les Frères ennemis*, which in turn derived from Euripides. The exact literary source is less important than the fact that in picking this model (the fruit of his wide and eager reading, since few people outside France are familiar with Racine's work, let alone such a minor early play) he had found himself a wider canvas and one much more amenable to choreographic treatment. Instead of concentrating on Antigone's defiance of the ban on burying her brother Polynices, he showed the family and political quarrels that led to the ban. The action still dealt with the acute moral crisis of the heroine, movingly played by

Svetlana Beriosova, but it carried also implications about the abuse of power and the causes of war that struck a chord in those days of Aldermaston marches for nuclear disarmament. The wider action also enabled the choreographer to provide outstanding roles for the two brothers: the conniving Etiocles (played by Gary Burne) and the mob-orator Polynices (David Blair). It was a bizarre mistake, when Rudolf Nureyev joined the Royal Ballet, to cast him in the former part, presumably because it had more jumps, rather than the latter where his expressive gifts would have been displayed. Once again John wrote big parts for older dancers, too: Julia Farron as Jocasta, killing herself in a vain attempt to shock her sons into sense, and Michael Somes as the usurping Creon.

John had a score specially written by Mikis Theodorakis, who at thirty-four already had some experience writing for ballet and films, although he had not then won his present international reputation. Theodorakis, explaining that he and John had chosen the subject because they "felt that ancient Greek tragedy is terribly modern in feeling", said they had tried to interpret it

> in the most modern manner, and in writing the score I've aimed at writing music for dancing and not symphonic music.... Both Cranko and I have broken away from tradition. For instance, the Chorus, instead of commenting upon the action, play an active part in the story, and Cranko has tried to create a truly plastic interpretation of the story. His choreography is dramatic and virile, and we have both attempted to make the action move along, without pauses, to its dramatic climax.

It was harsh, powerful music that supported the action strongly, and the stark designs introduced a new talent to the theatre, the Mexican painter Rufino Tamayo. Besides the influence of those gifted collaborators, another man of the theatre had a major effect on the way *Antigone* turned out. That was Jerome Robbins, whose company Ballets: USA gave its first London season while Cranko was rehearsing his creation. The vivid expressiveness of Robbins's choreography and the cool, relaxed excellence of his dancers won admiration on all sides. John went repeatedly to see them: at the matinée on their last day he speculated how he might get in to see the sold-out performance that night, and even joked about the practicability of hiding in one of the lavatories between shows. Under Robbins's influence he changed his own ballet from day to day. The most obvious example is that Beriosova's role, originally choreographed as a classical part using pointwork, gradually came down to be done in soft shoes, but more important was the sense of commitment built into the whole ballet.

Nobody could say there was anything committed about his next ballet, *Sweeney Todd*, created for the Royal Ballet's touring company and first given at Stratford-upon-Avon in December. He drew enthusiastically from the old theatrical tradition of gory and somewhat farcical melodrama to tell the story of the "demon barber of Fleet Street" in Victorian London whose customers had a habit of disappearing, while his neighbour Mrs Lovett was noted for the succulence of her meat pies. Among the comic incidentals were a chorus of policemen, apparently modelled on the Keystone Kops, and a table that walked from spot to spot thanks to someone hidden beneath. Donald Britton was allowed a whole-heartedly bloodthirsty manner in the title part and, once again, several young dancers were brought to prominence. Again, too, John had found an unknown designer, Alix Stone, who devised scenery and costumes in the style of the old Victorian "tuppence coloured" toy theatres; and Malcolm Arnold's score matched the choreography in its mixture of eerie and lighter passages. If the mood had been in John's favour at the time, the ballet would have been more warmly greeted, but although popular on tour it again received a cool welcome in London. *Sweeney* was not a great work, but it was fun.

It also turned out to be John's farewell as a resident choreographer with the Royal Ballet, although he retained the title for just over another year, covering the whole of 1960. It was a year in which he had not a single new ballet to make at home or abroad. The early months were spent working on *New Cranks*, a sequel that failed completely to match the quality or the success of its predecessor. It opened in mid-April at Brighton, a town often used for trying out a production on its way to London, and moved, towards the end of the month, to the Lyric Theatre, Hammersmith, where the original *Cranks* had played for a while: a theatre outside the main entertainment centre of London but with a good reputation and established traditions. The writing this time was less inspired. One couplet noted at the time as indicating its banality was

> I feel so marmaladed
> I must be getting jaded.

David Lee's music was not much admired, and there was a good deal of booing on the first night; the professional weekly *The Stage* wondered whether that was provoked by the excessive applause from some of John's friends or admirers. Whatever the reason, the show's death throes were not unduly prolonged.

Disappointment at this exacerbated John's gloom and perhaps caused him to muff his next commitment. This was to direct the premiere of Britten's new opera *A Midsummer Night's Dream*, on the occasion of the opening of a rebuilt and enlarged Jubilee Hall at Aldeburgh, where Britten lived and ran his own summer festival. The event was thus doubly important to Britten, who had devoted to it the months of careful planning that customarily went into his creations, in particular those that involved collaboration. This time Britten and his close friend Peter Pears had themselves adapted the libretto from Shakespeare's play; Piper was the designer. John, beset with other problems, arrived in Aldeburgh later than the punctilious Britten would have wished, and without having made himself acquainted with the music or even the libretto. Britten found that unforgivable. He was famed among those who knew him for the abruptness and finality with which he sometimes severed friendships of close and long standing, and that happened with John.

He did stage the opera, because there was no time left for making other arrangements. His robust comic invention for Bottom and his colleagues was enjoyed, but there was a general disappointment that the romance and subtle humour had been lost. That production was dropped immediately after its festival performance at Aldeburgh. When the opera was given at Covent Garden the following spring, it was in a new staging by John Gielgud, and the opera did not appear again at Aldeburgh for many years, when once more it had an entirely new treatment.

The rift with Britten was yet a further upset in John's increasingly precarious emotional life. It was also eventually the cause of *Pagodas* being lost altogether, because John came round to the thought that some cuts and alterations were needed, but felt unable to ask the composer for them. That was some years later, when he was thinking of reviving it in Stuttgart. It was *The Prince of the Pagodas* that actually got John to Stuttgart only a few months after the break with Britten.

The ballet company in Stuttgart was then directed by Nicolas Beriozoff, Svetlana Beriosova's father. He customarily (and contrary to usual German practice) brought in other choreographers to supplement his own productions, and readily accepted Svetlana's suggestion to have John mount *Pagodas*. It was also Svetlana who advised John to make himself known to Fritz Höver, a local man who ran the Noverre Society, a club for the Stuttgart Ballet's audience. According to Höver's account, John came to see him straight from the airport, before even going to the theatre, and asked to be briefed in detail on the company and its internal politics.

Only one incident marred the initial production. The company's leading woman, Xenia Palley, had been cast to play Belle Rose, but came to John during rehearsals and said "It's not my style", with the expectation that he would change the choreography to meet her wishes. His reply was "I'm sorry, but it's my style, so perhaps we had better find another dancer for the part" — which he did: the most junior of the women soloists, Micheline Faure, who was inexperienced and, from photographs, seems to have been quite unlike the tall elegant Beriosova, but was generally thought to have done well in the role.

The ballet was a great success with the Stuttgart audience and led the general director of the Stuttgart theatres, Dr Schäfer, to invite John to become director of the ballet in succession to Beriozoff. Accounts of exactly how this happened vary slightly but the general outline is clear enough. Fritz Höver says that it was Schäfer's then deputy, Badenhausen, who was chiefly concerned to replace Beriozoff, thinking that he had given as much as he could to the company. The working patterns of German ballet are different from those in most countries; each state of the Federal Republic, and many of the larger cities, have their own theatres, and it is not un-common for ambitious choreographers and directors to move from one to another, while the more ambitious managements for their part are always looking out for any potential recruit who might strengthen their fame. On the other hand, it is rare for the change-over to come in the middle of a season, which is what happened in this instance.

On the strength of what John had confided in him about his dif-ficulties in London, in his private life and in his limited prospects with the Royal Ballet, Höver let Badenhauser know that John might not be unwilling to stay in Stuttgart if invited. Schäfer, to whom this was conveyed, would hardly believe it at first, thinking there could be no chance to lure away so bright a talent, but he was persuaded to try. His account of their conversations is that John asked him "Are you serious, or are you just saying this?" and explained that he had already thought of coming to work in Germany, because the great waves of ballet history, moving from France and Italy to Russia, from Russia to England, had passed by, leaving Germany as virgin soil, waiting to be opened up. He had doubts, however, about the propriety of taking another man's job, but Schäfer was insistent and spoke to Beriozoff who, after some remonstrance, agreed there was no point in his staying if he no longer had the confidence of the director.

Among the motives that prompted John to accept the offer was his observation of the great possibilities offered by the German theatre system. He also said that he had been influenced by an occasion not long before when, full of doubt about what best to do for his career, he had come into a studio and seen a girl putting her feet into the rosin-box. That familiar act of preparation made him realize, with a rush of sentiment, that ballet was where his heart lay. On returning to London, he talked it over with de Valois, who was at first angry at the thought of his leaving but, after reflection, told him yes, he should take it, then he would have two companies, because he would always be welcome back to the Royal Ballet.

There was something else behind the decision to accept. What John told a *New York Times* interviewer much later is so revealing and unflattering that it has a ring of truth to it, however much he may have been exaggerating: "I'd lost confidence in myself. I'd atrophied from disuse. I finally took the job believing I could build a repertory and a company with ballets borrowed from Balanchine, Ashton, Robbins and others. I went to Stuttgart in the end not out of artistic need, but to exist."

It all happened very quickly. *The Prince of Pagodas* had its Stuttgart premiere on 6 November 1960. On 16 January 1961, ten weeks and a day later, John took up his new appointment. To the end of his life, London remained his home according to his entry in *Who's Who?*. But his London years, a third of his life, were over. He had not much more than twelve years left to bring about what was dubbed the Stuttgart "ballet miracle".

AMONG FRIENDS

JOHN Cranko always wanted to make friends of his collaborators, and collaborators of his friends. The former is more easily understandable than the latter. Even if many people, at the end of their working day, are glad to leave the office, shop, factory — or even theatre — and go home to a different set of faces, the nature of John's work enforced intimacy: using other people's bodies as the material of his art, needing other people's talents (as musicians, designers, ballet masters, or whatever) to help realize his own ideas. Even so, some people would have been glad to withdraw into a nest of privacy for part of the day. That was not his way. Ideas were for sharing, discussing, changing, developing. His conversation was never about the past, always the present or the future. The habit he formed as a boy, of grabbing anyone available and trying out his thoughts on them, persisted all his life: he "talks to everyone when he gets an idea", was how Alan Beale described it during one of the Stuttgart Ballet's American tours.

So if you worked with him, the relationship did not stop once the rehearsal or conference was over; it spilled over into life outside. Equally, and more unusually, anyone he met might be seized upon to join in. He had a belief "in the potential of everyone to have unique qualities which want to come out if only they are given a chance", and he wanted whenever he could to give them that chance. Hence the number of other choreographers, or designers, or outstanding dancers who began their careers with him. They went further than they might otherwise have done, partly because he saw potentialities in them which they had never imagined for themselves, and partly because he became so enthusiastic about any new discovery that they were fired to try harder than they would otherwise have done.

Not that he relied on flattery. When he invited Jürgen Rose to do his first ballet designs for the Stuttgart *Romeo and Juliet*, he started by explaining his ideas for the ballet, and when he saw the first sketches he was delighted. Beautiful, he said; just what I wanted. Whereupon Rose took great trouble over his working drawings, and was shocked by John's response, which was to fly into an absolute rage, rip them across and stamp on them. The explanation was that the original

133

concept had lost its spontaneity in the development, and in John's eyes that ruined everything. When Rose went back to his task with this new insight, he produced the designs that have been in successful use ever since, and his own view of the experience was that it changed his life.

But the process was never a one-way thing; John gained immensely from the collaboration, again and again. In the case of *Romeo*, to take only a minor instance, the carnival scene took on a character unlike that of any other production from having a German designer who based it on the German "Fasching" carnivals.

John's confidence in others also enabled him to delegate responsibility, and thus save himself for what he really needed to do. His faith in them was complete, and if it turned out that they could not do what was necessary, they had to be replaced but there was no malice or recrimination; nor was he interested in reasons or excuses. The most complex of such relationships was with Anne Woolliams, when she became his ballet mistress and chief assistant. Her temperament was in many ways the opposite of his, so combining their qualities for one joint purpose was a source of strength. But because they were both stong-minded and ambitious, they quarrelled too; they had fierce rows after which he would declare "I hate her, loathe her". One reason for that was that he recognized and did not like his own dependence on her. She had to do the unpleasant jobs that troubled his conscience: for instance, telling people if they had to be sacked. He found that too difficult, and questioned Frank Tait about how he ran an organization he was in charge of. "What do you do with a psychiatrist who's no good?", John asked, and when given the answer, "I sack him", his response was to ask "How can you *do* that?" In the last resort, the decision that somebody must go was his, but Anne herself commented that he could shut his mind to something he did not want to see. So he hated her, but at the same time loved her, for what she did.

He had a gift for education as well as inspiration, and that included self-education. The chance to learn always fascinated him; discovering on one occasion that Margaret Scott's husband, a research scientist, was going to Munich to visit an institute of behavioural studies, John dropped a rehearsal in order to accompany him. His ambitions were not just to do something new, but to base his work firmly on the discoveries of others: "to rediscover all the things that have been forgotten, and then go on to find things that were never discovered before." His own gift for teaching sprang partly from that knowledge, for instance in his lecture-demonstrations where, because he understood the work of his predecessors, and because his own

134

choreography was based on something more than instinct, he could show the public exactly why this step was used, and not that, or why a lift came at a particular point in the music rather than any other. He knew the value of a wide background; when he achieved his aims for the reorganization of the Stuttgart ballet school, he still wanted gifted pupils to have the opportunity of a scholarship to the Royal Ballet School in London: "It's important to have a year away from the family, new experiences, new influences."

In the early Stuttgart days, Marcia Haydée recalls, the learning process between John and his dancers was reciprocal: "We used to sit for hours, talking about how to build a company, how to develop dancers." She recognizes how "we all developed with him, we were handmade by him". They were also *chosen* by him; he knew exactly what kind of dancer he wanted — those who could "draw the public into them, not 'radiate' and sell themselves". That choice was a contributory factor towards the way he managed to make them grow without encouraging them to develop swollen egos: that, and the respect they had for his ability. Again, it was Marcia who commented "He doesn't direct through fear but through love. No one in the company is afraid of him. But when he walks into a class there's a sudden and complete silence." In fact, although they were not in awe of him, the dancers, in Fritz Höver's phrase "made too much a god of him. He did not want that, he was *immer menschlich* — always a man." So at dress rehearsals of his ballets he would make Höver sit in a box with him and ask him what he liked, what he disliked.

John concerned himself with all aspects of his dancers' lives: he was delighted when they became the highest paid in Germany, for instance, largely as a result of his constant nagging on their behalf. (He did not receive a vast salary himself: in 1968 it was the equivalent of $11,250 or about £4700, plus $1250 for each of three months he spent in Munich, although of course he continued to earn royalties on productions for other companies.) He wanted his dancers to take care of themselves — one remembers a dramatic lecture about the evils of drugs, which actually he never used. John had a great gift for putting a newcomer immediately at ease. Ashley Killar recalled arriving in Stuttgart to join the company, after a delayed train journey through the snow, and being told he would find Herr Cranko in the rehearsal hall. It was one of the final rehearsals for *Romeo*, but when he

> wandered in, very lost and "green" (straight from school!), John stopped the orchestra and came to greet me with all the warmth in the world. He didn't know me at all but must have sensed my bewilderment. He got one of the other dancers to

135

look after me and then went back to his rehearsal. The whole episode lasted for less than a minute, but I will never forget the impression that greeting made on me. I felt part of the company from the very first day.

One thing John insisted on was that "You must not remind dancers of their faults. Dancers are deathly afraid of their bodies. People who have never been dancers can never know what it is to look in the classroom mirror at this frail thing and think 'I have to make it work'. They can't call in the man from Steinway to fix the instrument. They *are* the instrument." As Marcia commented, dancers already know whatever is wrong — "the feet, the line, things like that". John gave her the confidence she lacked by "wanting me to do all the roles, creating the things for me. Because I admired him so much, I said well, if this man is doing everything for me, it's because I must have something. And he always gave me things to do when I wasn't quite ready for them, and that's what made me develop."

That "not quite ready" is the key phrase. Richard Cragun suggested to a reporter that "since John was never a good dancer himself, perhaps he doesn't realize what he asks of us". But John's response was "I know how hard my demands are — but you must always put the golden apple beyond the grasp". He worked by a process of experiment. Marcia again:

> We were all learning, John, Ricky, all of us. Because we didn't know what we couldn't do, we went ahead and did it. Sometimes when we were trying to work out something for a ballet, John would just say "Try this", making some gestures, and we would try and respond without knowing quite what he meant. Our lifts sometimes seem spectacular, but John always has a reason for a lift or a gesture, and when you know the reason, you can do it. Suddenly it becomes all right.

Of course he was not always vague in his demands; Egon Madsen remembered him, after setting a phrase of movement, asking "Can you do it backwards?", then when Egon had difficulty, getting up and showing what he meant, with the comment "If I can do it, *you* can do it!"

All this experiment was with one purpose only: the finished ballet. On the one hand, he defined choreography as "composing with human bodies in space and time", but on the other hand he said during a radio interview that works of art mean little if there is no "central unifying dilemma which springs from the heart, from being alive". Or, to put it another way, he was concerned with "movement architecture, plus everything that a body can express in movement".

136

He liked "the challenge of making a ballet work on two levels, as dance and as story. You fail only if the story becomes more important than the dance."

His belief was that inspiration came when he told himself to get on with the work, and that "it's cutting one's coat according to the cloth that makes one good at cutting coats". Again, "if one has the luxury to wait until one has a marvellous idea for a masterpiece, one will never do anything." But he could respond in that way because there were always so many ideas floating around in his mind; the question was only of choosing which one was ripe.

One of his enduring motives was to make ballets about "real people" — but he obviously applied to that the same principle as when he remarked of the settings for ballets that they should be "real but not realistic". He was always observing character and, as Myfanwy Piper remarked, his observation was "often witty and sometimes unkind". (Characteristically, he was fascinated by an account of a man researching facial expression and gesture who, in order to be able to take absolutely natural photographs of people in the street, had a camera that looked as if it was pointing in one direction while actually taking pictures from another). He put unusual characters on stage, not from eccentricity but because that was how he saw people, and because he did not want ballet to be confined to a traditional range of subjects. He always wanted, for instance, to make roles for women that were not sweet and beautiful; to free ballerinas from "perpetual virginity — then the woman will be free to be a woman, and the male dancers will be free to be men". He was interested in relationships that developed: hence his liking for making ballets that last a whole evening, with time for many facets. But the same approach, of giving movement a meaning, applied even to a single dance. When he came to make the duet "Feuilles mortes" in *Brouillards*, he said to Susanne Hanke and Jan Stripling, who were to dance it, "I like leaves lying on the ground and rolling over each other in the breeze", making hand movements as he said it; and that is exactly how the dance materialized.

An idea, and a piece of music, were his starting points; the dancers' bodies were his means, but what concerned him above all, in the finished product, was "the entire performance... total impression rather than only... the bravura of a pirouette or an arabesque". Dancers trying to explain what attracted them to join the company in its later years seized on that as the main factor: "There was a unity. Everyone seemed to enjoy what they did. There was an appreciation of the joy of dancing" or "something that goes from the heart across the footlights".

For that company, John had high ambitions, although he was not consistent in exactly what they were. He told me in 1969 that he would like, eventually, a big company based on both the Stuttgart and Munich companies, drawing even greater strength from the expanded scope that would be open to it as virtually a national company, and he said the same to other people. But at other times he said bluntly, "I hate national companies. I don't like their closed atmosphere". Or he would claim that Stuttgart was already the national company in all but name. Dieter Gräfe, who knew John's mind as well as anybody, thought he was really happy to stay with Stuttgart, although he would have liked the company to have its own orchestra and perhaps its own theatre to give it more independence.

Why expect a man so brimming with ideas to be consistent? He got where he did by always being ready to seize whatever opportunity presented itself. Besides, he himself drew an analogy, when discussing his own methods, with some African tribes who "have a parliament, and they discuss a question sober, then they discuss it drunk. And if they don't come to the same conclusion drunk, they try it again, sober, drunk, sober, drunk; blurred, sharp, blurred, sharp. In the process of getting it sharp, you get some super blurred pictures."

That comparison was more apt than it might seem, since John grew to drink far more than was wise, presumably as a refuge from his depressions. Yet it rarely incapacitated him: Martin Feinstein, who had a lot of dealings with him, observed that the more drunk he got, the more lucid he became. One of his closest Stuttgart friends, a dancer whom he tried to promote to posts of responsibility, also drank heavily and became unreliable in the process, so that in the end John was not able to shore him up any longer, and their paths diverged; but John himself, with the help that his friends gladly gave him, continued to cope. At his worst, he would spend most of the night playing records of the music he was working with, very loud, and drinking. Then during the morning he worked with the dancers at his new choreography; drank again during the afternoon and, unless there was a performance, returned to choreography during the evening. Drunk, sober, blurred, sharp — somehow it worked.

In the interview when he made the comparison with the African tribes, he also said, "I think one has to see the black side to do anything creative. Until you realize how awful people are, you can't begin to realize how beautiful they are. I don't really believe in God, but I believe very much in religious motivation. I think one needs that religious dedication. I'm in a constant state of doubt: the doubt that tells you there is no absolute way, but leads to other ways..."

And when challenged directly once with the question "What keeps you in ballet?", he answered,

> Well, if it's just steps, it's obviously not worth devoting one's life to. This will sound pretentious, but I really have to say that faith in one's work is a little like faith in God. If you believe that it's not wine and bread but the body of God in Holy Communion, well, it is. There's a limit to the amount of jumping around people can do. You can lift a girl only so high; she can spin round on her foot only so many times. One has to convert this extremely physical image — a physical way of expressing oneself — into a spiritual way of expressing oneself. In the great Balanchine ballets — *Serenade*, *Concerto barocco*, *Apollo* — the flesh becomes spirit while you're watching them. And the audience believes without entirely understanding what it is believing in.

Peter Wright asked John Cranko for whom he did his ballets. His answer was "myself", then, after a pause, "I think I really do them for God".

STUTTGART

Scene One
STARTING AGAIN

Scene Two
THE STUTTGART MIRACLE

Scene Three
A GREAT, ROARING, SHOUTING SUCCESS

Scene Four
CRANKO'S CASTLE

STARTING AGAIN

JOHN Cranko's appointment as ballet director of the Württemberg State Theatres took effect on 16 January 1961, and exactly two months later he presented his first new programme for the company, thus setting the pace for what became an increasingly hectic period of a life never much given to leisureliness. He also, during that time, had to make a ballet for a new production of *Die Fledermaus*.

In succeeding years, he would often remark that Stuttgart was a good place to work, then take the shine off that compliment by adding that he meant there were few distractions. Once, before he had learned the finer nuances of the German language and German thought, he spoiled the effect of his peroration to the Noverre Society by declaring that "The best ballet in Germany will spring from this dump". The city, with about half a million inhabitants, stands in hilly forested country in south Germany. The terrain, with steep hills hemming it in on three sides, has prevented the old city from sprawling over the neighbouring countryside as it grew; instead, there are small built-up areas scattered around it, many of which are inconspicuous until you are almost upon them. With energy and determination, it is possible to start in the centre of town and make a complete half-circuit around it on foot during an afternoon, walking through pretty woodland paths with frequent panoramic views over the town below.

There are vineyards on the hillsides, and the city is proud of its mineral springs and its standing as a publishing centre, but the main industry is the manufacture of automobiles; a huge revolving sign with the Daimler – Benz trademark, illuminated at night, stands next to the main railway station which, monolithically built of local stone, is one of the most conspicuous architectural features. The Schlossgarten, a public park formed from what used to be the palace grounds, runs beside the station and continues some way beyond it; the two state theatres both face the gardens at the far end. An artificial lake with fountains lies in front of the larger, older theatre, which is used as an opera house. In fine weather, audiences congregate in the open space between theatre and lake during intermissions.

The ballet company has its studios and offices in this theatre, but the first premiere evening of the Cranko era was given elsewhere, in

143

the main concert hall, the Liederhalle. John told the *Stuttgarter Zeitung* straight away that he meant the programme to be "light, cheerful, entertaining". He seems to have succeeded in that, although the evening showed signs of the haste in which it had to be thrown together. It consisted of four ballets, and John asked Kenneth MacMillan to provide one of them by mounting his *Solitaire*, an alternately wistful and vigorous mixture of comic and romantic dances to Malcolm Arnold's English Dances. John also revived his own *Pastorale* but presented it in a more abstract way as *Divertimento*, distinguishing the characters only as the Innocents, the Melancholy Ones and the Flirts. The new costumes by Richard Beer (who came from London to design the whole programme, and the poster for it) looked too pert and frivolous to have gone very happily with the Mozart music. One of the two new works was *Intermezzo*, set in a ballet studio where the dancers performed to a record album ("Latin American") by George Shearing and Peggy Lee: a return to the mood of the Stan Kenton piece at Henley nearly ten years earlier. *Family Album*, the other creation, was danced to the familiar music of Walton's *Facade*, using a selection very similar to the one in Ashton's ballet of that name, but in a different order. Each dance was (inevitably, with this music) a self-contained little sketch, and the idea of framing them as a series of pages from a family picture album may have come from memories of Dulcie Howes's *La Famille*, also to this music, back in Cape Town. The treatment, however, was a personal one. The show served its purpose of bringing a breath of fresh air into the ballet programmes, but John was aware of its shortcomings and none of the works remained in the repertory after that season.

Actually, at that time German ballet companies did not usually have a repertory in the way that is customary elsewhere. That was because of the way the theatres were organized. Every town of any size had its own theatre or, if large enough, more than one, with separate provision for opera and drama. They were subsidized by the state or city government, and operated a subscription system whereby a high proportion of seats were sold in advance to patrons who came to see each production. Once the demand for a work had been exhausted, it was dropped and another mounted. In any case, although even the most insignificant opera house would have some dancers on its payroll to appear in the operas, at the other end of the scale the ballet companies even in the greatest theatres were subordinate to the opera. The general director of the theatre was always a man whose main interest was opera, and that was true of his audience too. The ballet company's chief purpose, in their eyes, was to take part in opera-ballets, in return for which the dancers were allowed some performances on their own account, but very few, perhaps three or four a month in the major houses. The only company that managed to undertake a short tour each year was the one at the Deutsche Oper, Berlin.

Those were among the problems John had to overcome. The ballet company at Stuttgart was already one of the biggest and best in Germany, but only a few enthusiasts outside the area had heard of it, whereas the opera company there had an international reputation. The city had a small but respectable place in ballet history, thanks to two celebrated choreographers who had worked there briefly in earlier centuries: Jean-Georges Noverre, a famous reforming theoretician, for seven years from 1759, when some of Europe's most famous dancers came to work with him; and Filippo Taglioni, with his daughter Marie, for four years from 1824, shortly before his ballet *La Sylphide* made her the best-known ballerina of the whole romantic period. In recent years, however, the company had been led by directors of only local standing until Beriozoff's arrival in 1957. He mounted productions of the three Tchaikovsky classics (*The Sleeping Beauty*, *Nutcracker* and *Swan Lake*) that were popular enough to be given again in subsequent seasons and survived into the first Cranko year, thus helping to break the old habit of discarding ballets automatically. Thanks to Beriozoff also, the dancers John inherited were of a competent standard, and some enthusiasm had already begun to build in the local audience, helped by the founding of the Noverre Society in 1958.

On arriving in Stuttgart, John first stayed in lodgings, but soon made his first real home in an old, modest and rather uncomfortable house in Botnangerstrasse, on a hill overlooking the town from the west. It had fewer attractions than the house in London, but his life in Stuttgart was so entirely centred on the theatre that he probably had little time to notice any discomforts, and in any case, this first Stuttgart home was made cosy by the family with whom he shared it. They took care of him although all themselves involved busily in the arts. Salvatore Poddine was a member of the ballet company: a short man with the cheerful, wrinkled face of a puzzled gnome. Sardinian by birth, he had started dancing too late (aged 22) to become a strong dancer, but he had a sense of theatre that found a response in John, and it later made another career for him as a director. He had played the dwarf, Belle Epine's faithful servant, in the Stuttgart production of *Prince of the Pagodas*. Salvatore was married to a painter, Herta Zippel, a warm-hearted woman; Herta's sister Eva, a sculptor, also lived with them. John described the two sisters as "my antennae" and explained that "They keep me in touch with the

Germans. I tap their senses." They for their part treated him like family, and Eva was quoted at the time: "He is really our brother. Someone has to look after his shirts. He has no money, he gives it away to anyone who needs it." Herta Zippel had a daughter, Dorothee, then about fourteen or fifteen, who remembers with gratitude the "absolute sympathy this busy and important man had for a young child." Later she was to gain even more from his help in her career.

At the theatre, where he spent most of his waking time (he worked at least a ten-hour day), he made things materially less comfortable for himself, but in all other respects much easier, by not bothering to use the office provided for the ballet director. He claimed in jest that he could not find it in the theatre's long corridors. What actually happened was that, adopting, probably by instinct, the casual style that had served him when running the ballet season at Henley, he left the office to his assistants and set up his informal headquarters in the theatre canteen. It was in those days an austere place, with long wooden tables ranged in rows, and a counter at one end from which food and drinks were dispensed. Since John's death, a new canteen has been built, furnished and laid out in genteel fashion, that would not have served the same purpose at all. The bareness of the place was its attraction: like a school dining room. Visitors soon learned, if wanting to talk to John, to make their way there. Unless needed in the studio, he would often be sitting trying to solve a big crossword puzzle in German; he taught himself to speak the language fluently and colloquially, although with a heavy accent. He claimed to have known not a word of the language before he went there, but he did have the advantage of some knowledge of Afrikaans, a related tongue. He was helped by having a mind always interested in information and comparisons. He commented, for instance, on the different approaches of national types: "With an Englishman, you joke first and then get serious. With Germans, you must be serious first, then into the corner for a giggle." He said also "There are moments when I try to forget that I am a foreigner." When the critic Horst Koegler went to interview him quite early in his Stuttgart days, John already showed a sharp awareness of the literary and political overtones of certain words.

Between rehearsals, also before and after performances, most of the dancers poured into the canteen too. The ballet always occupied one side of the long room; conversation was general and nobody stood on ceremony. Consequently, any dancer with a problem knew that he could talk to his director without formality. Reid Anderson, who later became a close friend of John's, remembers arriving in

146

Stuttgart to audition for the company, when he left the Royal Ballet School. He went, with another boy, simply because he had been advised to, and knew nothing of Cranko or the company. Arriving at the theatre, he asked for Mr Cranko and was directed to the canteen. There, a man asked if they were from the ballet, and they answered yes, for the auditions. But they are not until tomorrow, the man said; do you have anywhere to stay? The answer being no, he told one of the other people at the table to get them somewhere for the night, and it was only then they realized who he must be, and that you could actually talk to the director. This freedom helped build the family atmosphere that was the hallmark of the Stuttgart Ballet. It also had another advantage: unlike most ballet directors, because he had no desk John stood no danger of being overwhelmed by paperwork. He left that to others. He even took his telephone calls on the instrument at the serving counter, and when he had business to discuss, that was generally done sitting around the canteen table amid all the hurly-burly. It must have horrified the German taste for correctness and method, but it left him free to concentrate on the things that most concerned him.

During the first season, his chief problem was to make sure that he surrounded himself with the right collaborators. He persuaded Peter Wright, who had been teaching in London and had established a high reputation (he was another of Vera Volkova's former pupils), to come as ballet master, arriving by the summer. Initially, Wright had Anneliese Mörike as his assistant, relinquishing her position as a solo dancer in the company. Georgia Hiden, an American, was put in charge of the school attached to the theatre, and Nika Milanova, from Munich, was brought in to help with the teaching. John was insistent on the urgent need to improve teaching standards because "when I arrived I found a number of faults that had to be corrected quickly, particularly in the dancers' turn-out and the placing of their feet. In their point work they were often on their knuckles, some of them apparently from the age of four." Although John did some teaching himself, too, in the early days, he had other matters needing his time, so he enlisted all the help possible. When Peggy van Praagh passed through Stuttgart and asked to be allowed *The Lady and the Fool* for the new Australian Ballet she was founding to replace Borovansky's now defunct company, John agreed on condition that she would come back and give the company some classes. John also arranged for the Baden-Württemberg Ministry of Culture to award an annual scholarship (on the recommendation of the Noverre Society) for a place at the Royal Ballet School in London.

Wright remained only three years in Stuttgart (although he

returned afterwards as a producer), but during that time his presence was invaluable. Like his successor, Anne Woolliams, he complemented John's qualities. John worked with enthusiasm at whatever interested him, but was easily bored by routine. Even when creating a ballet, he would complete the choreography within two weeks for a short ballet, or six for a full-evening production, then dislike the process of rehearsing it ready for performance. Wright and Woolliams undertook the more routine tasks of polishing and maintaining the dancers and the repertory, in class and rehearsal.

The other important need was to have the right dancers: those whose qualities he liked, and who responded to his way of working. The choice of ballerina to replace Xenia Palley, whose departure had been agreed already, led to the first of many crises between John and the theatre management. Marcia Haydée had been a member of the corps de ballet in the Cuevas company when John came to make *Cat's Cradle* in 1958. She adored him for his warmth and friendliness, and when she heard that he had taken over in Stuttgart she telephoned from Barcelona to ask for a place in the company. John did not really remember her but told her to come quickly if she wanted to audition. She caught a plane the next morning and was accepted for a corps de ballet vacancy after John had seen her take class with the company.

However, John had seen greater potential in her than she realized. He asked his leading man, Ray Barra, to rehearse the pas de deux from the last act of *The Sleeping Beauty* with her. Puzzled but full of enthusiasm, Marcia learned it and two days later they danced it on stage with the directors watching them. Told to wait in the dressing room, Marcia did so for an hour and a half before John arrived to tell her she was to be his ballerina. It had taken him all that time to convince Dr Schäfer that they should gamble on an unknown woman of twenty-two instead of going for someone with an established name. In the end, he succeeded only by saying that unless he could have her, he would not stay. Time and again in the following years he got his way by threatening to leave: Stuttgart always needed him more than he needed Stuttgart.

Marcia's determination must have been one of the things that made John choose her. It had enabled her to leave her well-to-do family in Rio de Janeiro and go to study at the Royal Ballet School; it enabled her to persevere when loneliness (she spoke no English at first), a strange climate and unfamiliar diet made her put on a lot of weight which she then had lose, not once but twice, to get into the Cuevas company: first before auditioning, then after months of frustrating wait for a vacancy. But there was something else: an individual quality to her dancing that he was able to detect in the inexperienced young woman as a portent for great things. It was the first, most crucial and most spectacular example of his ability to spot talent, as if by instinct. His later comment on her achievement was "Marcia was really there all along. I only helped her to set herself free." There was always a seriousness and concentration about her. She was never conventionally pretty, but had an alert and intelligent face that became beautiful when she danced.

Dancing the roles John made for her, Marcia grew to be one of the few incontestably great dancers of her generation, but even at the height of her career, the Stuttgart Ballet was never a one-woman company, and in early days there was even less temptation for that. Having had his way on the most important issue, John was prepared to let time help him towards ensuring that the rest of the dancers were equally congenial. There were nine principal dancers in the company he inherited, including two veterans for whom he soon found other tasks: Anneliese Mörike, as already mentioned, to teach, and Gerd Praast as stage director. Some turnover was usual at the end of seasons, and two others besides Palley chose to leave at the end of John's first season. There was at least one other leading dancer whose work he did not much care for, but he continued to find roles for her until she chose of her own accord to go two or three years later; equally, when one of his favourites, Anita Cardus, eventually decided she wanted to venture elsewhere for different experience, he did not stand in her way or even try to dissuade her.

Cardus, who joined in 1962, was one of several recruits to the company during his first couple of years; an even more important newcomer from the viewpoint of the way the company developed was Egon Madsen, a young man from Denmark who had already shown potential in the small touring Scandinavian Ballet but, between their seasons, had to be content to dance in the open-air Pantomime Theatre in Tivoli Gardens, Copenhagen; the Royal Theatre there was not interested in him because he had not attended their school. Some Danish friends in Stuttgart told him that dancers were needed; when he applied, John got his old teacher Vera Volkova, who was by then teaching in Denmark, to audition Egon. He joined the Stuttgart company in time to have a walking-on role in the first programme of John's second season, as the coachman in *The Lady and the Fool*, and within a year he was a soloist.

Accounts of John's time in Stuttgart, written in the light of his blazing triumphs or the gentler glow of memory after his death, tend to suggest that it was all a blissful progress from one success to another, with the rapidly emerging company cherished always by a

149

benevolent theatre direction. Nothing could be more misleading. There were fights all the way, and much harsh criticism at first until the company began to enjoy a rising reputation abroad. Neither was John the first to tackle these problems; only the most successful of those who made the attempt. An article by a special correspondent in *The Times*, prompted by his arrival in Stuttgart, pointed out that

> For more than a decade British dancers, teachers and choreographers have worked in the civic opera houses of this rich country and played a major role in the triumph of classical ballet over the firmly rooted "free dance" of the inter-war years. Now in Mr Cranko Stuttgart has seized from Britain one of the most creative minds our ballet has produced, someone who is capable of making a national, rather than just a local impact upon the world of German dance.

A few days later, *The Times* published a letter from Anne Woolliams, then teaching at the Folkwang School in Essen (the paper obviously did not believe her handwriting and therefore printed the surname as Williams). She reinforced the opinion that, "battling against opera strongholds, what has been achieved in little over ten years is a triumph for energy and enthusiasm, and if Mr Cranko finds the freedom he needs, he may well be able to coalesce the talent and achieve lasting results".

The Times article had announced that

> If plans are fulfilled, we can expect to see at Stuttgart ballets by Dame Ninette de Valois, Mr Frederick Ashton and Mr Antony Tudor, as well as those by Mr Cranko and choreographers from Germany and other countries. We can expect, too, the engagement of well-known ballerinas and premiers danseurs to lead the company as guest artists for longish periods. By this means the standards of the company will be challenged and raised so that the German dancers can be developed to take a proper place on the international stage.

The forecasts were based on statements by John, and corresponded in most respects with remarks quoted elsewhere, including the *Stuttgarter Nachrichten*, but in fact only one work by any of the choreographers named was mounted, and that right at the end of John's time. The report in *Stuttgarter Nachrichten* actually proved nearer to what eventually happened. In that, John promised to revive *The Sleeping Beauty*, said that he might mount *Giselle* and *Coppelia*, and certainly *Swan Lake*, because to do so was "not only the obligation of ballet to its own cultural history, but also the assumption for being able to attract prominent guests". He promised that he would bring no fewer guest dancers than Beriozoff had done, and lived up to that, but they came only for one or two performances, usually in the annual "Ballet Week" at the end of each season. He said there would be guest choreographers from London: MacMillan (to whom in fact he gave generous opportunities), perhaps even the great Frederick Ashton — which proved over-optimistic. But nobody should fear, he said, that Stuttgart would become a province of London; he wanted to create on the spot and to find and develop gifted young dancers.

The first part-season under John's direction ended in July 1961 with the Ballet Week of six performances in a row — something never possible during the opera season. There were three showings of *The Sleeping Beauty* and two of *Swan Lake*, both in Beriozoff's versions, to which John had made a few revisions of style and casting, and one performance of *The Prince of the Pagodas*. As guests for this week he had Rosella Hightower and André Prokovsky from the Cuevas company, Liane Daydé and Michel Renault from Paris, Annette Page and Ronald Hynd from Covent Garden; perhaps not so ambitious a choice as he would have liked, judging from later years, but respectable enough. That week also had a final performance of the Liederhalle programme.

Nobody could have guessed from the next season how well things were about to go for John and for the Stuttgart Ballet. There were three premiere evenings, comprising six one-act ballets by John, one by Peter Wright and one classic revival. From among all those, only one work took a firm place in the repertory. During the year, reviews were mixed and public response uncertain, so that Beriozoff visited Dr Schäfer and asked whether perhaps it would be better for him to take charge again. Schäfer answered no, but his feelings were less whole-hearted than they had been.

The first ballet evening that season was not given until November. John insisted on waiting until then (though naturally the dancers had to appear in the operas from the beginning of the season) so as to have two months of preparation to work up their standard. The quality of the dancing was duly admired, but some people, including influential critics, had reservations about the ballets, though two of them were revivals of works previously given in London. It must have been a surprise when some Germans found *The Lady and the Fool* trivial, especially as the Royal Ballet had included it only that summer in the programmes for their first visit to Russia, where the critic Natalia Roslavleva reported that it enjoyed a greater success than anything else they did except Ashton's *Fille mal gardée*. German taste responded differently from Russian and English to its mixture of comedy and pathos. That and *Antigone*, on the same bill, provided leading roles for Marcia; luckily she was not put off by the cool reaction in some quarters to what was almost her first big chance. (Late the previous season she had danced Belle Epine in *Pagodas*.) Luckily, too, the one creation on that programme proved more generally acceptable to John's new public. That was *Katalyse* ("The Catalyst"), in which he showed off the assertive personality and strong athletic technique of a new leading man, Gary Burne, who had joined Stuttgart — officially on leave from Covent Garden, though he never went back there. It was set to Shostakovich's Concerto for Piano, Trumpet and String Orchestra — music serious enough to please the Stuttgarters better than Mackerras's Verdi arrangements for *Lady and the Fool*, but still light enough to be readily engaging. A slight theme also helped to give the ballet respectability and theatricality: the leading man, in red, reconciled the opposition (expressed in smooth versus spiky dancing) of two groups dressed respectively in white and black; at the end there was a startlingly quick transformation of the whole cast into blue tights.

So 1961 ended under a cloud, even if *Katalyse* provided its silver lining, and most of 1962 proved no better. The new production of *Coppelia*, staged by John very freely after the traditional choreography, had to be put off from April until June, within a few weeks of the season's end, on account of technical problems. When it did arrive, it characteristically included one major change in the plot, namely that the heroine, Swanilda, was provided with a mother instead of implausibly living with no sign of parents; and the mother, presumably a widow, was married off at the end to the old toymaker Coppelius to give him a happy ending too. *Coppelia* was given with Stravinsky's *Scènes de Ballet* as a curtain-raiser in new choreography by John. This programme happened to be the first for which any of the London critics arrived in Stuttgart: Clive Barnes was on a tour of West German theatres as a guest of the government, and although he was convinced of the company's potential, it is significant that he more or less passed over the ballets themselves when writing about the trip. That cannot actually have cheered John very much; although preoccupied by his new life, he never cut himself off from his London friends and was always disappointed how few of the critics who had praised his work bothered to come to Stuttgart to see what he was doing there. Those who did arrive were welcomed warmly. That was partly because they brought news of people and events in a world he had inhabited and in which he was still interested, but also because his stubbornness in doing things his own way coexisted with a natural desire for approbation.

In 1962 John's mother, who had spent six weeks in London during 1959, went to Stuttgart to visit him. He received her well enough for

her not to complain at her treatment, but he certainly did not fête her
and make a great fuss about her. Otherwise Dr Schäfer would not
have been so surprised when John, years later, mentioned that a
book just published about him would please her. "Do you have a
mother?" Schäfer asked, and got the answer "Yes, Chief, everybody
has a mother. Mine, for example, lives in Johannesburg." On that
trip, she had resolved that she must speak to him about the past, and
how it came about that she and his father separated — something she
had never done before. Two things prevented her, she told me:
loyalty to the memory of Herbert, who was no longer there to defend
himself, and also the fact that "as John lived such a busy life, there
was never a moment available, so the opportunity was lost". They
never met again.

Another visitor that summer was a woman of an age to be his
mother, but one whom he respected and turned to in a way that he
could not do with his mother. Dame Ninette de Valois arrived for
four days of the 1962 Ballet Week. Her presence was a delight to him.
She had stood by him when he ran into adverse (or, as she described
it, "almost hostile") criticism before he left London, and she had
insisted that his works must be shown on the Royal Ballet's American
tours although their impresario, Sol Hurok, was worried about their
likely reception. John, in turn, found that memories of Dame Ninette
helped him with some of his problems when running a company
himself. He confided in her, and others, that when in a jam he would
ask himself "What would Madam have done?", and that gave him the
solution — even though, while he was a member of her company, he
would often disagree with her decisions.

In prospect, the Ballet Week — intended to sum up and crown the
year's activities — looked exciting. And so it proved, but not in the
way expected. John had been hoping for Fonteyn as guest, but had
to wait another couple of years for that; his thought of having Helpmann to play Dr Coppelius also came to nothing. However, he had
the French ballerina Yvette Chauviré, who had just danced *The
Sleeping Beauty* as guest at Covent Garden, coming to repeat the role
for him. He had two leading dancers from Vienna, Erika Zlocha and
Karl Musil, coming for *Coppelia* — not to dance together, but each
appearing with one of his own dancers, which added interest and
avoided hard feelings. To dance the title parts in his new production
of *Daphnis and Chloe*, too, he had invited guest stars: Carla Fracci and
the Danish Erik Bruhn, generally thought the finest male dancer of
his day. Unfortunately, things went wrong from the start. Fracci, the
fast-rising star from Milan, could not come, so Georgina Parkinson
was brought instead: a promising young dancer from Covent

Garden. Then, after only two performances of the new work, it was announced that Bruhn had fallen ill. The story widely circulated at the time was that his indisposition was precipitated by a personal emotional crisis, and years later, Bruhn confirmed the truth of that when talking to his biographer, John Gruen. Bruhn's explanation was that there was a lot of pressure arising from speculation and gossip about his friendship with Nureyev, who had come to Stuttgart also. That upset him, and on top of that he was worried about his role as Daphnis, even though it was his favourite among the parts created specially for him. He said that John

> somehow knew exactly what I could do, and in some ways it was almost too much. . . . John found qualities in me that just can't be taught and that cannot be analysed. It was amazing, because I didn't particularly enjoy exposing my facility — the tricks— but he loosened me up and gave me a freedom that scared me. The fact was that even I had difficulty in duplicating myself. . . . The first night was a miracle and the second horrified me. I simply could not repeat myself and it was a strange sensation.

Bruhn took to his bed but, when John came with Kenneth MacMillan to see him, and they obviously did not believe he was ill, he threw them out, got dressed, took his car and drove out of Stuttgart, in fact right out of Germany, without saying a word to anyone. John was left unable to give the next performance of *Daphnis*, and had to change the programme, hurriedly substituting an extra performance of the *Beauty* with, for novelty, a different woman playing Aurora in each act: Zlocha, Parkinson and Chauviré. The next night's gala also had to be changed and the revised version included Nureyev's unplanned Stuttgart debut. He learned the man's role in one of Chauviré's showpieces, *Grand Pas classique* to music by Auber, for this one occasion only. So everything ended in a mood of crisis and hectic improvisation, with a sort of triumph snatched from defeat. In spite of the problems, it was reported that the audience had "never clapped like this before", and the most respected, and feared, of German ballet critics, Horst Koegler, wrote in the *Stuttgarter Zeitung* that the company could look forward to a brilliant future if coming productions maintained the standards of *Daphnis and Chloe*.

Incidentally, another work on the new triple bill with *Daphnis* provided the first of John's Stuttgart choreography to be seen in London. He had made a big display ballet to Glazunov's *The Seasons*, and when Western Theatre Ballet were on tour in Germany the next

year he went to see them in Nuremberg and invited two of their
dancers to come back to Stuttgart and learn a pas de deux from it.
But that programme as a whole (it included also a work that Peter
Wright had created for the ill-fated Edinburgh International Ballet in
1958, *The Great Peacock*) did little to still a sense of unrest about the
way things were going.

Then, over the course of the next fourteen months, everything
improved immensely: not through a change of course, but because
what he had been trying all along was blessed with good luck where
before it had been bad. His ambition was still running ahead of what
was practicable, for instance in the remark quoted in a three-page
feature article, "The re-emergence of Herr Cranko", printed in a
Sunday Times Magazine in October 1962, that his next aim was for the
Stuttgart Ballet to make guest appearances in the other great German
cities. But perhaps such remarks helped soften up the management
to make some concessions when he demanded, as he did then, more
money and more help for the ballet in its home base.

The breakthrough in public and critical esteem came with *Romeo
and Juliet*, premiered on 2 December 1962. Returning to a subject
and music he had tackled before, he was starting with an idea of what
would and would not work in the ballet. For the Stuttgart company,
too, this was the second time of tackling *Romeo*: the German premiere
of Prokofiev's ballet had been given there only three years earlier,
with choreography by Werner Ulbrich. According to Schäfer, that
was not a bad production, and (especially in view of increasing press
comment on the unsuitable choice of ballet programmes) he was at
first against the idea of another *Romeo* so soon. Romeo and Mercutio
were even to be played by the same dancers as before, Ray Barra and
Hugo Delavalle, and other dancers had been in the ballet before
although now in different roles, for instance Gerd Praast exchanging
the role of young Paris for that of old Capulet.

John was obviously influenced by the Bolshoi Ballet's *Romeo and
Juliet* which had set a standard of dramatic intensity against which
other productions would be judged; in particular, he took their
powerfully tragic Lady Capulet as a model for his own, dominating
the end of the second act with her grief for Tybalt's death. For
that part, he used one of the company's senior members, Ruth
Papendick, with her basilisk stare, and for the nurse he found a
former dancer, Hella Heim, then already 60, whom he met,
recognized as an interesting personality and still a potential
performer, and persuaded out of retirement. Her Indian summer on
stage and Papendick's continuing career as a soloist (they both

remained active in the roles he made for them for another two decades) were owed entirely to the young director's interest in using dancers outside the conventional age limits.

Another artist also derived a great expansion of his career from his involvement in this production. John had used German designers for several of his Stuttgart creations and revivals, but without much success. He entrusted the designing of his *Romeo* to Jürgen Rose, then twenty-five, who had designed for the threatre in the small town of Ulm, about sixty miles from Stuttgart. John worked closely with his young discovery, who soon became a lasting friend. His criticism of Rose's first designs for the ballet, as detailed, frank and constructive as in his collaboration with Hanns Ebensten years earlier, resulted in a handsome practical decor for this production and the beginning of an outstanding international career for Rose, designing opera as well as ballet.

With a smaller, less experienced company, John had no chance of copying the detailed naturalism of the Bolshoi *Romeo and Juliet*, so he aimed for a bustling background of carnival and feuding, deftly and lightly sketched in, against which were set four major portraits. Some of them were to be much better done in later years by casts who had grown up under John's tutelage, but the coolly detached Tybalt of Ken Barlow (another ex-Royal Ballet soloist) still lives vividly in the memory after all these years, standing with his sword swinging provocatively as he waited for Romeo to fight him. The original Mercutio, Hugo Delavalle, made the character as nimble as a monkey and full of an insolent, practised humour, but some of his successors were to find in the role a feeling of poetry that was outside Delavalle's range. Egon Madsen told me that, when he began to dance the part soon afterwards, John worked with him a lot on the role, although his usual practice was to expect the dancers to find their own character from the choreography. Madsen, who had been the first-night Paris, later also played Romeo, to which he brought a marvellously moonstruck romanticism. His interpretations and, to a substantial extent, those of other dancers in those parts, revealed how much depth lay hidden in the production from the start, waiting to be dug out by the performers. Yet from the beginning, even without the richness and subtlety it acquired over the years, this *Romeo and Juliet* was a fine ballet. Many other choreographers have tackled the Prokofiev score since then, one or two of them with disastrous results, but most with some success, since the music itself was written so meticulously to order that it imposes its own structure. John's remains by general assent one of the best, and when Kenneth MacMillan came to mount the ballet for Covent Garden, he drew heavily on the Stuttgart staging, to an extent that disappointed John, who had hoped and expected to see a more original alternative treatment.

Ray Barra, the first Stuttgart Romeo, was outstanding in some aspects of the part. John had presented Romeo as a man of action, leaping a balcony wall as lightly as he kissed a lady's hand, and sweeping Juliet's nurse literally off her feet when he hugged her for joy at her message. Barra (an American dancer settled in Stuttgart since 1959) dark, assured and intense, gave the character an easy ardour. His strength and natural authority were valuable in the early Cranko days.

But Marcia Haydée's Juliet was, and remained, the wonder of the production. Leading roles in *Pagodas*, *The Sleeping Beauty* and *Coppelia* had given her experience of developing a character during a long ballet, and her parts in *Antigone* and *Lady and the Fool* tried out her gifts for drama; but she had not before had a role making such sustained demands on character and stagecraft. She rose to it splendidly in an interpretation that made her recognized, first locally and then in ever-widening circles, as probably the most gifted dramatic ballerina in Europe. Innocent, passionate and infinitely touching, her Juliet was a portrait to wring the heart and at the same time rejoice the spirit of those who saw her.

From that time, there was no longer any doubt about the potential of the Stuttgart Ballet, and when an invitation arrived for the company to appear at the 1963 Edinburgh Festival, John went to Schäfer and asked him to agree. Schäfer did so, even though he thought it was too soon. By cautious or even objective standards it probably was, but caution would certainly have meant missing opportunities that might never recur. It was only by rushing all the time that they got anywhere.

There were further premieres to come and at least one more crisis to weather before the company arrived in Edinburgh. The crisis was caused by Schäfer's absence in Vienna, where he was spending a season working with Karajan. His deputy, Rolf Badenhausen, had delegated authority for the one season only and could not take decisions for the following year. The delays and frustrations caused by that led John to announce that he would leave in the summer of 1963. Soon afterwards, apparently in an attempt to smooth over the difficulties that had arisen, the *Stuttgarter Zeitung* reprinted an article that Schäfer had written for a Viennese monthly, *Forum*, in which he gave his account of an Intendant's profession, with emphasis on a belief that everybody working in the house must feel at home there as in a family.

157

For the other two premiere evenings that season, John again called on Wright and MacMillan to share the burden. There was first (redressing the balance of the repertory after the strong drama of *Romeo*) what John described as an evening of abstract ballet, for which he made two new works. *L'Estro armonico* was set to some of Vivaldi's concerti of that title; his programme note said, "I personally would have liked best to choreograph all twelve, but so as not to bore the public I have selected three." That was a pure dance piece for three soloists and a small ensemble. Kurt-Heinz Stolze, who also conducted the programme, wrote a score specially for *Wir reisen nach Jerusalem* ("Musical Chairs"), six episodes of black comedy in which the chairs were used, in John's description, as "symbols of social position, political pressure and possession". Wright produced two works in the romantic style, which is usually popular but occupied curiously little of this company's time: *The Mirror Walkers*, a creation to Tchaikovsky's Suite No. 1, and Fokine's *Les Sylphides*. Another creation by Wright, a comic treatment of music by Ibert, was included in the other evening of new works, together with two ballets by MacMillan and only one by John: *Variations*, to another commissioned score, this time by a young composer named Yngve Trede. The music proved thick and muddy in texture, but rhythmically strong enough to support a series of solos which hinted amusingly at the sports field and also managed to parody a number of different dance styles. MacMillan's ballets, a revival of *House of Birds* and a choreographic adaptation of Lorca's play *The House of Bernarda Alba* under the title *Las Hermanas*, provided the dramatic content for that programme.

That year's Ballet Week to end the season included a constellation of guest stars: Violette Verdy and Arthur Mitchell from New York, Antoinette Sibley from London, Attilio Labis from Paris and Henning Kronstam from Copenhagen, all but Sibley learning new roles in the Cranko repertory for the occasion. Even the former Stuttgart ballerina Xenia Palley was invited back to dance *The Dying Swan* on the closing gala, which also included the Stuttgart premiere of *Tritsch Tratsch*.

When the company reassembled after the holidays, however, they set out for Edinburgh with only one guest, Kronstam, who was able to dance Daphnis, a role for which there was at that time no suitable dancer within the company. John's aim was to show off his own dancers. The repertory also was chosen to show what had been achieved in his time there, consisting entirely of works created for the company. Unfortunately it proved impracticable to bring *Romeo* (would John have accepted the invitation so eagerly if he had known that?) because the stage of the Empire Theatre, Edinburgh, temporarily restored from use as a bingo hall, was thought unable to cope with it. Consequently, the impact was a lot less than it might have been. Also, it was found that the second of the two programmes chosen was going to run too long (John must already have been getting used to the backstage conditions in German theatres and forgotten that standards were not everywhere so high). So he decided to drop one of his own ballets, the one with the chairs. Then, two of his works which were given were affected by an injury to Anita Cardus, at that time equally ranked with Marcia Haydée at the head of the company, their gifts complementing each other, one deep and dramatic, the other bright and classical. Cardus had to drop out of *Daphnis and Chloe* and was able to dance only the adagio section of the Vivaldi ballet that had been made for her. That may have suffered from having a substitute in the solos, but was not a great hit anyway. The gentle, ecstatic quality which Marcia brought to Chloe, on taking over the role, prevented the ballet from suffering similarly from Cardus's absence, but the work was inevitably compared, to its disadvantage, with Ashton's ballet to the same score. John's version had some nice touches, especially in the amusement that the seductive older woman, Lykanion, showed at her conquest of Daphnis; but the presentation of the pirates as toughs in black leather — and not much of it — seemed an unnecessary updating.

The outcome was that, although *Katalyse* and the parodistic *Variations* were quite well liked, John's own choreography did not achieve a great success in Edinburgh. MacMillan's *Hermanas*, strong drama with overwhelming performances, was widely admired, and Peter Wright had a fair success with the rhapsodic *Mirror Walkers*, but John's share of the praise was mainly for the way he had built up the company and its dancers.

Among them, already playing small roles, were two youngsters who were rapidly to become prominent among the Stuttgart stars, through John's time there and well beyond. Birgit Keil had just been promoted to be a soloist: at eighteen, the youngest in the company. Although not actually born in Stuttgart, she had moved there young enough for everyone to think of her as a local girl, which was a tremendous asset in boosting morale among the ballet supporters. She had joned the school at eleven, danced a tiny solo a year later under Beriozoff, and at sixteen auditioned for John and was accepted into the company. After one year, she was given leave of absence to go for a year to the Royal Ballet School in London with one of the Baden-Württemberg scholarships. She returned shortly before the end of her last term, in time to dance a solo in *Variations* and the sexy younger sister in *Hermanas* (MacMillan had specially asked for her to get back to dance that role). After only two more years, she was designated a ballerina, being not yet twenty-one. She was one of the people, growing up entirely within the company, who helped provide its public image and became, in effect, John's family. Another such was Richard Cragun, an American boy who had studied dancing (tap first, then ballet) in the United States and in Canada. He arrived in Stuttgart, again via the Royal Ballet School, in 1962, a little before his eighteenth birthday, with the intention of staying there only as long as it took him to save enough money to go to Russia for further studies. His robust strength and virile presence won him chances almost straight away, and he too became a principal at twenty.

At Edinburgh, those and other dancers who later won a big reputation were still fledgelings, but the spirit of the company was already high, its promise obvious. The gamble of venturing abroad so soon had paid off.

THE STUTTGART
MIRACLE

FROM these small beginnings, the next five years brought about what was dubbed in ballet circles the "Stuttgart miracle". It is the sort of phrase publicists love to seize upon, and ever since Clive Barnes first used it to express his enthusiasm in a report on the company's progress, it has turned up over and again. Of course it was an exaggeration, but an understandable one, as flair and hard work transformed what had been a reputable provincial company into one of the most famous in the world.

John was the leader and catalyst of the process. Without him it would neither have started nor ever succeeded. But it was not something one man could do alone. Anne Woolliams once remarked: "John is always trying to do the impossible. My job is to make it possible." She joined the inner circle of colleagues in the summer of 1963 and became increasingly important a year later when Peter Wright was persuaded by his wife Sonya that Germany was not the right country in which to bring up and educate their young children. He gave up the post of ballet master and returned to London to teach, concentrate for a time on television production, and eventually make a name as a producer of the classic ballets (enjoying his earliest success in Stuttgart) before himself becoming director of a company.

Anne Woolliams's path had already crossed John's on several occasions. They had both been pupils of Volkova in London; she had been a dancer and assistant ballet mistress with the St James's Ballet when he made *School for Nightingales*; and it was she who had written a letter to *The Times* about German ballet when he first went to Stuttgart. Anne's dancing career had been spent with small, mostly not very distinguished companies and in musicals, and it was as a teacher and ballet mistress that she had begun really to make a name. Since 1958, she had been the chief classical ballet teacher at the Folkwang School directed by Kurt Jooss in Essen. From there, she would sometimes visit Stuttgart, chiefly to see Peter and Sonya Wright, whom she knew better than she knew John. Wanting a change, she telephoned John and asked whether there was a job for her. He answered that there was a contract available for a dancer. "But I don't want to dance", she said, to which he replied, "Come anyway and we'll find something for you to do."

At first she was mainly Peter's assistant, teaching the company class. She also took over responsibility for what John nicknamed the "elephant class" at the school — the lumpy, less promising girls who had been on the role before the school was reorganized. She reasoned that they could not all be bad, and her hopes were justified, because from among them came Susanne Hanke, who rose to become a principal dancer. Georgia Hiden, who had been running the school, apparently felt her position was threatened by Anne, and left, whereupon Anne took over. On Peter Wright's departure, she became ballet mistress. In one sense, her remark about making things possible can be interpreted prosaically. In her book *Ballet Studio*, for instance, she mentions that John

> was particularly brilliant at devising, and making work, lifts that should rightly be termed impossible. Although the strength for these feats is often shared by the girl and her partner and by coordinating the use of the spine and plié, I found it beneficial to give daily shoulder limbering exercises in the Stuttgart boy's classes to counteract any tendency towards over-muscular shoulders.

Anne's domain was, strictly, the studios on the second floor of the theatre, where she was in charge of the dancers' daily training and rehearsals; and, as head of the ballet school, developing the next generation. Her functions actually went much further than that. She was an ambitious woman, never afraid of responsibility: after John's sudden death she became one of the acting directors who held the company together, then went to become for a time director of the Australian Ballet. John listened to her opinions and was often guided by them; but not always. She and others recount the story of an audition when several girls were seen for only one vacancy. John insisted on taking the one girl whom his colleagues agreed was hopeless. He explained that he had been taken by the way she blushed; behind the shy manner, he sensed an interesting personality.

Anne had another necessary function. John was given to extremes of emotion, freely expressed. Kenneth Barlow, a dancer during the early years, described to me how John, when in dispute with Dr Schäfer over something he wanted for the company, might go to him one day raging furiously, the next day in tears. Peter Wright has described the anger with which John could shout at anyone he thought to be acting stupidly. But John also had a tender side to him and hated having to bring sorrow or disappointment to any dancer.

So if there was bad news to give, that was Anne's job. Heinz Spoerli (now director of the Basel Ballet) recounted to me how he auditioned, in vain, for Stuttgart. John came up and thanked him warmly, leaving Anne to turn him down.

Another newcomer to John's team was unexpected but with time became indispensable. Dieter Gräfe was a young man working for a shipping company in Hamburg. About 1962 he was sent to Stuttgart for a year to get to know some of their inland customers. Through the gay nightlife there, he met Eddie Dutton, who introduced him to John. Eddie was a dancer in the company, an American, to whom John had become closely attached. This was before John had mastered the German language, and Dieter offered to help deal with letters and various official matters, fitting in an hour at a time whenever he could. As his usefulness grew and their friendship developed, Dieter came to be invaluable as one of John's aides, and after a couple of years the obvious course was for him to devote all his time to the theatre, although it was only later, after his presence had proved the need for such help, that he was officially appointed Ballet Secretary (a title actually first conferred for one year on Eddie Dutton). From then on, Dieter helped run John's official life and his private one too. To outsiders, he showed at the time a very reserved and correct manner, doing what was needed and not revealing publicly until much later (after responsibility as John's heir had thawed him) the shrewdness and humour that must always have helped endear him to John.

John's entourage moved from the first unsatisfactory house on one side of town to another, much better, in Neue Weinsteige, the road winding up from the plain towards the hills where Echterdingen lies — the site of Stuttgart airport, so everyone approaching the town from there knows the marvellous view from Neue Weinsteige over the city centre and its surroundings.

To cut the winding road up the face of the steep hillside had necessitated building walls on either side, which save the road from slipping down the ground that falls precipitously away from it, and hold back the ground that rises overwhelmingly above it. Consequently, the houses on the upper side, where John lived, have their foundations high above street level, and the passer-by can only peer up at the buildings high above him. There are fifty-two stone steps up from street level to the door of number 73B, John's former home, steps that can be treacherous in snowy or icy weather. Inside, a tiled hall leads to a multiplicity of rooms confusingly disposed on four main levels, one of them below the main entrance floor. The building is surrounded by trees, and the ground behind it continues just as steeply, so that a lawn in the small garden is at the same level as the top of the steeply pitched roof eaves. John's home was one half of a large house, so ugly that it can be thought endearing. It stands over a bend in the road making so sharp a blind corner that accidents are frequent, and a stream of traffic, including trams, rumbles or rattles by all day long; yet there is a vineyard only one minute's walk down the road. From below, the irregular shape of the building and the grey cemented finish of its walls give it almost the look of a fortress: inevitably, it was soon dubbed Cranko's Castle. This house was big, friendly and — like all his homes — full of objects recalling past and present enthusiasms. Though he needed time alone to devour books and saturate himself in music in preparation for his work, he was never one for a lonely life. As well as its regular occupants and visiting lovers, there was always a bed for someone in need, even on one occasion an entire theatre company from Cambridge University, the Marlowe Society, who were undertaking a vacation tour and were allowed to camp on the floor.

After Edinburgh, John's first new production was the promised *Swan Lake*. The most striking change he introduced was to the ending, about which he wrote,

> There have been "happy endings" where the lovers are reunited after death in "fairyland", but I believe that Tchaikovsky intended to write a tragic ballet. Consider the situation: Siegfried proves unworthy, he breaks his vow and unconsciously confuses outward appearances with inner reality ... He is a tragic hero and must be vanquished. The tone of the music, especially in the fourth act, is tragic... Odette and Siegfried are not the sort of lovers who can "live happily ever after".

By coincidence, Nureyev had a similar idea about the same time when preparing his production of *Swan Lake* for Vienna, and a while later Yuri Grigorovich tried to do something similar at the Bolshoi in Moscow, but was forbidden on ideological grounds. Obviously it was an idea whose time had arrived, but revolutionary and controversial when John thought of it. He invented, with the aid of Jürgen Rose as designer, a great flood conjured up by the wicked sorcerer, Rothbart, through which the hero Siegfried tries in vain to swim to save his beloved Odette, and the ballet ended with Odette once more transformed into a swan and Siegfried left dead as the waters subside.

If he had confined his changes to such logical production points, John's *Swan Lake* would have been acclaimed anywhere. But he had to work within the abilities of what was still a fairly small company, with strong principals but a limited number of soloists and an uneven corps de ballet. Partly for that reason, but also from preference, he chose to make new choreography for most of the ballet, retaining only the greater part of the famous second act, the scene where Siegfried meets the swan-maidens and their princess. Elsewhere he tried "to base my own work on the classic romantic style of Petipa, working freely and in my own manner, but not losing sight of the great man's direction". (Odd, considering how interested he was in the way ballet had developed, that he should forget that much of the traditional *Swan Lake*, including all of act two, was by Petipa's assistant Lev Ivanov.) John added, in the note he wrote for the programme, that "For the opening of the fourth act and the famous elegiac entry of the swans I have 'borrowed' from various Soviet productions. However, all the musical repetitions have been cut and the drama has been strengthened accordingly, so that the prince emerges as a living person who experiences a tragic ordeal, rather than being a human crane who simply lifts the ballerina."

As part of the process of making the hero more lively, his first appearance was changed from a stately entrance to a joky entry disguised as a fortune teller, after which he threw off his cloak and began joining in energetic dances with his friends. That sort of change was less enthusiastically received by traditionalists, although his German audiences at least had no such scruples.

One advantage of *Swan Lake*, as John had forecast, was that it helped in attracting guest stars: it provided Margot Fonteyn, for instance, with her first Stuttgart role, partnered by Nureyev. Even more important was the way it revealed, and extended, the growing strength of the company's own principals. Two ballerinas played Odette and her wicked double Odile from the start, Cardus being partnered at the first performance on 14 November 1963 by Egon Madsen, now seen clearly as potentially a very great romantic dancer. The next night (what German theatre usage regards as a "second premiere") Haydée took the lead with Barra (less romantic, but strong as a partner, dancer and actor) as Siegfried. Birgit Keil was prominently featured in a solo as a Russian princess, to music not then generally used in productions of the ballet; she was also soon dancing the ballerina role.

Swan Lake would have met some adverse comment if John had staged it for a British or American company, but in its context, as part of the process of building up the company, it was a solid achievement. His other creations for Stuttgart during the rest of the 1963 – 4 season were less ambitious, and his first premiere in the following season did not fall until January 1965. Consequently, 1964 looks a rather blank year for him on the Stuttgart calendar, but in fact he was kept as busy as ever because that was the year when, the first pioneering responsibilities of his new job safely behind him, he could look around and accept some of the invitations that were beginning to arrive for him to stage ballets elsewhere.

One of the first was from the Deutsche Oper, Berlin, where Gert Reinholm was ballet director and leading dancer. John agreed to produce *The Firebird* for them, but soon after beginning rehearsals he told Reinholm that he was not happy working with unfamiliar dancers after growing accustomed to his own team. They agreed that the best course would be for John to return to Stuttgart, create the ballet on his own cast (who were due to perform it later anyway), then simply teach the finished work to the Berlin company. One consequence was that Reinholm himself withdrew from playing the male lead, as he was not interested unless he could have the opportunity of assisting in its creation, but they remained on good enough terms for the company to have another Cranko ballet the next season — *The Lady and the Fool*.

Firebird had its Berlin premiere on 4 March 1964 (John's *L'Estro armonico* being given its first performance there the same night) and was first seen at Stuttgart on 20 May, when it was warmly received although the performance was interrupted by the failure of one of the scene changes, necessitating a disruptive break before the finale. Listening to the Stravinsky music as a boy had been one of the formative factors in making John a choreographer, and at that time he must have had his own ideas about how the story might look if told in movement. By the time he came to stage it himself, however, he had seen Fokine's original choreography, and decided to base his own on a free reworking of that, without trying to impose any personal reinterpretation of the myth or the music. He explained that he had made no bones about leaning heavily on Fokine's version "because there are certain things he did to the music that simply can't be improved". But John did adapt the Firebird's solo dances to give the ballerina some spectacular opportunities, and, though not developing the leading man's role beyond the usual acting and partnering responsibilities, he did make the duets more difficult because "now, in a purely motor way, we can make more exciting shapes than Fokine could produce in 1910". John also developed some of the stage effects (Fokine claimed that his own original intentions in that respect had been allowed to disappear when new designs were made). He used a trick he had first employed in *Beauty and the Beast*, of having a character appear and disappear through slits in a front-curtain, to provide a touch of drama during the hero's opening exploration of the magic garden (Jürgen Rose was again his designer). The ballet proved workmanlike; no more, no less. In Stuttgart, where a wide choice of more striking works by him was available, it has long since been allowed to lapse from the repertory, but the Berlin company still performs it.

John's next assignment was to mount *Romeo and Juliet* for the National Ballet of Canada, where Celia Franca (whose *Khadra* had helped him into Sadler's Wells) was director. He went to Toronto himself to stage it and, being, as many choreographers are, unable to remember all the details of his own choreography, made up fresh solutions to meet the same purpose. When Marcia Haydée arrived to dance Juliet as guest, she pointed out such differences as certain actions taking place on the opposite side of the stage. John joked that both versions must be correct as he had made them for the two companies. This was the first and last time John personally mounted one of his big ballets for another company; thereafter he saved himself from a time-consuming and unwelcome chore by having an assistant teach the steps even if he supervised the production. John was easily bored by routine tasks, but always found time to be interested in people and help them. Veronica Tennant, then a young dancer just about to join the National Ballet, was unable to take part in rehearsals because she was laid up with an injured leg, but she remembers with gratitude how he let her watch, and how he talked to her, an insignificant youngster, about his ideas, so that when she had recovered, she actually made her first appearance dancing Juliet and was able to bring a lively depth to her interpretation.

When *Firebird* went on in Stuttgart on 20 May the rest of the programme consisted of one of MacMillan's Covent Garden successes, *Diversions*, reproduced for a young cast headed by Keil and Cragun, and a new work by Peter Wright, *Entwürfe für Tänzer*, his last Stuttgart creation before returning to London. John's only tasks for the Ballet Week that year were to keep his guest stars happy (Fonteyn and Nureyev, dancing his *Swan Lake*, which of course they had to learn first; also Lynn Seymour as Juliet) and to stage a couple of showpieces for the final gala. One was in straightforward classical bravura style for Cardus and Delavalle, to music by Delibes from *La Source*, but the other was an exploration of the spectacular adagio tricks developed by Soviet choreographers. John had, as early as *The Prince of the Pagodas*, been experimenting with the High Russian lifts, holding the woman high above her partner's head; this time, in *Hommage à Bolschoi*, to Glazunov music, he made a dance entirely in that mode for Haydée and Barra. Fonteyn invited them to repeat it at her annual gala in aid of the Royal Academy of Dancing, given at Drury Lane that November, where it had a big success.

167

That same month, November 1964, saw another of the few creations which John made, during the German part of his career, for companies other than those with which he had a continuing relationship. This was *Concerti Grossi*, to music by Handel, for the Cologne City Ballet. As he never revived it elsewhere, it may be guessed as not one of the works close to his heart, but the genre, simply dancing to music, is one he kept returning to throughout his career, from the apprentice *Holberg Suite* in 1945 until *Initials*, to a Brahms concerto, in 1972. Most examples of the genre in its pure form, however, fall within a short time during the sixties: *Scènes de Ballet* and *The Seasons* in 1962, *L'Estro armonico* in 1963, *Concerti Grossi* in 1964, *Brandenburg 2 & 4* and *Concerto for Flute and Harp*, both in 1966. The first two of those were written (by Stravinsky and Glazunov respectively) specifically for dancing; in the others, John was matching his gifts against the challenge of classical music written by Vivaldi, Handel, Bach and Mozart for the concert hall. From remarks he made to me, I know that it was something he much enjoyed when he thought he had found a suitable score, but it is not the kind of ballet most associated with his memory.

The reason for that is simple. John always had a flair for making dances that showed off his performers; he had great respect for the classical tradition, and had analysed the way his predecessors achieved their results; he used virtuosity with zest, and was never afraid to extend his dancers to the limits of their ability, but he also knew the value of allowing moments of rest and simplicity in his works. Besides, his response to music ensured a slightly different approach each time, to match the style and shape of the score. Yet these were never his most successful works, because he lacked the deeper insight into musical structure that enabled his life-long idol, George Balanchine, a skilled and trained musician, to develop a form of plotless classic dancing that provided what the Germans would call its own dramaturgy (there is no exact and unpretentious equivalent in everyday English or American usage, because we tend to become embarrassed about discussing the arts seriously). In Balanchine's ballets, the structure springs so directly from the score that the analogy has been made of hearing the dance or watching the music. Consequently, the movement in its relationship to the music itself provides a kind of drama or, at the least, a recognizable theatrical form. Very few other choreographers have succeeded in matching him in that, and none consistently.

John was aware of Balanchine's outstanding gifts and took them as one of his models, with results that were highly beneficial — but mostly in those ballets where he was tackling something different, not venturing on Balanchine's own ground. He could succeed brilliantly with a suite of dances as part of a longer ballet (such as the pas de six in *The Prince of the Pagodas*), or with short display pieces to light-hearted and theatrical music. He also enjoyed great success with works where the chief interest lay in the dances, but with a touch of character or situation to fire his imagination and that of the audience: examples range from the early *Pastorale* to *Brouillards* in his later period. But in the kind of ballet that relied only on pure dancing to outstanding music, although he was at least as proficient as any of his contemporaries, John did not reach the heights.

He explained his method for such works in a broadcast when making *Brandenburg 2 & 4*, and in doing so he revealed his strength and weakness:

> I am passive to the music in the beginning. I let the music take over, and I form an emotional relationship to this music — I don't analyse it. Then, when I finally decide to do a ballet, is where I become active, and analyse and count out and start thinking of shapes that might fit, until the moment I get into rehearsal. And when I go into rehearsal, I've had, as it were, my experience with the music. I've got it intellectually defined; I know how many beats, how many bars, what phrases are coming after what other phrases. And then I try and stop thinking again, and make shapes on the dancer.

So the dancing in *Brandenburg* was the result of John's love affair with Bach's music, going back "a good fifteen years", during which he was listening "and wanting to do a ballet, but not letting myself do a ballet to them". After this long, cautious approach, rehearsals provided a new last-minute stimulus, trying with each dancer to give them "movements that they can do, finding movements in them which perhaps they didn't know about", and accepting also all the happy accidents that may occur as a departure from what had been planned: "All art's improvising. Even Bach improvised in the strictest fugue; the beauty of Bach is always the spontaneous action that is within this very strict discipline."

John caught the spontaneity in his choreography, but not always the discipline, and the separation of emotion and intellect in the stages of his preparation resulted in a less rigorous treatment than Balanchine's. He was clearly aware that his own strength lay less in pure form than in a casual informality. Consequently, in that same broadcast, although declaring that "I've been becoming more and more involved with pure movement", he went on to say:

> I cheat the public really — I have found a way of being invisible. *Jeu de Cartes*, for instance... is in fact an abstract ballet,

169

just like the Bach is. The kind of movement is different, but the public thinks it's not abstract because people are called Queens of Hearts and the Joker, and it's a funny ballet, so people don't in fact notice that it's not a story ballet. I like doing this kind of construction; I suppose it's a kind of myth-making, and this has been my general trend.

Jeu de cartes, which (as the radio talk implies) arrived in London about the same time as *Brandenburg*, was actually created in Stuttgart a year earlier, on 22 January 1965, immediately after *Concerti grossi*. It was done on a programme together with a short-lived piece, *Bouquet garni*, to Britten's Rossini arrangements "Soirées musicales" and "Matinées musicales", and two Balanchine ballets, *Allegro brillante* and *La Valse*. John had suddenly hit a winning streak, and during 1965 was to make three of his most successful and enduring works, each entirely different from both the others in structure, mood, manner and style.

Jeu de cartes was all the more creditable a success because previous attempts at staging it had always lacked something. The music was commissioned to form part of a Stravinsky triple bill put on by Balanchine and the American Ballet as a sort of manifesto of their intentions at the Metropolitan Opera House, New York, in 1937, and the ballet seems to have served a useful purpose in that context, but when that original version was revived in the fifties for New York City Ballet it proved thin, its humour laborious. The only other notable production was Janine Charrat's for Les Ballets des Champs-Elysées, with a marvellous role for the leading man but otherwise failing to make its point clear.

For his production, John seized upon the parodistic and allusive elements in the score as a clue to the right treatment. Each movement (or "deal") of the music has an accompanying plot representing incidents in a game of poker, with the Joker all the time trying to establish his superiority to the other cards. John succeeded in presenting these situations in such a way that the jokes were funny even to spectators unfamiliar with the game (Stravinsky, in writing the ballet, apparently overlooked the possibility that such people might exist). In the first scene, the distress of the proud Queen of Hearts — ousted by the Joker, who is able to form a winning hand with two Tens and two Sevens — provides the fun. In the third movement, the little Two of Diamonds, gamely but vainly trying to keep up with the Ace, King, Jack and Ten of Spades, is similarly excluded when the Joker turns himself into the Queen. Although both sections showed a woman dismissed from the game, the roles were so contrastingly cast and characterized that there is no feeling

170

of repetition. Only in the middle deal, when the Joker comes up against the camaraderie of a straight flush in hearts, does he meet his comeuppance — ignominiously bundled off stage by the others whose series of solos he tries to interrupt. When all the other cards turn against him in the last movement, he is still able to hold his own, and the ballet ends with a hint of further outrageous triumphs to come for him.

It was mainly a ballet for male dancers, with two fine comic roles for women (created on tall, elegant Keil, given something quite outside her usual range and bringing it off beautifully, and a tiny but plump soloist, Chestertina Sim Zecha). Apart from them, the honours went to the five men who danced the middle section, each with a show-off solo, and, above all, to Egon Madsen as the Joker — a role subsequently danced by many other fine dancers in many revivals and new productions, but never with more wit and flair. John had put something of himself into the role: his sometimes wild, bizarre appearance, his farouche humour and enterprise, his constant rebelliousness. There are several similarities between this irreverent, unscrupulous character and the accounts of John's own role as the Devil in *The Soldier's Tale*, including the disguise as a woman. But John also used to the full Egon's own irrepressible sense of comedy. Although his stage roles until then, except Mercutio, gave only limited glimpses of it, Egon offstage was the company's jester, assuming a theatrically camp manner and commenting on everything with a wry drawling cynicism. *Jeu de cartes* allowed him to bring his wit on stage. It also required a bravura technique as the Joker went whirling among the other cards with great flying leaps: not to mention the parody of the Rose Adagio from *The Sleeping Beauty* when, in skirt and crown as the Queen of Clubs, he was partnered by the two men and two women (the Ace and Ten) who make up the rest of the royal flush.

Was it perhaps a reaction from the effort of creation that led to a fight at the party after the ballet's premiere? It was held, as often happened, in a Greek restaurant much patronized by the company People kept coming up to Egon and offering him drinks until he became, in his own description, "absolutely pie-eyed" and started crying. John had also drunk a lot and wept too, embracing Egon. But then some of Egon's friends tried to take him home. John thought they were bad for him and started arguing, while holding Egon to stop him going. "Don't you talk to my friends like that, they're good people", Egon shouted, and a fight broke out. Luckily, both men had quick emotions but bore no grudge, so the quarrel did no harm.

John entrusted the scenery and costumes of *Jeu de cartes* to Dorothee

Zippel, Herta's teenage daughter, who was then just trying to start her career. It was her first designing job in the theatre, and at that time there were very few women designers in German theatres, besides which, it was unheard of to give such responsibility to somebody so young in bourgeois Stuttgart. But, she says, he "gave absolute trust, so you could do it". Her backcloth of a lady card-player's bust made an amusing setting, with the hand providing a hidden entrance for the Joker, and her card costumes were much simpler and more effective than earlier treatments of this theme.

With *Jeu de cartes*, John had made what is arguably the best of his many fine comic ballets; later that season he was to create the finest example of the long dramatic ballets at which he also excelled. In effect, this year provided most of the basis for the company's subsequent triumphs around the world; it also saw another achievement that was less obvious to outsiders, but vital to John's plans. This was the complete reorganization of the Stuttgart Ballet School.

To anyone outside the world of ballet, the importance that John always gave the school when talking about his work in Stuttgart must seem exaggerated. Stuttgart already had a ballet school attached to the theatre; the pupils used the studios during the afternoon while the company had its break between morning rehearsals and evening performance. There were other private dancing schools in the town and all over Germany; plenty of Germans were already following a dance career. Granted a wish to raise standards, some reorganization was understandable, but why anything more?

The trouble was that ballet had taken root in Germany so recently that parents had no idea how young a start was needed for best results. Also, professional organizations for maintaining standards, such as John had known in South Africa and Britain, did not exist. He often raged at the miserably unqualified teachers who practised without hindrance. He said it was like everyone who had completed an algebra course being able to put up a brass plate as a teacher of mathematics. And he complained bitterly about the results: "You should see some of the poor feet that come in and expect to dance."

If that angered him, his experiences in Cape Town, where the University Ballet School offered unique facilities, and with Ninette de Valois, whose school had been the origin and foundation of her company, had made him aware of the possibilities a good school could offer him as director and choreographer.

He was never himself keen on teaching, although in his first years in Stuttgart he did often take charge of the company class to help build up standards. Consequently, he tried to get good teachers around him and give them the facilities they needed. The first breakthrough came in the spring of 1965 with the beginning of an association between the ballet school and a long-established local school, the Werkschule Albrecht L. Merz, privately run but state recognized, where the philosophy was to teach the children not only academic subjects but music and handicrafts. For the ballet children, dancing would take the place of the latter, with classes every morning and afternoon as part of their curriculum. Any child under ten who showed promise as a possible dancer would be admitted without formality, and there were arrangements to accept them up to thirteen if appropriate. It was a help that the school could take boarders, and could also offer activities and meals from eight in the morning until six in the evening for those attending by the day but living too far off to get home in the midday break. This integration of a professional ballet school with another school was the first in Germany; it ensured (what had hitherto been difficult or impossible) that neither the academic nor the specialist training would suffer because of competing claims on the children's time and attention. John argued that "a ballet dancer must have it not only in his legs, but in his head too". A further benefit for the children was that those who, for whatever reason, failed to make the grade as dancers could be eliminated from the ballet course at any stage — as is common practice — and not have their education disrupted, as they could stay on at the Werkschule.

There was a further major change a few years later, when the ballet school became independent in its own building. Now, since John's death, it bears his name as a continuing memorial to his efforts in founding it.

During the rest of the 1964–5 season, there were quite a few new productions of Cranko ballets for various theatres around Germany: *Katalyse* (which had already been mounted in America for the National Ballet of Washington) for the Ballet of the Deutsche Opera am Rhein at Düsseldorf-Duisberg; *The Lady and the Fool* for the Deutsche Oper, Berlin (and that work was also mounted later in the year for the Capab Ballet in Cape Town); *Beauty and the Beast* for Wuppertal. John's reputation and influence were spreading more widely. But he sent assistants to produce the ballets; his own efforts after *Jeu de cartes* were concentrated on a new three-act ballet *Onegin*.

The idea of making a ballet from Pushkin's long poem had come to him years earlier when creating the dances for a production of Tchaikovsky's opera at Sadler's Wells. On one of the Stuttgart Ballet's American tours he told an interviewer in Boston, "The work struck me as being much more suitable for ballet". He liked the opportunity for large dance scenes in each act, in contrasted styles:

173

"We start with peasant dancing, then we have the middle-class at Tatiana's birthday, and finally the aristocratic ball in the last act. In the midst of this all, we have a very elaborate pas de quatre for the plot." To another American interviewer, he explained that he had read the poem while working on the opera, and that "What attracted me to *Onegin* is that that story is simultaneously a myth and a situation that is emotionally valid. You have a blasé man of the world who can't feel any more, who misses the point of the ugly duckling. When she turns into a swan, he suddenly wants her back, and she realizes how empty and bored he really is. And while her emotional side says 'Take him', her rational side says 'Don't take him'."

John told me that the piece of music in Tchaikovsky's opera that most attracted him was Gremin's aria in the last act, and he had envisaged this as a love duet when first thinking about the ballet. His idea had been to use an arrangement of the music from the opera, and there was talk of his creating the ballet at Covent Garden for Fonteyn and Nureyev, but the Board of Directors there would not hear of using opera music in that way and, as it turned out, neither would Dr Schäfer at Stuttgart. However, Kurt-Heinz Stolze undertook to arrange a new score from mainly unfamiliar pieces by the same composer, using not a single bar from the opera.

He explained how he went about it:

> My function was to provide large-scale musical forms ... to correspond on one hand with the dramatization of the plot ... while on the other they had to be composed of short musical numbers... for the purpose of interpretation through dance. Because of their simple form, Tchaikovsky's compositions for piano... lent themselves particularly well and provided about three-fourths of the music for this ballet. The piano cycle opus 37, *The Seasons*, was especially useful, and the opera, *The Caprices of Oxana*... (from which I used two arias, one chorus and a few instrumental numbers) yielded much of the music. A duet from *Romeo and Juliet* served as a sketch for the main theme in the Tatiana–Onegin pas de deux in the first act, whereas the second movement from the symphonic poems *Francesca da Rimini* takes up much of the pas de deux in the third act. The big numbers — waltz, mazurka, polonaise, etc. — have mainly been created from piano compositions. The dramatic structure of the ballet required a continuity, so that the different pieces had to be connected. For this reason some of the themes were used like Leitmotivs. On their recurrence, they are often changed harmonically and rhythmically. Some scenes are accompanied by free variations of themes used

earlier in the score ... I felt it was important not to depart too much from the typical Tchaikovsky orchestration. At the same time, I felt it was important to avoid all-too-frequent tutti effects. In line with the ballet's dramatic action ... and carried out almost exclusively by the main characters, I felt it was best to treat the orchestra in more chamber-music-like fashion than is usual in Tchaikovsky's ballets, and to reserve the use of the full orchestra mainly for the dramatic climaxes and endings.

The result, carried out with skilled musicianship, was a plausible recreation of a new Tchaikovsky ballet score: not of the same quality as *The Sleeping Beauty* and *The Nutcracker*, where the composer's own intentions are generally respected (*Swan Lake* has suffered far more from would-be improvers), but still far better than most confected or composed modern ballet scores, and ideally crafted for John's purpose.

The ballet tells its story clearly, without any need for audiences to be familiar first with Pushkin. One crucial problem, how to make the purpose of Tatiana's letter visible to audiences, was solved by a kind of dream sequence: the lighting changes, and Tatiana's imagination conjures up a vision of Onegin, looking far more romantic and ardent than he had done at their meeting, who appears in her room and dances a rapturous duet with her, disappearing before dawn when she completes the letter and gives it to her nurse to deliver. Although the plot is tragic, John followed Pushkin in providing many touches of humour; they relieve what would otherwise be the wearyingly sombre nature of Onegin himself, and they give a human warmth to the other characters, especially Tatiana, first seen in a most unballetic pose, lying on her stomach with her nose in a book. Among the many dramatic touches that John devised was that of having the sisters, Tatiana and Olga, play a fortune-telling game with a looking-glass, which is supposed to foretell future lovers; it is in that way that Tatiana, reluctantly drawn into the game, first glimpses Onegin who has come up behind and peers over her shoulder. Apart from the four principals (Lensky, Onegin's friend and Olga's fiancé, being the fourth), there are very few solo parts: the girls' nurse and their mother — roles made for the invaluable older dancers, Hella Heim and Ruth Papendick — and Prince Gremin, who married Tatiana. Yet there is so much action for the principals, and a large corps de ballet is so ingeniously woven into the action during each act of the ballet (providing the ballet's equivalent of the set dances in the opera) that the work never looks small-scaled.

The climaxes in the second act, and indeed the whole treatment of that act, are theatrical. At the party in Madame Larina's house, the corps de ballet (which elsewhere in this ballet is used for massed effects) is displayed as a collection of individuals, slightly comic. There are meetings, flirtations, sudden flurries of activity, little jokes going on in corners of the room. Against that animated background you see the recklessness and bored misbehaviour by Onegin that leads to the quarrel with Lensky, and the sudden chilling switch of mood that comes with the challenge. The duel is presented with a shadowplay effect, as if the two men were only dimly seen through a mist. After the almost naturalistic dramatic passages, the challenge and the duel, John included brief, strangely expressive passages of frenzied, grief-stricken movement for the two sisters: something quite unlike the rest of the choreography, and perfectly placed to make its point. The greatest moment in the ballet, as it should be, is the ending, a big duet for Tatiana and Onegin in which they have changed roles, he now the suppliant, she the haughty refuser — but managing at the same time to make clear how much in two minds she is, and how difficult, even tragic, she finds her actions.

The ballet was a particular triumph for Marcia Haydée, creating a character who grew all through the work and was in every moment entirely convincing as a portrait of an exceptional but credible person. But all the roles were observed and realized with exceptional clarity, giving great opportunities both to the original cast and those who followed them into the parts over the years. *Onegin* is perhaps the most successful original example of story-telling in ballet made in the present century.

After a work of this scale and quality, there was little time to rest, because the annual Ballet Week was being held earlier than usual, in late May and early June, and John had to make a couple of pas de deux (to music from Glazunov's *Raymonda* and Debussy's *Petite Suite*) for the closing gala. Straight after that, the company went into rehearsals for its second expedition abroad, again to a major festival, this time the one directed by Gian-Carlo Menotti at Spoleto, where they were to give eight performances of *Romeo and Juliet*. After that, although he had a poor opinion of Carl Orff's music, John was obliged to stage dances for a performance of *Carmina burana* on 10 July 1965, opening a week's festival in Stuttgart celebrating the composer's eightieth birthday. The ballet company, for all its growing success, had nothing like the independence it eventually won, and at that time John did not have another choreographer on his staff or among his dancers to whom he could have entrusted the task.

There was thought that John would be involved with an experimental opera evening a year later, when it was intended to do a work by Satie or Hindemith, one by Milhaud, and Ligeti's *Aventures* and *Nouvelles Aventures* — these last being the works proposed for a dance treatment. Nothing came of that, however. The 1965–6 season turned out to be notable largely for the development of the ballet company's touring — something vital if it was ever to break free of the opera. One other important occurrence went largely unnoticed at the time. Georgette Tsinguirides, who had been one of the soloists John inherited on taking over as director, was given a year's paid leave of absence to go to study Benesh dance notation in London, at the Institute of Choreology. This was a fairly new system of writing down dances, quicker to use than those existing before, and was beginning to catch on as a useful way for a company to ensure that choreography was not lost through being forgotten. John knew that the Royal Ballet had adopted it and it was his idea to send Tsinguirides because her dancing career was coming to an end, and she was an intelligent woman who might grasp the new skill quickly and be good at it. He mentioned this to her one morning and suggested that she might think it over; but by the afternoon he was already asking for her decision and she agreed to go. She thus became the person who, more than any other, is responsible for preserving many of John's ballets, with the advantage that, having seen them made and, in many cases, danced in them, she was able to pass on instructions about style as well as steps.

The season's first tour was to Leipzig, in East Germany, for the city's 800th anniversary celebrations. This was the first time any theatre company from West Germany had played in the East. They gave two performances of *Romeo and Juliet*, with great success.

Modestly, John had announced that he was going to create only a couple of opening works that season, but the first of them proved to be small only in size, not in impact. It was to music by Webern, *Opus 1*, given on the same night (7 November 1965) as MacMillan's *Das Lied von der Erde*, the great success of which temporarily masked, to some extent, the merits of John's ballet. It was an open secret that MacMillan had wanted to create a ballet to the Mahler score at Covent Garden, and had been refused because it was thought too great a masterpeice of modern music to be used accompanying a ballet. Consequently, two English critics with an equal interest in music and dance attended the premiere, both sending back enthusiastic reports which helped ensure that soon afterwards the Covent Garden management had to eat its words and invite MacMillan to mount it for the Royal Ballet also. It deserved its success, and John admired it as much as anyone. He had refrained from watching any of the rehearsals until the first complete run-through. Then

177

MacMillan asked him to watch and to bring a score to check that there were no discrepancies between the German text of the sung poems and the action of the ballet. Quite soon John closed the score and said that there was absolutely no need to check anything; in any event he could not take his eyes from the dancers. At the end of the run-through, he was in tears.

The curious thing is that, at the time, it was hardly remarked that John's creation for the same programme had a very similar theme: a poetic evocation of, and reflection upon, the continuing cycle of life and death. *Opus 1* has no ostensible plot but even those watchers who found its content enigmatic were aware that there was an implied content. The Webern music is a passacaglia, strict in form and scored for a large orchestra, very dramatic in its progression from a hushed opening to a climax of overwhelming volume of sound, almost back again, then another powerful crescendo before gradually returning to its starting point. The contrasts of mood, resigned or aggressive, are equally theatrical. The ballet used a cast of two soloists (Keil and Cragun) with a group of six women and six men, all dressed in plain tights, white or grey, with simple tunics for the women. Its choreography drew on elements from earlier ballets: the individual being born, exploring life and returning to his origins (as in *Harlequin in April* or, before that, *Primavera*), also the supportive group from the same source — the resemblance was close enough for *Opus 1* to be taken as an abstact reworking of the earlier theme, but there was also a strong element of the daring, almost gymnastic movement that had been included in the unsuccessful *Reflections*, with Cragun seeming to dive over the shoulders of the other men. Unconventional movement featured also in the relationship between the protagonist and the solo woman: Keil carrying Cragun's quite substantial weight in physical as well as emotional support, instead of the usual strong man/frail woman attitude of ballet.

German critics, more suspicious than the English ones about the propriety of dancing to Mahler, manifested some reserve about *Das Lied* and were more inclined to admire *Opus 1*, but its reception caused John to decide, reluctantly, not to give it to Covent Garden when he went there three months later at the invitation of the Royal Ballet. Instead, he mounted *Jeu de cartes* for them, in addition to the new work he made for them to the Brandenburg concertos 2 and 4. For the new work, he used many of the company's most gifted young dancers, eight women and eight men, and was very enthusiastic about the way they had developed since he last worked with the Royal Ballet six years earlier. He made more demands on their technique, as soloists and in duets, than they usually met, but set the virtuosity in a context of easy lightness, and they mostly enjoyed working with him as much as he did with them. His disarming comment about his intention in choosing this particular music was "I had tried Vivaldi and Handel; now I wanted to see if I was up to Bach". Unfortunately, the Covent Garden Orchestra was apparently not entirely up to Bach: although they played buoyantly, a decision was taken (quoting unspecified "established precedent") to substitute an E-flat clarinet for the high trumpet part in Brandenburg 2, presumably because it was safer. That took the edge off the music and detracted from the bravura effect of the men's dancing.

John decided to adapt *Jeu de cartes* (renamed *Card Game* for this production) to suit the Covent Garden dancers and their audience. He cut down some choreographic references to Balanchine's *La Valse* (which in Stuttgart had been justified by the presence of that work on the same programme, as well as by a Ravel allusion in the score), because it had not been seen in London for many years; but he put in some joke quotations from other ballets, including Ashton's *Les Patineurs*. He also adapted the men's solos in the second deal to suit the new cast. Unfortunately, *Card Game* did not remain in the repertory, perhaps because robust comedy was not to the taste of the Board (it was described, rather apologetically, as a "balletic farce" in their next annual report), and when the Royal Ballet wanted to give it as part of a commemorative programme after John's death, they had to get Georgette Tsinguirides from Stuttgart to mount it. Naturally, the version she had was the original one, so the English variant was lost altogether. *Brandenburg* also failed to survive, probably in large measure because replacement casts were unable to maintain the standard of the original team as they became, for one reason or another, unavailable. During the last years of his life, John's ballets were given very little in London. That was in spite of the fact that Princess Margaret (who is President of the Royal Ballet) remained one of his warmest friends and admirers, even to the point of coming to watch his ballets in rehearsal. As she turned up on a day when the Covent Garden press office had invited critics to come and meet John during a break in rehearsals, she also attended the press conference and photographers were hurriedly sent for to record the occasion.

Opus 1 was not performed on stage in London until after John's death, but its inclusion in a BBC television programme a year after his Royal Ballet premieres brought it to a wider public and helped to keep attention on John during his absence. Meanwhile, his Royal Ballet connections were to be of immediate benefit, because during a short tour of German cities, Ray Barra had suffered a serious injury

179

while rehearsing. The policy of having more than one cast for most of the big roles now paid off, and luckily Cragun had matured quickly enough to be able to step into such parts as the man in *Lied von der Erde* (where he had originally taken one of the smaller solo parts), but there was nobody in the company immediately available and suitable to replace Barra as Onegin. Donald MacLeary was fetched from London to learn and play the part, and over the next few months was to commute to and from Stuttgart whenever needed for it.

John had said he would revive his Cologne ballet, *Concerti grossi*, for the next new Stuttgart programme, due only six weeks after his *Brandenburg* premiere and five weeks after the first London *Card Game*. However, he decided to create a new ballet instead. The rest of the programme was to consist of *Giselle*, because, although John confessed himself quite out of sympathy with that ballet ("I don't like the music, I can't stand the silly story with its pathos"), he recognized that as a state-supported repertory company "you have to show the past as well as the present. If you're in repertory theatre and choose not to do Shakespeare, the audience can still go home and read Shakespeare. But you can't go home and read *Giselle*." Also, perhaps even more important, "You can't educate a ballet company that do not know what *Giselle* is... I can say I don't like Giselle because I know what *Giselle* is". So it was to be mounted by Peter Wright, who was an enthusiast for the romantic style. He took great trouble preparing a version that drew intelligent lessons from all the other major productions in finding its own path, and finally made his name internationally as a producer of the classics on the strength of it. Even the Royal Ballet in London soon asked him to stage his Stuttgart version of *Giselle* for their touring company.

Because the men, three or four soloists excepted, had little to do in *Giselle*, John decided to make a ballet mainly for the male dancers, to Mozart's Concerto for Flute and Harp. It featured two female and two male soloists, with a supporting ensemble of ten men, no women: just the opposite of the usual corps de ballet. A pleasant, lively work, it remains in the Stuttgart repertory to this day.

There were still some choreographic chores in store during the rest of the season: a pas de quatre, to the *Ruslan and Ludmilla* overture, full of swift bravura dancing for Haydée, Cardus, Madsen and Cragun to give at the Ballet Week gala — even earlier that year, in April, again because of touring plans — and the dances for a production of *The Trojans* by the Stuttgart Opera. However, the most important developments during the rest of that season happened off stage.

Reports began to appear in the press that Dr Sellner, director of the Deutsche Oper, Berlin, was trying to lure John there to take charge of perhaps a joint ballet company serving that theatre and Stuttgart as the basis of a national ballet. Sellner had been seen sitting in Dr Schäfer's box during the Stuttgart Ballet Week. It was no secret that John was unhappy that, in spite of all the progress made in his time, the Stuttgart Ballet still gave only fifty or sixty performances in a whole year at home, brought up to seventy-five by touring. He had been at pains to increase the company's stock by pointing out, on returning from London, that while there, people had been more interested in asking him questions about Stuttgart than about what he was doing in London. He had reached the point where it was no longer necessary to invite guests for the Ballet Week except for the final gala, which had a Royal Ballet contingent dancing pieces by Ashton and Bournonville. Understandably he was restive.

Contradictory accounts were published of just what was in mind; ranging from a complete merger to some cooperation between two separate companies. One commentator in a cultural magazine published in Stuttgart, *Dabei*, complicated the issue by suggesting that a Stuttgart/Berlin merger would not work, but a Stuttgart/Munich one might. Much was made, by commentators for and against a change, of the frequency with which Berlin airport was closed by fog, of the cool reception afforded by the Berlin audience to *The Lady and the Fool*, of disparaging remarks John had been heard to make about the standard of dancing in Berlin and, on the other hand, Gert Reinholm's claims of a transformation in the standing of the company and its individual style.

Government departments had to be involved on both sides, since much of the money for both companies came from public funds. Eventually an agreement was reached whereby John got at least part of what he was after. How far his heart was in any sort of merger plan is doubtful: it may all along have been, on his side, a lever to gain benefits for his own company, although he certainly liked Berlin as a city. In the event, Berlin engaged Kenneth MacMillan to take charge of the ballet's artistic policy, and John signed a new three-year contract in Stuttgart. Both men were to produce works for each other's companies, although not a great deal actually came of that. The official name of the Stuttgart company was changed from Württembergische Staatstheaterballett (Ballet of the Württemberg State Theatre) to Staatsballett für Baden-Württemberg (State Ballet for Baden-Württemberg), the whole "Land" — one of the constituent members of the Federal Republic — of which the former Kingdon of Württemberg formed part. Dr Schäfer was given the commission of discovering what could be done to provide more performances for the ballet in Stuttgart and in other cities throughout Baden-Württemberg.

Amid all these excitements, work went on. The season ended with visits by the company to Luxembourg in May, then in June to Munich, Vienna and Kiel. The most important of them, both for prestige and for its effect on the future, was to Vienna. The outcome could have been disastrous, because Barra had already decided to give up dancing altogether as a consequence of his injury (he went to Berlin as a member of the ballet staff), and then Cragun fell ill. Attilio Labis, one of the stars of the Paris Opéra Ballet, who had previously danced Romeo as guest in Stuttgart, was engaged to dance in Vienna, but he too was injured while rehearsing the day before departure. Consequently *Romeo and Juliet* had to be dropped. The company proposed to offer *Giselle* instead, as the audience was expecting a big ballet with a story, but the orchestra engaged to appear with them at the Theater an der Wien said there was no time to prepare the music. *Las Hermanas* was considered, too, but again there was nobody available to play the man's role. So it was impossible to give any narrative work at all in either of the two programmes, making their balance completely unrepresentative of the company's usual manner even though all but one of the works given (Balanchine's *La Valse*) had been created for Stuttgart. Public goodwill was saved only by the tact of John's curtain-speech before the performance began on the opening night, assuring them that the complete decors of *Romeo and Juliet* and *Giselle* were behind the scenes, and that it was misfortune, not bad faith, that prevented their being given.

The other works given that night with *La Valse* were *L'Estro armonico* and *Jeu de cartes*. A second programme consisted of *Concerto for Flute and Harp* and *Opus 1*, together with *Lied von der Erde* — this last being made possible only with the help of a member of the British diplomatic corps in Athens, who managed to find Donald MacLeary in that city, where he was on tour with the Royal Ballet, and arranged for him to rush to Vienna and perform.

Fortunately, the company made a good impression in spite of all the difficulties, especially on a member of the audience who was to play a key role in its further development, a gentleman named Martin Feinstein, from New York.

___A GREAT, ROARING,___
___SHOUTING SUCCESS___

MARTIN Feinstein was vice-president of the Hurok organization. Sol Hurok, with a reputation as America's leading impresario for dance, knew the great centres himself — London, Paris, Moscow, Leningrad — but he wanted to diversify and sent Feinstein travelling around Europe with a brief to find out what was new and promising. Seeing the Stuttgart Ballet for the first time at those Vienna Festival performances, without *Romeo*, without Barra or Cragun, he was at least able to catch three of the best ballets that had been made for the company (*Opus 1*, *Jeu de cartes* and *Lied von der Erde*). He arranged a meeting with John, at which he said that he thought the company was not yet ready for America but "there's something there; I guess three years". John's reply, as Feinstein remembers it, was "That's exactly my timetable".

It is a safe guess that if Feinstein had said one year, John would have agreed as readily. He once told an interviewer from *Newsweek* that when young dancers came to him with problems, "I usually tell them 'Do what you think best'. They think that's wonderful. All I really do is give them the courage to be afraid." He himself always dared to be afraid, to take risks. If a New York season had been set for the summer of 1967, it would not have been in his nature to refuse, and the intervening twelve months would have been spent working hard on preparing for the visit. Having three years in hand, he obviously gave himself the luxury of letting things develop naturally, and the only pattern that emerges during that period is one of diversification, experiment and spreading his energies rather than consolidating or concentrating them. It is as if some instinct had taught him to apply to his life generally the lesson he learned earlier from his ballets: "If you try too hard, you don't succeed."

So far as repertory was concerned, with one important exception (a very important one, admittedly — *The Taming of the Shrew*), the period from summer 1966 to summer 1969 added very little to what they actually took to New York. John undertook only one other big ballet during that time, a characteristically individual new version of *The Nutcracker*. As he remarked, "Even the purists, who insist that the original choreographies of the nineteenth century ballets should not

183

be altered", must admit that this case was different. He pointed out that only fragments of the original choreography survived, that important characters had little or nothing to do, and added more controversially that the children featured prominently in traditional stagings are "meaningless", and the "endless divertissements" of the second act "tasteless and stupid". He argued that the music was the ballet's only virtue, and even there he thought there first act too long, the second too short.

His solution to the problem of making a more interesting plot, while still relating to the music (which is so well matched to Petipa's original specifications that it resists too much alteration of context) was to treat the young heroine, not as a child but as a girl "at a difficult age, too young to count as a woman, too old to be a child". That is something which most other recent reinterpreters of the ballet have found for themselves (John's version was seen too little abroad to have been widely influential), but at the time it was an innovation. With that as his starting point, he invented a story in which Lene (as he renamed her) is in love with a young soldier, Conrad, but he is more fascinated by the worldly charms of a French singer and a Russian dancer. Luckily, Lene's godmother happens to be a fairy (an unconventionally mature and stolid one, Fitzliputz by name, played by the usually stern-looking Ruth Papendick with an unexpected twinkle in her eye) who is able to put a spell on both divas and give her protégée a magic nutcracker with hair remarkably like Conrad's. Naturally, in Lene's dreams he turns out to be Conrad, a nice fellow but unable to save her from being abducted by rats. He has enough sense to ask Fitzliputz for help, but she sends him to look for Lene himself, amid realms of snow and ice, guided by a star, until he finds her hidden at the heart of the rose which he had sent for her birthday. Although the dream has to end when the lovers have found each other, there is an epilogue in which Conrad rejects his earlier loves in Lene's favour.

With an extra interval to divide the first act after the party scene, some extra pieces of Tchaikovsky music to supplement the action (including a comic "Moorish dance" for men, after the big pas de deux), fuller roles for its principals, and both more comedy and more classical dancing than conventional versions, this *Nutcracker* was not to everyone's taste and has long since vanished, but it did at least get praised in an anonymous report to *The Times* as "both choreographically and dramatically superior to any of the various productions we have sen in Britain", and a selection of dances from it, presented just as a divertissement, was taken to New York for the company's first season.

The Prince of the Pagodas: Svetlana Beriosova and David Blair

John's "office" in the theatre
canteen at Stuttgart

RIGHT *Romeo and Juliet:* revival for
National Ballet of Canada, with
Veronica Tennant as Juliet

Onegin: Marcia Haydée with Ray Barra

Jeu de cartes: Egon Madsen as the Joker

John at the filming of *Die Befragung* for television (Egon Madsen at left)

ABOVE RIGHT *Présence:* Reid Anderson (in Bull's head) as Roy, Christopher Boatwright as Don

The Taming of the Shrew: Marcia Haydée
and Richard Cragun

Rehearsal at
Stuttgart: Juain Reyn
on John's left,
Marcia Haydée,
Alan Beale and
Richard Cragun on
his right

John in 1970

ᴇꜰᴛ John at
ʜhearsal: Jiri Kylian
ᴄing him, Jan
ᴄripling at right

On tour in Russia: broadcasting with Galina Ulanova

LEFT Dr Walter Schäfer and Frau Schäfer (left) with John at the opening of the new school in 1971

The Stuttgart Ballet on tour at Athens airport: Egon Madsen, Marcia Haydée and Judith Reyn on John's right, Birgit Keil and (behind) Heinz Klaus and Suzanne Hanke on his left

On tour in Russia: with Gadina Panova

John in his late Stuttgart days

In the studio, May 1973,
immediately before the
American tour

A late portrait

After the *Nutcracker* premiere in December 1966, John waited more than two years before undertaking another big ballet, although he did rework *Onegin* in October 1967 and intended to revive *The Prince of the Pagodas* in April 1968, but abandoned the production at a very late stage because he was dissatisfied with it as it had been and could not have approval to changes he thought necessary in the score. There was also, in June 1967, an attempt by Peter Wright to stage a new version of a long-lost nineteenth-century ballet *Namouna*, with music by Lalo and a melodramatic plot. It did not work out well: among other problems there was a solo in which Keil had to smoke a cigarette, and her "puff, puff, puff" on the beat caused amusement; feathers from a headdress fell loose and scattered all over the stage during a pas de trois; and the use of a couple of body-builders as extras during one scene made even Cragun's powerful musculature look puny. There were only two or three performances, and plans to revive it the next season and try to tighten it up fell through: John thought it not worth the bother.

What obviously interested John more during this period was branching out into experimental forms. First came *Die Befragung* ("The Interrogation") on 12 February 1967. The occasion was the company's first performance in the Kleines Haus, the smaller newer theatre adjoining the Grosses Haus, and used until then mainly for drama; appearing there was one of the means found for giving the ballet more performances. John said on various occasions that a prime inspiration of *Die Befragung* was the work of the painter Francis Bacon: a wish to capture in movement the frightening power of his paintings where a figure is seen in torment and alone. He had in fact more than once spoken to Bacon, whom he knew well, about the possibility of the painter's actually collaborating with him on a ballet, but Bacon said no, he did not want to supply a background. The only way he could accept would be by being active in the choreography, and he did not know enough about ballet for that. John's eagerness to work with Bacon came from the idea that his pictures "are pure choreography, because there is always a figure, always a naked figure, mostly a tormented form. And at the back is a curtain or a sheet of glass." He described *Die Befragung* as having been "generated" by Bacon's work. If he did not also have in mind consciously the novels of Kafka, then they must have worked their influence in the background. And the ballet took its shape and essence from the music of a strongly individualistic protagonist of modern music, Bernd Alois Zimmermann, whose Sonata for solo cello was played for the ballet by Siegfried Palm, to whom it had been dedicated at its composition four years earlier.

185

John described Zimmermann as a "dreamy, slightly bizarre man". The composer was full of theories about the relation of both music and dance to the other arts. He argued that "the ballet of the future will be a very complex one. All elements of the theatre of movement, including film, sound, speech, electronic music, must be mobilized into one great space-time structure" which would be regulated "by music as the most general form of temporal order". John could never have accepted that as a working rule for ballet as a whole, but it was nearly enough in accord with some of his own theatrical experiments for him to go along with the composer in trying to realize some of the ideas — although rather more in their next collaboration than this one.

There are three main characters in this ballet: a woman in a brown dress, a man wearing sweater and slacks, a girl in a white dress. At the begining they are clumped together in a knot; then a faceless crowd (they wear oblong gauze masks completely hiding their features) confronts each in turn. Some kind of crime, perhaps even murder (a man is seen lying still as if lifeless), may have been committed: the nature of the accusation and the guilt is not made clear, but an overwhelming sense of anxiety and despair is created. Some reviews described it as a "non-ballet", but it was a powerful piece of dance-drama, original and unforgettable, which survives also in a television adaptation with the original cast of Ilse Wiedmann, Egon Madsen and Anita Cardus.

The night of its premiere also brought a modern classic into the Stuttgart repertory: Balanchine's *Apollo*, staged and danced by Heinz Clauss, a new and valuable recruit to the company, the only one of its stars, after Barra's departure, not to have grown up under John's regime. Clauss was born in Esslingen, a small town only 14 kilometres from Stuttgart, and began his career there before trans-ferring first to Zürich, then Hamburg where he became a principal dancer. It was there that he learned *Apollo* and satisfied the choreographer sufficiently with his understanding of the work that he was allowed to restage it. His return to Stuttgart (initially as guest: he joined full-time after the summer break) was important in two respects. It gave the company its second German principal dancer, after Birgit Keil — a sensitive issue, sometimes, in its internal relations as well as its public standing — and it completed a team of three men — Clauss, Cragun, Madsen — each eminent in his own manner but totally different from one another, who among them could match each of the many-sided qualities of Marcia Haydée.

Clauss's presence was invaluable in the preparation of the revised *Onegin* later that year, since he could convey the world-weary

186

cynicism of the early scenes and, equally well, the abandoned romance of the idealized version of him seen by Tatiana in her dream, with the combination of those qualities helping to make the character's final capitulation credible. Before that, however, came three further creations.

One of them was a treatment of Messaïen's *Oiseaux exotiques* in a world inspired by Tinguely's strange animated sculptures, with Haydée as a human who meets various birds in situations with associations from Aristophanes to Hitchcock. That opened the Ballet Week on 5 May 1967, and it closed on 13 May with a gala including the other two Cranko premieres. *Holberg Pas de Deux* used music from the suite John had choreographed in Cape Town, but this time for a swift-moving show-piece for Keil and Clauss. *Quatre Images* was made to music by Ravel. The title is explained by a claim in the programme that the work presented "four separate episodes, each complete as in Ravel, but in their juxtaposition making a choreographic whole". That may have been literally justifiable, but anyone who knows of the difficulties put by the owners of Ravel's copyright in the way of using his music for ballets will recognize its evasive purpose. John was familiar, from having Balanchine's *La Valse* in his repertory, with the fact that the prologue of that work, danced to the *Valses Nobles et Sentimentales*, has to be set out on the programme as if it were a separate ballet, to satisfy the owners of the Ravel estate. So *Quatre Images* it had to be, even if many spectators thought that it had a story as clear as, and very similar to, that of *Ondine* — a ballet that John had been urged to tackle. Actually, the plot (a prince fleeing from his dusty court, meeting a mermaid and, through her, his doom) was even closer to a work by Andrée Howard, formerly in the Rambert repertory, called *Mermaid*, which used two of the same pieces of music (Introduction and Allegro, and Alborado del Gracioso). That ballet eventually had to be withdrawn because of the copyright difficulties John was ingeniously avoiding. John himself had also used the Introduction and Allegro, back in his Johannesburg days, for a puppet show based on *The Little Mermaid*. It seems likely that one or both of those earlier productions, at least as much as *Ondine*, put the idea into his head. His own ballet on this theme was substantial and attractive enough for him to mount it in Copenhagen when invited in 1971 to provide a triple bill for the Royal Danish Ballet.

Those pieces were not really out of the mainstream, even if *Oiseaux exotiques* looked deliberately strange; but for his next group of Stuttgart creations, a year later (the gap is explained by the diversion of rehearsal and production resources to reworking *Onegin*), John was

187

right out on a limb. This was a triple bill first given at Schwetzingen, a small town in the north of Baden-Württtemberg, for their annual festival. For this, he made three works, given together with the first professional ballet of one of his young dancers, John Neumeier.

The closing work on that programme found few defenders. Called *Kyrie Eleison*, it was danced to an orchestration by Stolze of Bach three-part inventions, with a cast listed as a woman, a man, an angel, and people. Its simple movement was generally thought far too naïve. The opening piece, *Fragmente*, to music by Henze, fared a little better, but it was another work to music by Zimmermann (the composer of the music used in *Die Befragung*) that really caused a stir.

Zimmermann did not compose any scores exclusively for ballet, but a dozen of his orchestral or instrumental works were meant to be suitable equally for the concert hall or the ballet stage. *Présence* was one of them, a "concerto scénique" for violin, cello and piano. The composer identifies each of the three instruments with a famous character from literature: Don Quixote (violin), Ubu Roy (piano) and Molly Bloom (cello). But they are named just Don, Roy and Molly, and he did not want the ballet treated in a literary way. He even described it as a "ballet blanc". That is understandable — what story could you tell using those three characters? However, to make clear who they are is difficult without introducing some dramatic action. John's solution was to introduce a comic episode before each of the five sections of the score. They are performed with the cast wearing identifiable costumes, and to a mixture of various sounds — extraneous music, incidental noises and some speech (with John's own voice, introducing a fictitious news bulletin, recognizable on the recorded soundtrack).

Don, the dreamer, hankers after his ideal woman, though she proves only too willing to remove her clothes (silhouetted behind a screen) for the benefit of bull-headed Roy. The latter, true to type, tries to destroy anything that gets in his way. Molly has a fantasy of sinking voluptuously into a living sofa that swallows her whole, and another of singing an operatic aria while a surgeon extracts a series of increasingly unlikely objects from her belly.

Between such farcical episodes, the characters strip down to plain leotards and tights with an identifying initial on their chests, and dance an abstract version of their wishes and relationships. An ingenious setting by Jürgen Schmidt-Oehm, which among other devices allows characters to pass through an apparently solid screen, adds to the fun. The ballet's mixture of knockabout comedy and philosophical abstraction, both based on eternal types of human nature, disconcerted many people, but John described *Présence* as his best ballet, which is a view that can be defended on grounds of originality, depth and creative collaboration, if not of wide accessibility to the public that his big narrative ballets attracted.

One of John's own comments on *Présence* was, "I don't know if it should be called musical theatre, or ballet, or what. I try to keep away from intellectuality. Art consists in doing it." His way of doing it, because of that attitude, never involved the exclusive and relentless exploitation of one approach, but a wild variety that could look capricious to theorists although it made sense in the context of his pragmatic theatricality.

Consequently his next creation, premiered only two weeks after the Schwetzingen programme on 1 June 1968, was a frivolous trifle, the *Suite from "Salade"* for a cast of three women and one man. When it was shown in New York on the company's second visit, even so sympathetic a critic as Clive Barnes described the choreography as "cute", which was not meant as a compliment. Perhaps the most interesting thing about *Salade* was the choice of cast, in which Birgit Keil, still only twenty-three although by now one of the long-accepted Stuttgart stars, was joined by three dancers of the new generation coming up in the company.

Judith Reyn, Keil's exact contemporary, was a Rhodesian who had joined the Royal Ballet, showed some promise, but become thoroughly dispirited by the lack of opportunity and encouragement she found there. John chose her to cover one of the roles in *Brandenburg*, and she enjoyed the experience so much that, instead of giving up ballet as she had thought of doing, she asked if she could join the Stuttgart Ballet. She arrived later that year, becoming a soloist the next season and, before long, beginning to share the big roles with Haydée and Keil. Susan Hanke was only nineteen and had joined the company the previous year with Reyn: from East Germany, she had come to the Stuttgart Ballet School and been sent for a scholarship year (like Keil) to the Royal Ballet School. She too came quickly to prominence in solo roles. The man in *Salade*, Bernd Berg, also came from East Germany and had escaped in 1963, aged twenty, joining Stuttgart a year later, and soon taking his place only just behind the trio of male stars.

Another important recruit was Alan Beale, a former dancer with the Royal Ballet who had to stop dancing in 1965 because of an injury. He turned to teaching and, after very little experience, was invited by John to join Stuttgart as an assistant ballet master in 1966. He soon began participating in other ways in the company's creative activity: as designer of *Quatre Images*, for instance, and choreographer of a pas de six to music from Khachaturian's *Gayane* for that same 1967 Ballet Week.

John's "family" of dancers and other colleagues with whom he had a long-term close relationship was growing. At the same time several of them were begining to develop talents for activities other than dancing — talents which in some cases were to cause them to leave and follow their fortunes elsewhere. This was largely thanks to the "Young Choreographers" programmes which John had incited the Noverre Society to institute. By the time the society celebrated its tenth anniversary in January 1969, it was able to claim that no fewer than eighteen would-be choreographers had been given chances through its special matinées. For the souvenir programme of the first decade, John wrote a short article explaining their purpose:

> Many people have asked me, how one begins to be a choreographer. The answer is "Education, talent and luck". First, one needs to have graduated from a really good school in which every style of dance is taught. Then one needs the opportunity to watch first-rate dancers at work and also great choreographers bringing their ideas to reality....
>
> But there is a fourth and more important proviso. There has to be a beneficent organization that is prepared to put opportunities for rehearsals, and a stage, at the disposal of dancers. Ballet has to be seen; it does not exist if it is not seen (it simply is not there). This last paradox was always very painful for me, when I was young and had to fight my way through. We envied painters, composers and writers who could express themselves on a piece of paper. A Bach can die and leave behind his Brandenburg concertos for a world to come. A choreographer is lost forever.

Before John's arrival in Stuttgart, the Noverre Society had presented lecture-demonstrations, by Beriozoff and others, on different styles of dance and mime. John continued those, taking as his subjects the anatomy of the dancer, the choreographer's vocabulary, or the analysis of choreography. But these talks and demonstrations were given only as the first part of the programme in which young choreographers presented their work. A surprising number of them went on to make a career as choreographers (and quite a few of the others, having realized that choreography was not for them, turned their gifts of enterprise, initiative and leadership to other activities in the theatre, as ballet masters, directors or producers). At the time of the tenth anniversary, one of the Noverre young choreographers, John Neumeier, was on leave of absence to

make a ballet for the Harkness Ballet of New York; he and Jiři
Kylian, who made his first choreographic attempts a little later, are
the most spectacular successes of the organization, now directing
their own companies in Hamburg and The Hague, but Ashley Killar
and Gray Veredon from John's day also made careers for themselves,
and some others who came on later.

Neumeier and Kylian, before branching out on their own, both
made their first professional ballets for Stuttgart after John had seen
what they could do at the Noverre matinées. They have both
acknowledged the effect of John's influence on their development, in
remarkably similar words. "The climate of creation was exhilarating.
I learned that the act of creation itself was celebration", Neumeier
wrote. Kylian told an interviewer, "Just to be in that creative atmosphere was exciting. John gave people chances and made them
grow. He had a tremendous ability to build people."

Ashley Killar was more specific about the kind of help they all
received. He wrote,

> John was the only choreographer I have met who had the gift
> (or indeed the will) to criticize the work of "aspirant"
> choreographers constructively and without bias of any sort. I'm
> not sure what the knack was, but his probing questions (always
> with gentleness and humour) made one think in new channels
> for oneself. Sheer enthusiasm when listening to one's ideas
> played a large part, I think. He recognized the quagmire of
> emotion a young choreographer is apt to wade in, and made it
> his business to know the "essence" (if such a thing existed) of
> what one was "getting at". This was *before* one has progressed
> very far with the work — rather different from the familiar
> "policy" of non-interference. Once or twice Cranko did suggest
> to me certain dancers he thought I ought to use. Not much else.
> After the performances were over, there was little in the way
> of a post-mortem — but one would feel that one's next ballets
> would be judged against the merits or failure of the previous ef-
> fort rather than by any other scale. My main memory,
> however, is of the generous encouragement John always had
> ready for each of us.

John's own comment to Fritz Höver, who was running the
Noverre Society, was, "The most important thing you can give a
young choreographer is the chance to blame himself".

The time for the New York season was growing closer, but meanwhile John had spread his energies wider by taking on new
responsibilities in Munich. The ballet director there, Heinz Rosen,
was retiring in the summer of 1967 and on 9 August the *Stuttgarter*

Zeitung speculated on the possibility of John's leaving Stuttgart for Munich, or perhaps even for London to succeed Ashton as director of the Royal Ballet. John wrote in reply denying any discussions about the latter, and saying that he would not become director of the Munich Ballet but that he would make ballets for them. Not until 31 October however was it confirmed that he had signed a contract as chief choreographer. That same day a not very tactful interview with John quoted him as saying that he did not like Munich as a city, thinking everything there imitated, with no atmosphere of its own. He much preferred Berlin, "in spite of the Wall and the uncertainty. This city fascinates me with its pulsating life." Asked what he thought about the possibility of a Stuttgart/Munich merger, he replied "Nothing! Nothing at all! The difficulties are already big enough in Stuttgart ... the bureaucracy in Germany is a problem."

A few days later, Dr Schäfer made a statement explaining that John's Stuttgart contract was due to run out at the end of the 1968–9 season, and John wanted a clause in the renewal stipulating that it was valid only while Schäfer remained as Intendant, but the latter had advised him against this. John then told Schäfer and others that he would go. Afterwards, the Munich direction had raised the question of a possible merger, but Schäfer talked them out of that. It was then that John agreed to stay in Stuttgart but take the Munich engagement too. He told Schäfer, "I promise you, Stuttgart will not be short-changed", and said he would cut out other guest engagements. Schäfer was convinced that agreeing to this was "the only way to keep him". John, meanwhile, had written to the *Stuttgarter Zeitung*, saying "There is neither in Stuttgart, nor anywhere else in Germany, an independent ballet company, performing every day, which could take up my full artistic activities. So next year I shall choreograph in Munich instead of, as before, London, Cologne, Berlin, Hamburg, etc.".

In spite of his expressed dislike of the city, John enjoyed some aspects of Munich life, especially the night-life there, on a bigger and freer scale than in Stuttgart. But the Munich Ballet has long had a reputation for being one of the most difficult to manage, with a degree of intrigue and politicking far above the average, let alone by comparison with the unusual atmosphere of sweetness and light in Stuttgart. Even though his responsibilities extended only to providing them with ballets, John had to tread warily. When he came to mount *Romeo and Juliet* there, for instance, he told Kenneth Barlow, who had been his first Tybalt (and a very good one) in Stuttgart before moving to Munich, "I've got to act politically, so I can't put you as Tybalt. I must give that to Hallhuber and cast you as Paris." Barlow wondered whether perhaps the Munich direction were expecting John to be difficult and insist on changes. He thought that if John had fought there as he did in Stuttgart, he could have succeeded — but to fight that kind of battle over again was expecting too much. So John just settled down to putting on his quota of new productions.

If, as seems inevitably to have been his motive, John hoped for artistic satisfaction from the chance regularly to make works for another group of dancers, he was soon disappointed. He started with two creations, given on 23 February 1968: *Begegnung in drei Farben* ("Encounter in three colours") and *Le Chant du Rossignol*, both to Stravinsky music. Already he found that the dancers did not give him much inspiration, and so it continued. For the rest of that year he mounted only revivals in Munich: *Katalyse* in May, *Romeo and Juliet* in November. During 1969 he made a more intensive effort with four creations. *Triplum* and *Grund zu Tanzen* were to music by living German composers, respectively Fortner and Grund; the latter's name provided that punning title, which translates as "Basis for dancing". They and *Fête Polonaise*, to Chabrier's music, were all given in May, right during the run-up to the Stuttgart New York season. Then in November came *Fête galante*, to a score by another modern German, Werner Egk. Also that year he gave Munich his Henze *Fragmente*, his *Daphnis and Chloe*, and one of his English ballets which had not been seen in Stuttgart, *The Shadow*. But thereafter he made only one further original work in Munich, *Ebony Concerto*, which needed a cast of just three dancers, and seems to have been the best of his Munich ballets, since it was the only one he thought worth taking into the main Stuttgart repertory. Apart from that, Munich got *Swan Lake* (in a revised version, incorporating a new role as a jester for a remarkable Hungarian dancer, Ferenc Barbay), *Orpheus* and *Présence* during 1970, all transfers from Stuttgart. In 1971, John relinquished the post of chief choreographer in Munich, but the following year, 1972, he mounted two further existing works there at the request of the new ballet director, Ronald Hynd: *Quatre Images* and *Onegin*. A Cranko creation, to music by Killmayer, was announced for the 1972-3 Munich season but not given.

Thus Munich gained far more than John did out of their association. They had the obvious immediate benefit of working with a lively choreographer of the highest repute, who provided many novelties to keep the dancers busy and the public happy. They also acquired a much longer-term benefit, since three of the Cranko productions were major works — *Romeo and Juliet, Swan Lake* and *Onegin* — which, more than a decade later, are still pillars of the repertory there.

John for a time had the excitement of trying to build a new connection, but that soon faded. He had hoped also to solve one of his personal problems. Eddie Dutton, one of the close friends who shared John's home, had begun to drink to an extent that interfered with his work as a dancer. There were increasing quarrels between him and John, and between him and Dieter Gräfe, who was also one of the occupants of the house on Neue Weinsteige. Eddie was sent to live in Munich as John's personal representative there, and joint ballet master. Unfortunately the hope of rallying him with this new job proved vain, and with the greater responsibility his difficulties in turning up on time for rehearsals became more crucial.

With the Munich connection, John had the commitment of commuting between two cities more than 200 kilometres apart. There were good autobahn links, but the journey often had to be made late at night, and he found himself sometimes having to rush to Munich just when he was busiest in Stuttgart, since both ballet compamies had to fit their premieres into the schedules of a theatre that was primarily an opera house, so clashes were difficult to avoid. There was a little complication about John's journeyings, too. He once drove past a traffic light when it was red. The police stopped him and took a breath test, which turned out to be eighty per cent above the permitted alcohol level: John joked to Dr Schäfer that "they could not have found a more favourable night for me". He lost his driving licence as a result of this infringement, and there was a story current among some of his friends that Schäfer, afraid of losing his ballet director through a fatal accident, had pulled strings to ensure that John did not get his licence back when he became eligible. The story as Schäfer himself tells it, however, is more amusing and quite in character. The procedure for restoring a driving licence after a period of being banned from driving included a visit to the police station for an oral examination. John arrived with his dalmatian hound, Artus, and was told that dogs were not allowed in the station. When he returned alone, he took out a cigarette and was told that smoking was not permitted, either. "In that case, please keep your driving licence" was John's response, and he left with a polite goodbye. Thereafter, he always had to be driven by a friend — which anyway suited his passion for talking or reading, rather than having to be at the wheel himself.

The roads between Stuttgart and Munich saw a lot of John

during the time of his engagement in both cities, but his travels with the Stuttgart company were also becoming far wider and increasingly frequent. After the Vienna Festival engagement of summer 1966, there was a December visit to Nancy, conveniently placed in the part of France nearest to Stuttgart, and then in January 1967 a further tour to East Germany, playing this time in East Berlin and Dresden. In the latter city, the greatest of modern Russian ballerinas, Galina Ulanova, was in the audience to see *Romeo and Juliet*, his version of the ballet in which John had first seen her dance in London. He was thrilled and when the applause for the ballet went on and on, with nobody from the audience leaving, John made a curtain speech saying how proud they were, not only to be the first ballet company from the West to play in East Germany, but also to have Ulanova there — whereupon she touched him even more by vacating her box so as not to rob the dancers of their applause.

Summer 1967 found them visiting Vienna again, followed by trips to Hammamet in Tunisia, Spoleto once more, and Athens. Tunisia and Greece thereafter became two of the countries John was enamoured of and went back to as often as he could, not as a tourist but mixing with loyal people. A couple from Stuttgart, on holiday in Tunisia, once passed a man in Bedouin robes, barefoot and carrying a staff. Suddenly the wife told her husband to stop the car: she had recognized Cranko's nose under the Arab costume. He had rich friends there, but made friends of ordinary people, and upset some of his acquaintances by embracing waiters with as much warmth as he did them.

There were even more exotic invitations for the following summer: to Lebanon, where the company played in the historic open-air theatre for the Baalbek Festival, and after that to Marcia Haydée's homeland, Brazil, for a season in Rio de Janeiro and São Paolo. Less glamorous, but carrying no less prestige, was an engagement at the Paris International Dance Festival in October/November 1967, playing at the Théâtre des Champs-Elysées.

There was a major task remaining before the New York season (apart from such minor matters as having new, bigger, grander scenery made to expand *Onegin* for the bigger stage, and rehearsing the company like athletes so that they would peak at the right time — actually, the excitement of the occasion would help them there). But first, there was another big premiere to come: *The Taming of the Shrew*, completing John's trilogy of full-evening narrative works.

Juliet and Tatiana had provided Marcia Haydée with great tragic roles, but her sense of humour, so keen off-stage, had been little used

195

in her dancing, since the comic ballets had tended to go to other members of the company. She was alarmed when John picked her for Kate

> because it was a comic role and I had always found my way with dramatic roles.... I remember, when we were sitting in the canteen, John told me he wanted me to be Katharina. I said, "John, I think you've chosen the wrong person". He said, "Nonsense, you'll find your way". And he used to give me the steps and then just leave me alone to work out the role. It took a long time; then suddenly at one rehearsal I got the thread, and at that moment he said, "That's it, now you have it".

The secret, of course, was that she acted the part as seriously as any of her tragic parts, and in fact that she put an element of tragedy into the plight of the young woman who is thought a shrew because her intelligence and pride made her rebel against subservience. John remarked, "Marcia is so funny because she is so sad", and he drew parallels between her performance and Chaplin's in his films, where the comedy came from the terrible and the sad things that were happening to him.

John picked on this subject, he said, because "I was reading *The Taming of the Shrew* one day, and I suddenly asked myself, why has no one made a ballet of this? It's so visual". It also happened that the time was ripe in that he had an ideal dancer on hand for Petruchio, and this (more than *Onegin*, more than *Romeo and Juliet*, although the men in both of these had been important) was a subject where the leading man was crucial. Barra, in the company's early days, would have been tough enough to play it, but Richard Cragun at twenty-four had exactly the right temperament and a blossoming virtuoso technique too. He had created roles in shorter ballets by John and others, and he had danced many of the bigger roles besides, but this was the first time (discounting the ill-fated *Namouna*) that anyone had built an evening-long ballet around his talents, and it turned out to be a part in which he was uniquely outstanding. John drew on Ricky's strengh, as a partner and a solo dancer. Alone, he hurtled breath-takingly high above the stage, whirling round three times before coming down again (most dancers, even good ones, are content with two). In the duets, he and Marcia threw each other around — literally, since they often had to end with a bump on the floor. The battle of the sexes acquired a ferocity new to the ballet stage, yet a gentle tendernesss peeped through long before the reconciliation at the end.

John claimed that the essential plot of the ballet was conveyed in their three big duets. In the first, Kate is the stronger; by the second,

Petruchio has the upper hand; and in the third, they find a balance. By this development, and by his sympathetic treatment of Kate, John disarmed at least some of those who find Shakespeare's play unforgivably anti-feminist. John's Kate was a more modern character: a free woman who chooses her own terms for life.

There was, however, a great deal more to *The Shrew* than just those two roles. As usual, John adapted his source considerably when turning it into dance. Many irrelevances were stripped away, including the prologue of the tinker, Timothy Sly, which John admitted "I could never understand" — in common with most readers and most producers of the play. On the other hand, he added a sub-plot about Lucentio's tricking his two rivals for the hand of Kate's sister, Bianca, into marrying a couple of whores in the belief that it is Bianca herself they are wedding. This looks so convincingly Shakespearian that most spectators, unless closely familiar with the play, probably take it as authentic. One of the whores was played by Ruth Papendick as a big, blowsy older woman, but for the other, John cast Leigh-Ann Griffiths, a tall, good-looking young woman who was the daughter of Lillian Graham, for whom John had made the ballerina role in his Holberg ballet before leaving Cape Town.

Susanne Hanke, in the second female lead as Bianca, like Ricky Cragun was enjoying her first major creation. Her admirers were played by two of the company's leading men, Heinz Clauss and Egon Madsen, with the rising soloist John Neumeier. All were given rich inventive comedy, notably Egon who played Gremio as if suffering from a cold the whole time, with neatly choreographed sneezes in his solo. John put in a private joke for Clauss as Lucentio, playing his guitar under Bianca's window as if it were Apollo's instrument in the Balanchine ballet so closely associated with him. The switch from comedy to romance for the main love duet between him and Bianca was an example of John's skill at mixing and contrasting moods.

With all its virtues, *The Taming of the Shrew* had one serious limitation. Scarlatti had long been one of John's favourite composers, but it was actually Schäfer who suggested using his music for this ballet. As for *Onegin*, Kurt-Heinz Stolze made a score based on a selection of short pieces by the old composer, in this instance from among his 550 keyboard sonatas, freely adapting the music when necessary, as well as arranging it for orchestra. Although skilfully done, it disturbed some music-lovers simply by being done at all, and even for those happy to accept it without complaints of sacrilege, there was a sameness to the score that prevented it from enjoying a full success.

During the three years since he first saw the company, Martin Feinstein had been in and out of Stuttgart preparing the way for their trip. He was there for a week, for instance, in October 1967 when the revised version of *Onegin* was first given. During the performance, he made notes of points that he thought might with advantage be amended, and afterwards went backstage where he found John as usual in the canteen, surrounded by dancers. He was nonplussed to be greeted with the words "Well, Martin, what did you think?" — he was accustomed to discussing such things only in private. However, he said he liked the ballet but had a few suggestions for changes. "Well, tell me what you think", John replied. "If I agree with you, I'll make the changes. If I don't, I'll hit you." Luckily they did not have to come to blows, and several changes (but not all those Feinstein suggested) were agreed on the spot, including one to the music after Stolze, who was conducting that night, had been brought into the discussion. "Will it work?" John asked, and on being assured that it would, "Fine". The most important effect of Feinstein's intervention was probably a heightening of the differences between the bourgeois party in Madame Larina's house and the grand ball at Prince Gremin's palace: John gave Jürgen Rose some ideas that sparked him off.

There were to be twenty-four performances during the three-week season at the Metropolitan Opera House, opening on 10 June 1969. Most of them were devoted to the big-scale story ballets: opening with *Onegin*, which took up no fewer than eight of the performances, the *Shrew*, with another seven. By the time they had given three showings of *Romeo* and two of *Giselle*, there were only four performances left for the triple bills of shorter ballets. Although New Yorkers would have a chance to see *Présence*, *Opus 1*, *Jeu de cartes*, the Mozart concerto, *Holberg* duet and a divertissement from *The Nutcracker* (quite a representative selection of the repertory, in fact), the image of the Stuttgart Ballet was clearly presented as depending on one aspect of its work. That was what Feinstein had decided would sell at the Met, and he was right. Having insisted on a (more than token) representation of the shorter, more experimental works, John did not dissent from the decision. It was during the final preparations for New York, when new grander versions of the *Onegin* and *Romeo* decors were got ready, that John told me, "Some people think commercial success is wrong, that somehow there is more prestige in attracting only a tiny audience, in order to prove how artistic you are. I could never agree with that. It must be because I have the theatre in my blood — I always want people to enjoy themselves."

It was his idea that *Onegin* should open the season, holding *Shrew* until the third night. That meant that their American principal dancer, Richard Cragun, would not appear at the opening. Thinking of his spectacular performance as Petruchio, Feinstein asked John, "Are you sure you're opening with the right ballet?" But John had his reasons: show Marcia first as a great romantic actress, he argued (knowing that people would enjoy the comedy of her Kate all the more by contrast), and hold Ricky unseen to surprise everybody. The strategy worked.

Looking back on that season, Clive Barnes (whose notices in the *New York Times* had helped to crystallize public opinion — although he could hardly take any credit for the first-night cheers) wrote that "No one is a small success in New York — you are either a great, roaring, shouting success or a dismal failure. The Stuttgart Ballet completely won over New York, partly with its ballets, partly with its dancing, but most of all with its spirit." John loved the audience response. He wrote, "Americans tend to express themselves outwardly, verbally, more readily than European audiences ... German audiences were trained from opera and concert-going not to applaud an act, or even between movements in a concert work. I like them to respond. I like them to laugh when it's funny or cry when it's sad."

Right up to the last minute, everyone in the Stuttgart party had been concerned about their New York reception, because they knew that, whatever successes they had enjoyed in the past, this was the engagement that could finally clinch their international standing. During the flight, John was outwardly calm, busy doing the puzzles in a German magazine and complaining how hard they were for a non-German. Marcia spent part of the flight talking cheerfully to a journalist, and when she had finished, Schäfer asked her, between themselves, how she *really* felt. "In one word," she answered, "I'm scared." Hurok himself met them at the airport. So did the German Consul-General, who greeted Schäfer with the remark "I hope you realize that you are in the most anti-German city in America". Fortunately the Cultural Attaché, Heide Russell, was more encouraging, and only later admitted that she had been as anxious as everyone else.

The dress rehearsal was a disaster, so much that Hurok asked Feinstein, "What kind of company have you brought me?" John managed to remain outwardly cheerful, even making jokes to a reporter from *The New Yorker* about the five tiers of boxes at the Met: "They look like giant molars just about to gnash. If they don't like the performance, I'm sure they go *snap*." But when asked directly about his feelings, he admitted that he felt "Numb. Absolutely numb."

On the opening night, it took time for audience response to build up. The ballet starts quietly, with a muted autumnal mood, a cosily domestic setting; and Heinz Clauss, in the title part, was a dancer of quiet, reserved manner. But as the drama developed, so did the applause, and the last impassioned duet between Haydée and Clauss brought the roar of cheering. After that, and the even greater triumph of *Shrew*, they were fêted all the way. When they arrived back home (their plane was delayed, and instead of landing at 3 p.m. did not reach Stuttgart airport until 10.45 p.m.), John's comment to the waiting reporters was that it had all been "Wonderful, wonderful — but I'll never say again, Stuttgart's too quiet".

John's holiday that year could hardly have brought a greater contrast to the urban excitements of New York. Enamoured of Greece ever since the company's tour there two years earlier, he went there — not to stay in any of the resorts, nor even (like many dancers) to visit the islands where there was nothing to interrupt a life of sun and sea bathing, but to live with goatherds up on the hills, as one of them. Unfortunately he broke his foot, and had to be carried down to the nearest town for treatment, so that it took two days before he reached a hospital, where his new friends were surprised to learn that he was actually a distinguished man.

CRANKO'S CASTLE

AFTER the triumphs of New York, nothing was too much for Herr Cranko in Stuttgart. Now at last he won a kind of independence for his company, freedom from the tyranny of the opera; he won new facilities for his precious school; his dancers became the best-paid in Germany; he was able to lead them to new foreign conquests, including Russia, the old homeland of classical ballet. Even the long desired but always frustrated wish to show London what he had achieved seemed to be in his grasp. Seen from outside, the four years of life remaining to him were a continuation and enlargement of his aim, a time to reap the benefit of the long struggle.

His status was confirmed in public regard by a move to a new home, at Solitude, about seven or eight kilometres due west from the city. He could reach it by road in twelve minutes if conditions were good, twenty minutes at most even if the city streets were congested before arriving on the motorway at the edge of town. The point about living there was not only the tranquil situation, with open country on all sides and marvellous views of meadows and woods; it also carried prestige because these were historic buldings, and disposal of them was in the hands of the city administraiton. The centrepiece of the development was Schloss Solitude, a "castle" or pleasure palace built between 1763 and 1767 for that same Duke of Württemberg who invited Noverre to be ballet master in Stuttgart. Behind this stand two curved rows of houses, known as the Kavalierbau, where the duke's followers lived when the court was in residence. It was one of those "knights' houses" that John occupied: his was house number 7, but at the time of his death he was due to move into another that he was having restored and adapted. That was necessary because the houses, although attractive in appearance, had been poorly built (the work was carried out by the Duke's soldiers). John's intended new home had been completely rebuilt inside and restored outside. It is occupied by Dieter Gräfe and Reid Anderson, who shared the first Solitude house with him, and they have furnished what was to have been his bedroom with his things from along the road. Any expectations of grandeur from the historic surroundings are far wide of the mark. It is a tiny room in one corner of the ground floor, with a small simple bed. Pictures, photographs and dolls fill every available space; they alone prevent it from looking austere.

Even in the sitting-room that takes up the rest of the ground floor, the furnishings are relatively sparse but good, in a mixture of styles. Among the pictures on the walls (two Pipers, two Picassos, a Miró) hung a wall carpet made by John during an illness, birds and bushes on a gold ground, signed $\frac{JC}{52}$. The kitchen and dining-room were down in the basement; the "boys", as John always called Dieter and Reid, had the upper floor. Here at Solitude, John was a familiar figure to the other residents, often out walking his dog Artus (the German equivalent of Arthur), wearing blue jeans and wooden shoes.

Unfortunately those final years, when everything seemed to be going well, were the time when the depression that had long been part of his nature took its firmest hold. During that time he continued to make some outstanding new ballets, but there were others that proved sadly below his own standard. Another developing problem, that John recognized before anyone else, was that the apparent advances of the company were often consolidation rather than real progress. But in the aftermath of the first American triumphs, nobody could have been expected to see the gathering clouds.

The importance of the organizational changes that followed the American success is best explained in John's own remark that, from being in effect the Stuttgart Opera Ballet, they suddenly became "the Ballet-Ballet". The difficulties of having to provide dancers for the operas had long been a complaint of his; he told an American interviewer, for an article that appeared in *Opera News*, "I can't say I'm happy to see some of our first soloists hopping around as extras in *Rigoletto*." In the early days, when there were fewer ballet nights in Stuttgart and few or no tours for the ballet, the opera obligations did have one compensating advantage: they justified giving the dancers year-round contracts and paid holidays (something that is usual in leading European companies, but even today is not universal elsewhere; among the reasons for a pay dispute in American Ballet Theatre, one of America's two leading companies, during 1982 was a claim for holiday pay to be introduced). However, as the number of ballet performances increased, at home and away, it became increasingly tiresome to have to fit in with the rehearsal and perform-ance schedule of the opera company.

The solution that was found was to institute a separate second company to take over all the opera-ballet commitments. But, since "no really good dancer wants to stay in an exclusively opera-ballet", they were also to be allowed some independent ballet nights when the mother-company was away from Stuttgart. In this way, John hoped to form "a lively and creative new company, which can have different

202

qualities from the original one". He obviously had the old Sadler's Wells Theatre Ballet in mind as a model, and he eventually used the new company, as Ninette de Valois had used that one in early days, to develop new choreographers and young dancers. But, remembering how often that had been thoughtlessly and hurtfully referred to as the second or junior company, he wanted a distinctive name from the start for his new company. Taking his cue from the well-established success of the Noverre Society matinées of new works, he named the new venture the Noverre Ballet, since one of the functions it would serve was the similar one of giving young choreographers a stage for their works, although John remarked that at first he might need to "pep up" the repertory with ballets by established choreographers. He also meant to give promising dancers from the corps de ballet of the big Stuttgart Ballet the chance to show what they could do with solo roles.

All this was agreed during the 1969–70 season, although the Noverre Ballet did not officially come into being until the 1970–1 season and, in practice, soon proved a disappointment, lasting only three years before it was agreed to kill it off. In prospect, however, it brought hope: much needed, because while everyone else was rejoicing at the New York triumphs (repeated in the autumn of 1969 when the company returned to America for a cross-country tour of sixteen cities), John told Fritz Höver, in a taped discussion, that "it's only a beginning". As well as being "the slave of the opera", the ballet had too little money for its activities and, in particular, the dancers were paid less than the singers. A ballerina would stay with lower pay only if all other conditions were good, and he pointed out that Marcia, Egon and Ricky were "world stars".

They were also, as it happens, sufficiently devoted to John personally, and to the company and repertory in which they had grown up, not to want to stray. Each of them by now was receiving more invitations to dance as guest stars elsewhere, Marcia quite often to dance with Nureyev in the classics (he had first partnered her in *Giselle* and *Swan Lake* as guest in Stuttgart), and Cragun to appear with Fonteyn. But they came home after their expeditions. An example of how the dancers thought about their director was provided that season during the preparation of one of the new works, *Poème de l'Extase*. John had been quoted as saying that he would like to have the men dancing nude but thought Stuttgart would not allow this. One of the leading dancers told me that if other choreographers asked them to do so, they would refuse, but "if John wanted it, we would know that it was artistically necessary, so we would do it". In the event, it turned out that they were to wear fine, one-piece tights

203

in flesh-coloured material with a pattern painted on them; and with the amount of lifting and carrying of their ballerina involved in the ballet, to appear without their athletic support-belts would hardly have been feasible anyway. But for a time, the rumours ran wild.

That was a year, 1970, when a great deal of talk was going on in Germany about the supposed need for the arts to be "committed" — to a political or social purpose, that is. John was invited to be the guest at one of a series of "meeting point" talks and discussions organized by the *Stuttgarter Nachrichten*. He began with a talk, illustrating with demonstrations by Susanne Hanke and Bernd Berg, about how a choreographer works, but when it came to question time the paper's arts editor, Jürgen Offenbach, and even their dance critic, Heinz-Ludwig Schneiders (in spite of being a good friend of John's), grilled him in what seemed an attempt to get a nice newsworthy indiscretion, but the nearest they got to this was that he said one of the points they made was "shit" — a less outrageous expression in German, as in French, than it is in English, but this did at least give them something to write about. That apart, John adroitly sidestepped all political questions by turning them into a discussion of art.

This was in March, between the premieres of *Brouillards* and *Poème de l'Extase*, given only sixteen days apart. *Brouillards* had been hastily created as a curtain-raiser for a new ballet by Kenneth MacMillan, *Miss Julie*, which led to a rift between Kenneth and John. There had been some tension throughout the rehearsal period because Kenneth insisted on bringing with him, to play Jean, a young dancer, Frank Frey, from the Berlin company he now directed. Frey was embarrassed by the situation, since although he had a strong personality and technique, those qualities were not exactly missing among the Stuttgart principals, so he was aware that his presence could hardly be welcome. Then there were difficulties about Barry Kay's designs: a cumbersome setting that took a long time to put up and remove again afterwards, and costumes which the dancers found to impede their movement, or even detract from credibility: for instance, in having Julie seduce Jean while still wearing her full riding-habit. John for once tried to suggest a change, but that was not kindly received. Two days before the premiere, Barry Kay called a press conference to announce that he was dissatisfied with the way the Stuttgart workshops had made up his designs and also because some costumes were not yet ready (a circumstance that arises quite frequently in the theatre). He therefore withdrew his name from the production and left town, accompanied by MacMillan. The dress rehearsal was consequently held without the creators, and John authorized some changes, including Julie's leaving the scene for a while and returning without her outer garments for the seduction on the kitchen table. The ballet caused so much misery that Marcia was physically ill after dancing the title part, and it soon disappeared from the programmes. Unfortunately, that also meant an end to MacMillan's Stuttgart activities for the time, and that lasted until after John's death.

Brouillards was made, to a selection of piano preludes by Debussy, to provide a lyrical and comic contrast to the melodramatic intensity of *Miss Julie*, and to give the soloists who were not in that ballet something to do. No money had been budgeted for costumes or scenery, so it was danced in white tights on a bare stage. In a prologue and an identical epilogue, the whole cast came spilling on stage from one corner, tumbled and whirled in a bright circle of light, then spun away into the darkness they had come from. Except for those episodes, each section used only a few dancers, generally two, three or four. Among them were a solo for Egon Madsen that revealed an almost incredible ease, strength, delicacy and lightness, for instance when he leapt over his own outstretched leg in a high rivoltade, then sank to the ground so gently that it was difficult to trust one's eyes until he did it a second time. Richard Cragun's number, "Hommage à S. Pickwick, Esq.", had him wearing a black hat and carrying a furled umbrella for an evocation of phlegmatic British imperturbability, continuing gamely about his business while a clutching, rolling, ensemble of men impeded his progress more and more and eventually overwhelmed him. Character, drama, mood or comedy illuminated each of the dances. In structure, the ballet reverted to that of some of John's early experimental pieces, and the contents were just as original, but now handled with an assured skill that made every one work successfully.

While *Brouillards* was almost improvised, John's other ballet made at the same time was the achievement of a long-held ambition. He had wanted to have Margot Fonteyn dance some of his early works, but when he asked for her (at the Covent Garden restaging of *The Lady and the Fool*, for instance) he was refused. Now he was able to create a work for her. He wanted to get away from the little-girl image to which ballerinas are mostly confined, playing sixteen-year-old princesses, adolescent peasant girls and similar characters. He thought it a pity that dancers were unable, like actresses, to graduate to different (and often more interesting) roles as they matured, and decided to create a part for the fifty-year-old ballerina that would make the most of her experience instead of trying to hide it. His first idea was to treat the story of Medea, but he came to the conclusion that the story could not be made clear enough in dancing. After that, he adopted Colette's novel *La Naissance du Jour* as his starting point, although the countrywoman recalling her past was transformed in the ballet into a famous actress, flattered at first by the attentions of a much younger man who falls in love with her, but then, as she recalls her former loves, realizing that this part of her life has already been fulfilled and so rejecting the young man.

Scriabin's music, with its accumulating torrents of emotion, suited the concept perfectly, and to match it, John and Jürgen Rose made the whole ballet visually an evocation of Gustav Klimt's paintings. After a realistic prologue to establish the situation (Wolfgang Fortner orchestrated Scriabin's Sonata no. 9 to accompany this), the ballet became a phantasmagoria of the boy's aspirations and the woman's memories, with four men — Jan Stripling, Bernd Berg, Heinz Clauss and Richard Cragun, each sharply differentiated in character — severally and then collectively coming between the two figures. Without the cloaks they wore for part of the time, the "memories" did in fact look almost naked, except that their flesh-coloured tights were painted with little jewel-like patterns. Two huge, multi-coloured curtains dominated the stage during the main action, providing a coup de théâtre at the beginning, as they tumbled down into position, and another, even more striking, at the end, as the past lovers seized a corner each and ran diagonally over the stage and off, causing the curtains to fall billowing down, across and out of sight as the music reached its last orgasmic climax. Yet the ballet essentially made all its points through dance, ranging from simple gestures to tumultuous patterns of movement.

It was, above all, a triumph for Fonteyn, even though John had felt it necessary, when she arrived to start rehearsals, to make sure that a photograph of Marcia Haydée embracing her appeared in the local papers, since by now his own dancers were held in such jealous esteem by their audience that a guest ballerina, even one as illustrious as Fonteyn, would encounter some ill-feeling without such an endorsement of her welcome. Fonteyn caught the Jugendstil feeling of the choreography with absolute assurance, right from her first entrance with hands held at a slight angle, arms curving gently down, hip thrust a little to one side so that her dress also flowed curvingly, and head alertly poised. She brought out the depth of emotion implicit in the role, not by opposing a natural humanity to the artificial conventions of the period, but by finding the expressiveness that underlay those conventions. All the same, it is a measure of the strength to which John had now brought his company that in Stuttgart it proved possible to present the work successfully with other dancers taking Fonteyn's place, whereas a revival for the Royal Ballet at Covent Garden two years later flopped, even with Fonteyn, because that company could not cast the male roles satisfactorily.

After two such hits as *Brouillards* and *Poème de l'Extase*, John's next ballet was a miss, but an interesting one. He wanted to present the trilogy of "Greek" ballets composed by Stravinsky. Balanchine's *Apollo* was already in the repertory, and he arranged without problems to be allowed Balanchine's *Agon* also, recognized as one of the greatest modern ballets. He was not happy about Balanchine's staging of *Orpheus*, however, even though the music had been written to Balanchine's specification, and decided to make a new version. Unfortunately his own proved even less satisfactory, although it does leave two vivid impressions in the memory. One is the vision of hell as a vast grey place (the stage was opened up to its full extent and many extras used) like a concentration camp; the other is the ferocity of the maenads tearing Orpheus to pieces with their bare hands and, when they turned from the plinth from which his body had disappeared, revealing their white costumes soaked in red.

That was on 6 June 1970, and he made two more small pieces for a gala later that month to end the Stuttgart Ballet Week, one of them bearing a title deceptively like one of his early works. But *Cous, coudes, corps et coeurs* was a new piece, still to Stravinsky's music but for four dancers only, who were given daringly difficult adagio tricks to perform. At the end of July, John completed a productive season (dominated by Stravinsky in its latter half) by remounting *Orpheus* in Munich together with a new work to the same composer's jazzy *Ebony Concerto*. The costumes by Sylvia Strahammer made the dancers look like brightly painted wooden marionettes with huge wigs, and the work, for three dancers only, was successfully transplanted to the Stuttgart company early the next season, having its premiere in Tel Aviv during a tour of Israel.

There was great uncertainty about the visit to Israel, right until the very last moment. The political situation in the Middle East was tense, and to add to other factors, this was the first German company to go to Israel since the war; there was some fear of attack by Germans who did not approve, as well as the other risks. Yet there was more exhilaration than anxiety once the Lufthansa Boeing had actually landed at Tel Aviv. Fourteen performances were to be given in different locations ranging from the Mann Auditorium in Jerusalem to the stage of the Kibbutz Ein-Gev, and naturally there was intensive sight-seeing and party-going too. At one party, when young people from many different countries were present, John remarked that about twenty different nationalities were represented

207

in the company and made everyone say a few words in his or her own tongue. Language fascinated him: on another occasion, Margaret Scott remembers him at a dinner party engaging for an hour in a discussion on the finer points of the history and usage of the German language.

It was about this same time, in the winter of 1970–1, that John suddenly developed an enthusiasm that seems extraordinarily capricious. One of the Stuttgart Ballet's American admirers, Donas Jean Russell, told him that a well-known collection of books and other material on dance, assembled over a period of forty years since 1930 by Doris Niles and Serge Leslie, was for sale. By John's account, this consisted of 2100 books, the oldest of them dating from the fifteenth century, 200 scores, and a dozen original costume designs. Librettos by Bournonville, Petipa, Nuitter and Saint-Léon, great choreographers of the nineteenth century, were among its treasures. As an historical archive, it was of interest, perhaps to be added to one of the existing dance archives (in New York, Paris or London, for instance), where it could be consulted by scholars and some of the material possibly published in modern version or facsimile. It is difficult to see how a strong case could be made for needing it in Stuttgart, however keen one might be on the idea of ensuring that the dancers and students had access to material for learning about the background of their craft. Somehow, John managed to convince Schäfer that it really was not only desirable, but so valuable to the city and the theatre that the price being asked for it, $80,000, somehow had to be raised. It is a tribute to John's standing by then, and to the way he could communicate his own enthusiasms (as also to Schäfer's organizing skills), that the money was found: half of it from the Baden-Württemberg Ministry of Culture, one third from the City Council, and the balance from a local bank, the Girokasse Stuttgart. The five huge chests of material arrived in February 1971 and were formally handed over to the Landesbibliothek, the state library.

Such an extreme enthusiasm, in John's temperament, was matched by extremes of depression. In this instance, there was plenty to provoke such a mood. In the summer of 1970, one of his closest long-term collaborators, Kurt-Heinz Stolze, was found dead in a dwelling in Munich. Stolze, a gifted musician, had worked on two of John's biggest successes, *Onegin* and *The Shrew*, choosing, arranging and supplementing the music by Tchaikovsky and Scarlatti respectively. He had composed one of John's early Stuttgart ballets, *Wir reisen nach Jerusalem*, had orchestrated *Les Sylphides* and *Kyrie Eleison* for the company, and had conducted all those and many other

208

ballets. In August 1970, aged thirty-nine, he travelled to Liechtenstein, where he was able to buy a pistol without needing to show a licence, went back to Munich and shot himself. The sudden loss of a dear friend and congenial colleague (a man even younger than himself, too) upset John greatly. Coincidentally, another musician he had worked with, Bernd-Alois Zimmermann, whose scores inspired *Die Befragung* and *Présence*, had died only a few days earlier, aged fifty-two.

There was another sad and unexpected death to come, giving John even more cause for grief. Salvatore Poddine, who had danced in the Stuttgart premiere of *Pagodas*, had helped his wife Herta look after John in early days there, and had subsequently begun a new career in drama, becoming director of the Chamber Theatre in Tübingen, a small town forty-six kilometres from Stuttgart. He had great successes there, and somehow those successes themselves brought difficulties which in the end proved too much to bear, and he hanged himself.

John's closest friends do not like to talk about the time that followed, but acquaintances in the town speak in whispers of an attempt at suicide, a doctor being called and John's life being saved. There is no great secret about the fact that he did begin to receive treatment for his depression. The medication he was given brought his despondency under control, but at the cost of subduing all strong feelings, so that he lost the joy of life also. For two years he was in a state of unnatural calm, painful to those who loved him. While receiving the drugs, he was forbidden alcohol, tobacco and sex, a radical change for a man who drank all the time and functioned well with it, who was rarely without a cigarette even when rehearsing, and who found new boys all the time to share his bed with him.

The deaths of friends were not the only reasons for his despondency during 1971. The early months of that year brought disappointments in his work too. First came another big story-ballet, *Carmen*. John said that he would never have thought of attempting it if he had known only the opera, with its heroine shown as a nymphomaniac, or a huntress chasing men. It was reading Prosper Merimée's novel that made him see her in different light, as an outsider, reacting to oppression. He saw in the situation of a gypsy woman, humiliated by Spanish attitudes, a parallel with a black woman in a white society today, or a Jewish girl under the Nazis. Don José, similarly, had a political or social motivation in this concept: a respectable Basque middle-class young man, like a tamed animal, who finds an urge to freedom within himself when he sees freedom embodied in Carmen.

The ballet became not a story of sexual passion but a study of two complex and fascinating people and their effect on each other. Carmen (Marcia Haydée, of course) began as a savage creature, first seen disrupting the cigarette factory with her rebellious disobedience and, in a quarrel with the supervisor, ripping the latter's dress open to carve a bloody cross on her back with a dagger. Gradually, making use of Don José, the gang of smugglers and the stupid, arrogant torero played by Richard Cragun, she wins her freedom by disguising herself as a lady, walking proudly in fine clothes. José (Egon Madsen) meanwhile suffers the opposite fate, turning from a smart young officer into a wild-eyed, unkempt rebel and outlaw. These were marvellous roles, given by their originators, and by later casts, with great power and impact.

In spite of that, the ballet was only a partial success, largely because of the music. John asked Wolfgang Fortner to write a score, and was at first refused because, although he saw the attractions of forgetting the opera libretto and working from Merimée's material, Fortner thought it impossible to compose another *Carmen* after Bizet. But then Bizet's music would not go out of his head, and he eventually had the idea of making collages and variations from it, which he did with the help of an assistant. The resulting score, however, was not especially distinguished; it also proved too short, so that the ballet *Carmen* could not stand satisfactorily on its own as had been intended. Like more or less everything the company did at this period, it was indulgently received by the Stuttgart audience, but when it was given in New York that summer the first ovation did not come until Cragun's big solo, more than halfway through the ballet. At the end, cheers for Haydée and Madsen were mixed with a few boos, which became a chorus when John came on stage. He was already dissatisfied with the work before then, and after only a year in the repertory he decided to drop it until the ballet could be reworked, musically and choreographically. He died before that could be done, and a revival some years later was in fact amended by Marcia and her colleagues from the original cast in a way that they thought John would have wished.

There followed, in quick succession, several new productions. First, a triple bill of existing works (*Quatre Images*, *Opus 1* and *The Lady and the Fool*) for the Royal Danish Ballet. Next, a new version of *The Seasons* to give the Stuttgart Ballet a big display number for their second New York season, which occupied six weeks at the Met during April and May. Heinz Clauss and Richard Cragun were in it, but not Marcia or Egon; instead, many of the young dancers were featured, including his new American virtuoso, Joyce Cuoco, and the choreography pushed the dancers to the edge of their strength for big,

210

bold dance effects, some more successful than others but all exciting.

Immediately before the company's departure for New York, the Noverre Ballet gave its first independent performance. Anne Woolliams, Alan Beale and another teacher, Fay Werner, had been working all season with a "studio group" of advanced students from the school, who had also been appearing in the operas, starting with *Aida.* John had said he thought of producing *Coppelia* for them, but in practice Beale was mainly responsible for staging it, with some help from John. Many of those involved enjoyed new oportunities. There were new designs by Wolf Bauer, a Stuttgart textile designer whose work John had seen at a design centre exhibition; and Dr Coppelius was played by Ulrich Behrisch, a former member of the corps de ballet making a come-back as a guest artist. The other leading parts were given to youngsters, Cuoco and Andrew Oxenham. Cuoco, who was born and grew up in Boston, appeared as a child prodigy on television shows and at Radio City Music Hall, where she displayed her ability to turn apparently unlimited numbers of fouettés. This astonishing technique was accompanied by a childish appearance; when she joined the Stuttgart Ballet in 1970 she was seventeen but looked pre-pubescent. At her audition, Anne Woolliams had doubts about her value to the company but John insisted "She will grow with love", and he proved right.

The acquisition of new dancers from many different sources was both a benefit and a problem. John was forcefully opposed to what he called the "closed atmosphere" of national companies drawing their dancers from an attached school. His open attitude had brought him almost all his leading dancers, and as the company toured more widely, the numbers turning up in Stuttgart and applying for jobs were supplemented by others who saw the company in their own town and wanted to join. The competition for places ensured a steadily growing standard, and although the recruits did not have the uniform style that comes from having studied at the same school (as with the leading Russian, American, French and English companies), John did not worry about that. His attitude was that the company should be able to adjust totally to the style of the choreographer and the ballet they were working on at any moment. He went so far as to say, "We have no style. It's a personal thing, like playing Mozart. It depends on what you think Mozart wanted. You don't play Brahms in the same way."

The other side of the coin was represented by a letter published in the *Stuttgarter Zeitung* in 2 April, shortly before the New York trip. This complained that "in what is perhaps internationally the best-known German ballet company, German dancers are dying out. In the Stuttgart ensemble of about fifty members there are exactly five female and five male German dancers." All ten of those felt obliged to sign this "cry for help" from an enlightened public: Birgit Keil, Susanne Hanke, Bernd Berg, Heinz Clauss, Jan Stripling, Dieter Amman, Hedda Twiehaus, Ruth Papendick, Gudrun Lechner and Ulf Esser. Many of them were dancers whom John particularly favoured and advanced, which must have made it harder for them — and him — to accept the necessity for such a public gesture. In fact, only three of the ten were in the corps de ballet, the others all being principals or soloists, which gives rise to the thought that it should have been possible, and would certainly have been tactful, to ensure that a few more Germans were recruited at the lower levels. All the more so, as it was now ten years since John had taken over responsibility for the Stuttgart Ballet School along with the company; and besides, at that very time (only two years after the school moved in with the Werkschule) a sum of DM 2,200,000 was being spent on preparing a building for a further, even more drastic and ambitious reorganization by which the ballet school again became independent, functioning as an academic high school (what is called in German a *Gymnasium* — nothing to do with the English meaning of that word) in the mornings, with dance classes all afternoon. It was the first ballet school in Germany to accept boarders, and the city had agreed to meet fifteen per cent of its running costs. It began functioning in October 1971, although the official opening ceremony was not held until 1 December, when John's speech, in informally colloquial German, said that "the little home has been built, now it's work, work!" ("Das Häusle ist gebaut, jetzt heiszt es schaffe, schaffe!")

By then, the company was back from a further visit to America, for a ten-week tour (again separate from the New York season), and John himself was back from creating one of his most unusual ballets, *Ami Yam Ami Ya'ar*, a Hebrew title generally translated as *Song of My People*.

John had received many requests to make a ballet in Israel, and the invitation he eventually chose to accept was from the Batsheva Dance Company, which was the least balletic, having been founded in 1963 with Martha Graham as its artistic adviser, and drawing its dancers and choreographers largely from those who had come under the influence of her style of contemporary dance. John told Domy Reiter-Soffer, an Israeli dancer and choreographer who was in Tel Aviv working with the rival Bat-Dor company, that he thought it would be challenging both to him and the dancers to do something different. The work he produced was quite extraordinary, like no other, and extremely moving.

He visited Israel first to watch the dancers at work and to decide what to do for them. He had no preconceived ideas and spent some weeks finding out as much as he could about the artistic interests and experiences of the Israeli people. That led him to the conviction that it was in words, literature, and specifically in poetry that they expressed themselves most deeply and truly. He asked to be shown as much poetry by modern authors as possible, anything that was written in English, French or German, and translations from poems in Hebrew. As usual, he read voraciously, and he had a literary adviser Israel Yuval, to explain the poems and the background and to help with the final choice. It took some months to achieve the final selection which gave the ballet a theme which the programme note defined as "A nation and man move in parallel cycles from death to regeneration". Seven writers were finally represented, two of them living, the others all having written in this century, except for a passage from the *Song of Songs*. Rahamin Ron, a dancer closely involved in the creation of the ballet and its later preservation, told me that they were very familiar poems which a child learns at school and "no Israeli choreographer would have dared choose something so familiar".

Although he spoke no Hebrew, John wanted to work to both the sound and sense of the text, and decided that the poems should be recorded. He chose Chana Maron as the narrator, thought by many to be the most accomplished and versatile of Israeli actresses. She had been shot by terrorists in Munich airport only a year earlier, and had to have a leg amputated, but that coincidental connection with one of the cities where John worked, although it might look significant, was not the reason for choosing her; it was her deep husky voice and the way she used it that moved John, who described her speaking as "music from the soul". One poem, beginning "I know, I know, that soon I must die", was sung by a soprano in a setting by Erich Sternberg, a German-born Israeli; other spoken sections had accompanying music for percussion and flute by Ruth Ben-Zvi, whose own playing of an oriental jar-drum, a folk instrument she had made her own and developed to concert use, also accompanied the only section without words, an exhilarating dance for men. But it was primarily the resonant, varied and expressive voice of Chana Maron that took on the quality of music for the ballet, and John laid down that her recording must always be used and never replaced by a translation.

When he came back to Tel Aviv to make the ballet, he worked quickly and sympathetically with the dancers. Rahamin Ron said,

> I have worked with many choreographers, and almost all gave you the idea that there was something wrong with you, something you couldn't do. John never gave any sign of that.

I thought, he is used to working with this wonderful company in Stuttgart, but he seemed to look for what each person can do and what their nature was. "All right, you can't do five pirouettes but there's something you *can* do."

Ron explained that the solo he danced was "very much me — I'm very patriotic, I do forty days in the army every year. It's a boy who is born in Israel and is happy because the sun is his, the air is his, the landscape . . . then other men are born from him and become an army." That dance was made in just one rehearsal of one and a half hours, and nothing changed afterwards. John originally set all the male solos on Ron, but later took the other ones away and gave them to different dancers. Ron was very hurt and asked Israel Yuval why, getting the explanation, "He liked you and wanted you to do it, but then the people would look at you and see the dancer, not the idea". The importance of the ideas is indicated not only by the general shape of the finished piece, but by the fact that when actually making the dances, John would ask which was the exact word that meant something.

The ballet begins with a scene that shocks an audience and even shocked the dancers in rehearsal. The words describe a man brought "to the mound of corpses that was in the snow in the foreign field", screamed at by a German officer to undress, hesitating in his white underwear, his socks and his white skullcup, then struck between the shoulders with the officer's weapon, and falling with "a groan that was like the finishing of a last prayer, after which there is no more prayer, only a clouded sky, a heap of corpses, and a live officer, smoking in the snow-covered plain" — the snow "melting, reddening, because of the blood that came out of his mouth, from his burst lungs". John had the men enter, one by one, take off their coats, shoes, trousers, then walk forward and fall, forming an ugly mound. The text makes the point that the man "in all his days . . . had not stood naked in his underclothes beneath the dome of the sky", and although the tights they wore were as substantial as their usual costumes, the dancers at first felt embarrassed with the undressing, but then thought, "Well, it was like this, that's how it happened, so why not show it on stage?"

Women lament the dead, but their dance is very sharp, containing the idea that on the day this thing happened, the sun shone, the breeze blew through the trees, mothers took their children to play. There was a strange dance for the company's finest dancer, Rina Schenfeld, in which (enveloped in a white cloth, and with left arm outstretched and right arm held bent against her) she represented a white bird with only one wing, and also stood for the spirit that receives the souls of those who are ready to die.

The image of a man born from within a group, a recurring one in John's work from the earliest days, found a new development in this ballet. Ron, after raising up the prone figures of his comrades, was himself born from them. There was a marvellous visual metaphor in which couples rushed together, two by two, to embrace, and his head squeezed successively between the bellies of each couple in turn, like a child emerging from the womb. At the same time, John found entirely new resources. For the men's dance to drum music, he wanted strong steps from folk dance. The men showed him the debka. He chose steps from it, and added Graham-style jumps to go with them. Another element at once new and old was the use of hands. For a poem about "The Hands of Israel" he stood dancers exactly one behind the other to give an illusion of multiple arms from a single body; it was the sort of trick he would have delighted in during his days of staging revues, but this time he used it seriously.

With hindsight, people have read a premonition of John's own future in the emphasis on death, but the ballet was equally emphatic in its presentation of love, from the frankly erotic dance for women ("Night after night on my bed I have sought my true love") to the celebration of "God lives", which found proof of that belief in opposites, the harshness of life as well as its pleasures. Perhaps the poem closest to John's own beliefs was the last:

> I always want eyes to see
> the beauty of the world and praise
> this wonderful faultless beauty
> and praise Him who made it so praiseworthy
> and full, so full of beauty.
> And I don't want ever to be blind
> to the beauty of the world as long as I'm alive.
> I'll give up many other things
> but I'll never have enough of seeing
> this beauty in which I live. . . .

The title of the ballet, *Ami Yam Ami Ya'ar*, generally translated as *Song of my People*, should more correctly be *Song of my People-Forest, People-Sea*. It becomes clumsy out of Hebrew, because the idea it expresses is strange to us. In the poem from which it is taken, the image is of a man calling out in the forest and hearing his voice answered by an echo, but if he lifts his voice by the sea, "The sea never answers, the water goes on flowing". The poet complains that his people, a forest to the peoples of the world, who come to chop down the trees "for pillars and cills and roofs of palaces", is like "a sea unanswering" to its own prophets.

During the making of the ballet, John was sick in body and spirit. He became restless in the heat, drank a lot, and developed a painful rash, for which tablets were prescribed that ought not to be mixed with alcohol. Yet he continued working with energy and vigour, like a man possessed. One evening, in a restaurant at Jaffa, he suddenly dropped his glass and broke it. He had just noticed that the waitress, a women in a white, light dress, had a number tattooed on her arm. He kept watching her movement, the way she was serving, then turned to Domy Reiter and said, "God knows what she must have gone through during the war. Maybe she lost all in the concentration camp, not only her best years and family, but dignity. But look at her: she is life itself, she wants to live in spite of everything. She looks like a dove having served in hell." A week later, he choreographed the dance of the woman wrapped in a white cloth — a wounded dove trying to fly, hovering above the ashes of bodies.

As the days went by, he became more possessed and restless; his rash grew worse, and he drank more heavily. He spent most of the night listening to a tape recording of the poems and music. Then when he had time to spare, he would sit in an open-air bar watching the people go by. On one such occasion, he burst out,

> Look at these people! God, they look as if they are not in a state of war and constant danger; they ignore reality. God, I hate them! What state of mind must they be in? How can one run from one's problems? These fucking people — I hate them — in fact, what the hell am I doing here at all? God Almighty, why should I care? These people don't mean a fuck to me!

He grew more and more angry, then turned to Domy Reiter and said, "I'm going", left the table and disappeared in the crowd. His companion sat embarrassed, finished his drink, and was getting up to go when John returned, red-faced but calm. Domy Reiter offered to take him home, but he said no, he wanted to sit. After a long silence, he said,

> Do you know that I have Jewish blood in me, in fact a lot of Jewish blood in me, too much Jewish blood in me to ignore that part of me; and the strangest thing about it is, here I am in Germany promoting and helping to build dance in the very country that helped to exterminate that part of me. In fact, if I was living in Stuttgart then, I would have ended in some goddam oven.

Then he went on to talk about how much he cared for the dancers in his company. At one moment he was asking "How can I bear to live and work in Germany?", at another he said, "I don't belong to any nation, I don't belong to any country, I don't belong to any creed. I'm a choreographer, I'm an artist, I belong to everybody. But I have a conscience."

In spite of his troubles, John completed his work on *Ami Yam Ami Ya'ar* so quickly that he had time to teach the company his Stravinsky *Ebony Concerto*, too, which they danced with the women in soft shoes instead of on points. It made a frivolous contrast to the serious work and helped the success of the programme.

Actually, John never saw the new ballet complete. The men were having difficulty with the rhythm and speed of their warlike drum dance and could not perform it strongly enough, so before the first night he said to take it out, but that he wanted them to put it in again when they could do it strongly. However, about that time the Batsheva company had a number of caretaker directors, who instead of restoring that dance, decided that the ballet was too long and started making further cuts, choosing just the bits that looked good. The result was that the work, carefully planned for a particular purpose, no longer made sense. Luckily, a new American director, Paul Sanasardo, arrived a few years later and saw the video tape of the ballet. He realized that "It may be long, but it is properly shaped. Cranko knew what he was doing." Rahamin Ron, by then rehearsal director, managed to put the whole work together again, to last fifty minutes instead of the twenty-five it had been pared to, and in that form it no longer seemed long because its parts supported each other.

Sanasardo commented, "There is a lot of talk about doing Israeli ballets, but actually *Ami Yam Ami Ya'ar* is the one that I think has the greatest feeling for the country and its traditions." It was he who told me that John gave the ballet to Batsheva in perpetuity without a fee. Another example of his generosity, in a different way altogether, is that although he could certainly have designed the very simple costumes himself, he found two young boys in the company, Ya'akov Sharir and Yair Vardi, who were eager to work and advance themselves. One day he used them to help in a rehearsal where he experimented with cloth for the effect he eventually obtained of the wounded bird, and after that he asked them to go ahead and try designing the ballet, which they did.

After the premiere, he said, "Well, I can go now. I've done my bit, I've done what I needed for that part of me which belongs here." Yet that part of him did not interfere with his developing a passion also for Arab people and culture. Contrasts and contradictions flourished within him, another example of this being that, immediately after the depth and quality of his work in Israel, the first work he made on returning to Stuttgart, *Into the Cool*, was shallow and boring. Presented by the Noverre Ballet in the Kleines Haus on 19 December, it was a suite of dances, to music by Stan Kenton, in a jazzy manner that lacked invention, punch or humour.

Yet his next creation for the big company, which was given exactly one month later, was one of his big successes: *Initials R.B.M.E.* The music is Brahms's Second Piano Concerto, each movement of which was inspired by a different personality (himself, his violinist friend Joachim, and Clara and Robert Schumann). Similarly, John created each movement of the ballet around one of the friends who had been with him since the earliest days in Stuttgart: Richard, Birgit, Marcia, Egon. Each of them had a supporting group of dancers, but they also appeared in one another's sections — not necesarily to play any very active part, but just to be there, evoking the real-life situation where each was a strongly defined individual with a life of his or her own, but all helped and sustained by their friendships. There was no need for the public to be aware of this; the ballet was developed as a plotless classic ballet, full of very demanding choreography, but the underlying idea helped the performers to give it a sense of being something more than just display. Cragun tells the story of dancing it during the Russian tour that they undertook soon after the premiere, and because of other problems losing himself until the other friends came up to him as always at that point, but with genuine concern for him, whereupon he recovered.

The tour in Russia was an occasion of extreme contrasts. On the one hand, John more than anyone else was conscious of the honour of leading his company to the city that had been the undisputed world capital of ballet when it was still St Petersburg, and even as Leningrad still held supremacy as a centre of perfection in classical dancing. Moscow, too, was a special challenge because of the great influence the Bolshoi Ballet's visit to London in 1956 had exerted on John's own way of working. On the other hand, all his hatred of oppressive regimes was stirred by some of the things he found there.

There had been seemingly endless negotiations with the representatives of Gosconcert, the official Russian agency handling the tour, about what works to bring. John insisted on opening with *Onegin*, which Russians in the United States had praised, saying that it caught a true Russian spirit. Gosconcert said no, Pushkin was a kind of saint, a holy figure to be handled only with kid gloves. Schäfer would have accepted their advice, but John dug his toes in: *Onegin* or nothing. He similarly insisted on taking some modern works in a mixed bill, also against advice, and had the satisfaction at the Stanislavsky Theatre, Moscow, of seeing sixteen people crammed

218

into a box for eight persons, so great was the demand. However, the Russians did not altogether approve of *Onegin*, and criticized it for missing a true understanding, although Marcia's performance as Tatiana was so ecstatically admired that the reception was a warm one. *Shrew* was a more complete success, and the applause one night went on so long that the last duet was eventually encored, although by then the orchestra had already left and it had to be danced in silence. On the mixed bill, that began with *Brouillards* and ended with *Initials*, the central part of the evening was given over to short numbers, among which the duet *Hommage à Bolschoi* was particularly appreciated. That programme had great success in Leningrad, too, where the tour began at the Maly Theatre, before moving to Moscow by way of the opera house at Riga.

There had been no great enthusiasm before the company's arrival. People thought that, coming from a small German town, they could not be much good. After the dress rehearsal, word spread quickly that this was something special, and there was a rush for tickets. Even so, some people left before the end of *Onegin* (and thereby missed the best of it). With reservations about that work, praise was lavish. Ulanova, in a television interview with John, praised the technical strength of all the dancers, the way each was in command of his or her own body, and said she found no strain anywhere.

Off stage, however, not everything was going so well. One problem in Moscow was that while some dancers had luxurious apartments at the Metropol Hotel, others found themselves in miserable little rooms; Susanne Hanke had to go to the doctor after spending three days without central heating in her room. A report sent back to Stuttgart said, "The kids can talk of nothing but eating". There were other frustrations, too. John wanted his dancers to meet Ulanova, but they were escorted everywhere by men from two ministries, foreign affairs and culture; when one said, "Tonight we shall go and see Ulanova", the other revealed that actually a different expedition had been laid on for them; and the next time they simply swapped roles in that little exchange. Finally John lost his temper, burst into tears, and said "No! Tonight we *shall* go to see Ulanova" — which they did.

Naturally they were taken to ballet schools, tours of the cities, all the obvious sights: churches, museums, the Kremlin, the Metro. There were embassy parties and official receptions. But John managed also to get involved with artists of all sorts outside official circles, including those opposed to the official line. The most crucial friendship he struck up was with the Kirov Ballet dancer Valery Panov, already disaffected, wanting to leave Russia, and within a few weeks

219

of publicly declaring that intention. Panov took John to meet other friends; they spent three nights talking and drinking until dawn, and spent a last day together in the country, walking and singing in the open air, taking a steam bath, drinking again. Panov criticized *Onegin* for not being Russian enough, and was not immediately impressed when John replied, "I wasn't making it for Russians", although he saw the force of that once he himself got to the West. To his astonishment, John actually invited him to Stuttgart after Panov had spoken at length about his ideas for ballets and his desire to leave Russia. John told Panov, "I'll give you dancers to work with, I'll correct your choreography, in two years we'll be able to show your work everywhere." Panov was hurt at first, thinking John was mocking him, but realized he was serious when he asked for a pen to draw up a contract on the spot. John promised to badger the Russian Ministry of Culture to let Panov come to Stuttgart, and also to get the Israelis to send an invitation.

In Moscow, too, John met artists away from the official receptions. One such party came about because a Stuttgart fan of the ballet company, who had travelled to Russia with them, met a young Bolshoi soloist during an intermission at the Stanislavsky Theatre one night. Invited to the dancer's home, he offered to take John with him. They arrived bearing vodka; their host already had caviar, and the informal feasting and talking went on until three in the morning. Other guests were a tenor and a journalist. John told the Russians in English how to make a ballet. Before he left, the Russians gave him as souvenirs a cross and a gramophone record. John also managed to meet an "underground" painter and bought several of his pictures.

Although he found much to enjoy in Russia, John was in a black mood when he flew back to London (leaving the company, then returning to join them there again) for the Covent Garden premiere of *Poème de l'Extase*; Peter Rosenwald remembers him very miserable at the party after the performance. Yet he brought a present of twelve Russian eggs made of marble from the four St Petersburg palaces — different colours but, John joked, no white "because they would not be able to find it in the snow".

When the ballet returned to Stuttgart, there was a big gala to honour their success. Tickets were at a premium, so there was some consternation at the theatre when a telephone call was received on the actual day of the performance: Herr Ministerpresident Goppel would like to come. Naturally they promised to try to find tickets, and in due course rang back the number given to report success. It was arranged that a chauffeur would come to collect them. A young man, fair-haired, called for them, and there was some surprise when he was later seen sitting in the box with another young man. It's all right, he explained, the president was suddenly ill; he was his nephew. A further call was made to the "chancery" and this time the response was from a private name. Consultation with the telephone directory revealed the correct number, where it was learned that the president was not ill and had not requested tickets. The incident suggests the unusual lengths to which some admirers were prepared to go in order to be present.

The Russians, for their part, decided that they would like to cement the newfound links with Stuttgart. Gasconcert offered not only to supply two Bolshoi dancers as guests for that year's Ballet Week, but also to send two singers to appear in the Stuttgart Opera's production of *Eugene Onegin*. By the time the offer arrived, however, Valery Panov and his wife Galina had applied to leave Russia and in consequence had been put in public disgrace. John had grown fond of his new friend, to the point of handing over his own Star of David medallion, a parting gift to him from the Batsheva company — or rather, not himself handing it over but, in an attack of shyness, getting one of his colleagues to do so. He was now devoting himself, by all means he could, to the campaign to win permission for the Panovs to leave (it succeeded only after his death). Without waiting even to discuss the matter with Dr Schäfer, John sent a telegram to Moscow that, while his friends were suffering, and until they could visit him in Stuttgart, no Soviet dancers would appear there. That was the end of the Russian dancer guests, and to nobody's surprise it turned out that the singers were also unable to come because one was reputedly ill.

John continued to keep up pressure on behalf of the Panovs in every possible way, and a year later, one of the works on the last new programme he made before his death was *Spuren* ("Traces"), a ballet to the adagio of Mahler's unfinished Tenth Symphony, which treated the theme of a woman whose life had been shattered by an authoritarian society; it was dedicated to Galina and Valery Panov.

That Mahler symphony was to have been the basis of a new ballet with Fonteyn which had been announced for presentation at Covent Garden in mid-February, but towards the end of December John changed his mind and said he would revive *Poème de l'Extase* instead. While rehearsing it, he was in a far from happy state. One night, for instance, he had been invited to dinner by Nureyev, and at about 8.30 rang the friends with whom he was staying to say that he was in Kensington with a boy he had picked up, and would they come to rescue him? He turned out to be already almost incapacitated with drink. It appeared that he did not know just what the arrangements were meant to be that night, and that he did not have Nureyev's telephone number. Eventually he managed to get that from somebody at Covent Garden, but when he rang, Nureyev's housekeeper announced simply that Mr Nureyev was at the theatre, and put the phone down. Instead of ringing again and explaining, John decided it did not matter, they would all go out to dinner at a restaurant he remembered from years back. The restaurant had declined and the meal proved disastrous. Eventually it was established that the Nureyev party was still on for after the performance. Down to Sheen they went, thinking it would be a big affair with many guests and a buffet, only to find the table laid for a small formal dinner, at which their host politely kept getting up to fill their glasses, and thus seeing the uneaten food they tried, by moving candles or spreading their cutlery, to hide on their plates. The party was not a success, and John at the end was so drunk that he turned up for rehearsal the next morning wearing a knitted suit, inside out — to which Fonteyn's comment was "That's lucky".

During much of 1972, John was feeling played out. What he would have liked was a sabbatical year, to go off somewhere far away, possibly to India, without any responsibilities for a time. Lacking that possibility, he said he would restrict himself to one new ballet for the 1972–3 season, to Mahler's Tenth Symphony, the music he had thought of using at Covent Garden and put off. Apart from that, he said in May, he would bring in revivals of several existing works: *Swan Lake*, *Présence* and *Quatre Images* among them. By then he had, fortunately, a strong "back list" of ballets to rely on, and his contribution to the Noverre Ballet's new programme in June was again a pair of revivals, although both new to Stuttgart: *Pineapple Poll* (which proved too English in its humour for some German tastes) and a revised version of his Munich *Song of the Nightingale*. As intended, new choreographers were also making works for the Noverre company, and Jiri Kylian in particular was beginning to reveal the sure and original talent that afterwards took him to make his reputation as director of Nederlands Dans Theater. Fonteyn had been sufficiently impressed by one of his early efforts to arrange for it to be shown in London.

There were new pieces by John for the annual Ballet Week, but none of them very substantial: a couple of duets, to music by Wieniawski (Marcia and Ricky had already danced this a little earlier at a gala in Munich) and Chabrier; also a curious work entitled – *1* + *6*. This had actually been announced for January but postponed. The music was the first movement of Haydn's First Piano

Concerto, but with the solo instrument removed (– 1) and its rhythms replaced by tap-dancing from a cast of two women and four men (+ 6). It began under "black light" so that only the white tricots and socks worn by the dancers were visible, and although performed by leading members of the company it enjoyed no great success.

Another work John did undertake that summer was a new version of *Children's Corner* for the children of the ballet school, the cast this time including snowflakes, a little frog, and an ape as well as dolls. It was given a public showing on a Sunday morning at the beginning of July, when some senior students and recent graduates also danced an extract from *Onegin*. Something had obviously set John thinking about works from his earliest days, and he made a new version of *Tritsch Tratsch*, too, for Marcia and Ricky to dance on television.

That summer, Walter Schäfer returned from directing the Stuttgart theatres and Hans Peter Doll succeeded to the position. Although John had initially expressed some reservation about staying, he had signed in June 1971 a further five-year contract from 1972, after discussing with Doll what his plans would be. Schäfer explained at the time that John's attitude had never been "I'll stay while Schäfer is there, then go", only "While Schäfer is there, I'll stay whatever happens. After that I can't say at the moment." It had taken time, and not a little disputation, before the trust between ballet director and general director had been built, and consequently John was fully aware of how important the relationship was. It is difficult to be sure how far it was weariness that made him say again in October 1972 that he wanted to leave, and how far he was using his own strong position as a lever. On 30 October, the *Stuttgarter Nachrichten* reported him as saying that he had been anxious about money for the company during the past three years, but had been too loyal to say so. He said that the company was stagnating in its development; that he found himself in a creative crisis, with no ideas coming to him any more; and that the performance of the ensemble had become quite crazy, with no interest in devoting themselves to the proper discharge of works by his other choreographers. He would like to invite guest choreographers but had no money for that. Whatever motivated that complaint, it was quickly remedied, because the next day the rival paper, the *Stuttgarter Zeitung*, was able to announce that Cranko would stay. He had been promised for 1973–4 the 200,000 Marks he had asked for, and was off to London to talk to Jerome Robbins about coming to mount a ballet: one of the pieces which John remembered from way back, or possibly even a new work. Glen Tetley was going to come to Stuttgart, too.

Now began a great change in John's mood. It began when he met

223

old friends in London, and he even became enthusiastic enough about life to start talking of buying a house in the English country-side. "When would we go there?", Dieter and Reid asked him, to which there seemed no answer, but the eagerness was real, if unrealistic. Another cause of pleasure was that it seemed he would at last be able to bring the Stuttgart Ballet to London. They could have come sooner if they had been prepared to appear at the Coliseum, which (as friends continually urged on him, and as became apparent on subsequent occasions when they did go there) would have suited the company excellently. But John always insisted that they must go to Covent Garden, and only there: he wanted to make a point to his old colleagues about what had been achieved in Stuttgart and about the company's standing. Eventually he was persuaded at least to talk to Lord Harewood, director of the English National Opera, which held the lease of the Coliseum. The night he went there, sitting in Harewood's box, the Covent Garden general director, John Tooley, was in the audience and saw them together. By what might be thought a happy coincidence, an invitation arrived only a couple of weeks later for the Stuttgart Ballet to appear at Covent Garden in 1974.

Back in Stuttgart, John threw himself with restored energy into plans for the future, and during January and February was able to reveal his ideas not just for the season to come, but for the three years ahead — something unprecedented in Stuttgart or, probably, in any other ballet company. For the next season, 1973–4, a ballet by Jerome Robbins was "as good as sure", he said, perhaps *New York Export, Opus Jazz* or *The Cage*, both early works, dramatic in style; and there would be further ballets by Tetley (whose *Mythical Hunters* had just been mounted for the Noverre Ballet) and Balanchine. John himself would create, for premiere in February 1974, a work based on the novel *Le Diable au Corps*, by Raymond Radiguet, who had died when only twenty, having been for five years the great love of Jean Cocteau. From the way he went into the background, it seems John was thinking of it as biography more than fiction. The provisional title was *Preludes* and he would use music by Rachmaninoff, with designs by Jürgen Rose. Then in the following season he wanted to do a three-act ballet of *Othello*, to have designs by John Piper. He had asked Andrzej Panufnik to write music for it, but feared that "it probably won't come off because he is very busy and hardly has time for a long work. He would need as long as it takes to write three symphonies." For the year after that, he intended to mount a new production of *The Sleeping Beauty*: "It's necessary for the public, who can gain a historical perspective from it. A Stravinsky would be impossible without a Bach, a Picasso without a Velasquez, a modern choreographer without Petipa."

His ideas did not stop there. He got in touch with Hans Werner Henze and proposed to him a breath-takingly ambitious project: a sequence of three long ballets on the subject of Tristan. Although Henze calculated that the project would take between seven and ten years to write, he was interested enough to invite John to visit him and discuss it, and the choreographer's enthusiasm seems to have been infectious, because on 8 May 1973 John was able to write a characteristically impetuous letter following up their talks:

Dear Hans,

I think with great pleasure of our four days together. Herewith *Travels with My Aunt*, which I think could make a marvellous "sweet-and-sour" opera, but anyway, I am sure you would like reading.

As to *Tristan*, I hope you are still excited by the project. I have done a scenic breakdown which I think is interesting but shows signs of being done in a hurry. I do not know if I have stressed enough the Mark–Tristan relationship, and I do not know if the sacrifice of Tristan at the end is strong enough. Anyway, I thought at least it would give you a rough idea of the way I am thinking. The visual style of the whole should be fluid and dream-like; just as *Satyricon* was a hallucination of Rome, so I think our *Tristan* should be a hallucination of the Middle Ages.

I have given some musical examples as they occurred to me, naturally not expecting you to copy them, but to give you an idea of the weight and feeling required. I have also not divided it yet into acts, or the numbers into minutes, but would like first to know if you like/hate what I have done.

We go to America on Sunday, and I can always be got at Hurok Concerts Inc., ... and get back to Germany on 26 June. I could gladly then come to you for further discussions, perhaps by then I will have the incident in scene 5, number 4.

Much love to you, the whippets, the chickens, the ducks and everybody else. Doll is very enthusiastic and is writing to you himself.

Again love.

On a second sheet the letter abruptly resumes:

I have an idea for the musical construction which I think would be interesting, and get away from the Wagnerian "Leitmotiv" idea.

The first ballet has as its basic element WATER, i.e. the

225

voyages, magic bath, etc. It is also the birth of the tragedy and the love of Tristan and Iseult.

The second ballet, which would be concerned with the sexual relationship and wanderings of Tristan and Iseult, has as its element EARTH.

The third ballet, which would be concerned with the other Iseult and Tristan's madness, would have as its element FIRE.

This might help you to get a foundation and unity of conception in the three ballets.

Third time: love,

John

The scenario of the first *Tristan* ballet is printed as Appendix B.

That schedule of new ballets to be made from scratch would have been enough to occupy some people, but not John. On the American tour that summer he was discussing further non-ballet projects. The company's last engagement was at Philadelphia, where the producer Moe Septee wanted to stage a "Cranko year". The idea was that John would restage *The Merry Widow* first, opening in Philadelphia, then going on a national tour. Septee wanted a New York revival of *Cranks*, to be done in an off-Broadway theatre, and a new musical too. John's idea for this was to base it on *Steppenwolf*, and have the music written by Anthony Bowles, whom he had invited to become music director of the Stuttgart company. He said he would go to London as soon as he got back, and speak to Anthony Newley about starring in it. Septee in turn got carried away by John's enthusiasm and "felt that if he could get together with Leonard Bernstein, something great would happen, and I'd begun trying to make that arrangement. I was so taken by his genius, that I felt that if it were ever unleashed on Broadway it would be something entirely new."

Too late. John had already made his last production. His mood that year was not simply and entirely euphoric. He had, for instance, agreed that the Noverre Ballet must come to an end. Although it did have some value in bringing on young dancers, and had allowed Kylian to prove his fast-growing talent for choreography, the company did not satisfy the local audience as a substitute for the Stuttgart Ballet during its absences on tour, and many of the productions (including at least one of John's) had not been good. So it was decided in January 1973 that the Noverre Ballet should be integrated into the big company after the end of that season, thus providing a larger company, more easily able to meet the needs of the operas as well as the larger-scale ballets. During tours, only an ad hoc ensemble would stay behind. John described the decision, although it meant the end of something he had struggled for, as bringing "an improvement in the artistic quality of the Stuttgart Ballet's work and the solution of problems of personnel within the company". Its last programme, premiered on 6 May 1973, just before the main company left for New York, included a revival of *Présence* and also (twelve years after John had first said he would be adding ballets by Ashton to the repertory) the only Ashton ballet ever danced by the Stuttgart dancers, *Les Patineurs*.

A month before that, on 7 April, had been the premiere of the last Cranko programme. Starting with a revival of *L'Estro armonico*, it included two new works. *Green*, which ended the evening, enjoyed no great success and there were some boos at the end. Set to Debussy's Fantasy for Piano and Orchestra, with Birgit Keil in the lead and a cast including several of the promising young women, it was thought too much like "fitness training" with its handsprings and rolling on the floor for it to make sense of its intended theme (derived from a poem by Verlaine which also provided the title) about fruit, flowers, leaves, branches and the condition of the loving human heart. Presumably it was meant as a playful contrast to the programme's centre-piece, *Spuren* ("Traces").

This was the awaited ballet to the adagio that is all that exists of Mahler's Tenth Symphony. John drew attention to the contrasts in the music between "the Viennese lushness, the lovely tunes and the sensuous strings with their gorgeous melody and then suddenly, in the space of a few bars, the most agonizing torment that one's ever heard, and the climax of the symphony as a scream of agony". Dedicating the ballet to Galina and Valery Panov, then still only hoping to be allowed to leave Russia, he took as his subject a woman who "has escaped from a totalitarian state. Now she must start a new life. First, however, she must forget all the horrors she has experienced in the past." Marcia was the woman, Heinz Clauss the stolid, careful man who tries to comfort her, Richard Cragun a monster-headed creature representing the past. With a mixture of realism for the new present and fantasy for the feared past, the ballet reached its climax in a moment that recalled both the hell of John's *Orpheus* and the waitress with a tattooed arm he had seen in Tel Aviv. The stage was opened, by pulling aside curtains, to its full depth; on it stood a large congregation who turned, dropped the wrappings they wore around their shoulders, and revealed a number seared into each back. The response to the plight of his Russian friends was unexpected, imaginative and compassionate.

That American tour was a new experience for John. He had always before, when the company went to New York, been so scared that he spent all his time in an alcoholic haze. Now for the first time he was sober enough to see his own success. He came back from one party quite astonished, saying, "There were so many stars there, and everyone wanted to talk to *me!*"

They played at the Met for three weeks from 15 May, then went to perform in Washington and Philadelphia. At the end of the tour, some of the dancers went straight on holiday in the United States or, in the case of Marcia and Ricky, at her family's home in Brazil. The rest of the company embarked on a Pan American flight from Philadelphia back to Stuttgart on the evening of Monday 25 June. John had dinner, watched the movie, then in the small hours of 26 June he went to his seat at the front of the aircraft to sleep. He had been prescribed a mild drug, chloral hydrate, to help him sleep; it is so mild a sleeping aid that it is the one generally chosen by doctors for children. Very rarely, it can have a side-effect of causing the person to vomit. That night, it did so to John Cranko, but at the same time the effect of causing him to lose consciousness was so immediate that he choked on the vomit. When Dieter came forward to join him, John was obviously unconscious and, as was established later, in fact already dead. The pilot of the aircraft asked permission to make an unscheduled landing at Shannon airport, on the west coast of Ireland, but a strike there made it impossible so he flew on to Dublin instead, where John was taken to hospital and death was confirmed. An inquest found that the cause of death had been asphyxia by stomach inhalation while under the effect of the drug. Referring to reports in German newspapers that he had committed suicide, the coroner emphasized that the drug was a relatively safe one, that the amount taken was nowhere near a fatal dose, and that the death was purely accidental.

EPILOGUE

THEY buried him with a ceremoniousness that would surely have surprised him. After the inquest in Dublin, the body was taken back to Stuttgart. Those dancers from his company who had already scattered far and wide hurried back to join those who had flown back with him from America. Friends and former colleagues came from all parts. The mother for whom John had found so little time in life came from South Africa and was received with a degree of honour she had never known before.

Four days after his death, on 30 June 1973, the Intendant who had invited John to Stuttgart, Walter Erich Schäfer, spoke in his memory in the theatre that had seen his life's work crowned with so many creations, so many memorable performances, the growth of a great company. Professor Schäfer began with a protest that it was against nature for him to have to memorialize a man almost thirty years younger than himself, but drew comfort from the thought that John's life, though short, had been lived at a faster pace than others', enabling him to achieve so much, so quickly, so young. Then the mourners went, on that bright Saturday midday, to the chapel at the Waldfriedhof, full of brightly coloured summer flowers. There were more speeches: from the Baden-Württemberg Minister of Culture, Professor Wilhelm Hahn; from Hans Peter Doll, the new Intendant who had succeeded Schäfer; from Dr Arnulf Klett, Oberbürgermeister of Stuttgart. So city and state and theatre assembled to pay their homage and give thanks for their enrichment. Among the mourners was Dr Hans Filbinger, Minister-President of Baden-Württemberg and a neighbour at Solitude, who afterwards recorded how the news of John's death had reached him during a meeting of the state cabinet, and how all around the table had fallen silent.

The next week, with only a few close friends present, John's ashes were interred in the burial ground near his home on the hill at Solitude. But that was not the last of him and his work. Walter Schäfer, in his memorial address, had claimed to speak on behalf of the company's dancers and staff when he declared rhetorically, "We have now all become John Cranko and shall work on as if he were still here among us before our eyes". At the service Marcia, for all her own sorrow, had found strength to embrace the other dancers with a gesture of comfort like a mother's.

Without the leader whose inspiration had drawn them together, the dancers might easily have dispersed, and they would have found no difficulty in obtaining engagements elsewhere. Memory and loyalty, however, together with the friendship of shared work, held them together. John had always said that if anything should happen to him, Marcia ought to take charge of the company, but she was reluctant to believe in her own ability to do so. For the next year, therefore, Anne Woolliams and Dieter Gräfe provided an interim direction. Dieter was the chief beneficiary under John's will and inherited the rights to John's ballets. His administrative skill and experience, and Anne's similar qualities in the studios, ensured stability for the time being.

The mood among the dancers was one of holding on to links with the past, but they kept enough of John's spirit to insist that the company must not become a museum of past glories: a continuing policy of creation was essential. So for the first premiere of the following season, Glen Tetley came (as already planned in John's time) to make a new work as part of a programme that would also include new productions of one of his existing ballets and Kenneth MacMillan's *Concerto*. Feeling the sense of mourning in the company, Tetley chose Poulenc's *Voluntaries*, a piece for organ and orchestra, and created an abstract ballet that reflected its mixture of liturgical and theatrical elements, with many images of grief. Even the movement incorporated many of the steps and lifts most favoured by John in his choreography. A cast headed by Marcia, Ricky, Birgit, Jan Stripling and Reid Anderson responded to the ballet in a singularly heartfelt way, and by a general consensus it was decided to invite Tetley to take over the company's direction.

At the end of that season, the Stuttgart Ballet at last played in London, opening at Covent Garden on 24 July 1974 with the British premiere of *Onegin*. The fortnight's season included also *Shrew* and five Cranko one-act ballets, of which only *Card Game* had ever been given in London before; *Voluntaries* was the only work not by John. The company enjoyed a success as great as any of their earlier triumphs.

Immediately before coming to London, the company had given new pieces by two of the Stuttgart alumni, Jiři Kylian and John Neumeier, during their Ballet Week, thus maintaining a link that proved valuable when, after a comparatively short period, relations with Tetley grew strained. It was recognized that he was pushing the standards of pure dancing within the company to even higher levels, but some of the established dancers felt that they were being supplanted by new recruits who were more apt to the lithe athleticism and speed of Tetley's style, although often not so well suited as the older generation to the more expressive style of Cranko's ballets. All the same, John's principals (except for Heinz Clauss, who retired from the stage and took over the direction of the school) continued to hold their own, even in the new repertory. It was the public that found more difficulty in adapting to the Tetley era.

Some of John's ballets had been as original and as far from the mainstream of conventional taste as anything Tetley did in Stuttgart, but John knew how to sugar the pill, how to ensure that even his most "difficult" ballets had a theatrical quality, and that they were presented as part of a varied total repertory with a preponderance of straightforward dramatic ballets. Tetley was more uncompromising, and dissatisfaction began to grow to the point that the management felt obliged to ask him for a more conventional production with a plot and pretty costumes. The honeymoon was over, and both sides realized that the match had not proved a happy one, in spite of initial raptures. After only two years, Tetley left.

It was then that Marcia Haydée agreed to become artistic director, adopting a policy based on what she had learned over the years from John. Her first year was devoted primarily to building up the strength and quality of the dancers, with a new *Sleeping Beauty* as the biggest production, and her second to trying to find new choreographers, while continuing to invite outsiders with an established Stuttgart connection (MacMillan, Neumeier, Kylian) to return and create or revive ballets. Those aims of renewing and maintaining the dancers and the repertory have remained the pillars of the Stuttgart policy ever since, with the surviving stock of Cranko ballets as its firm foundation.

One of the formal ways found of honouring John's memory was renaming the Stuttgart Ballet School after him. Also in Stuttgart, a John Cranko Society was founded, to hold monthly meetings of local supporters, to organize occasional exhibitions, and to award an annual medal for outstanding services to the Stuttgart Ballet in general, and Cranko's oeuvre in particular. The first, in 1975, went to Anne Woolliams, followed by Marcia Haydée, Walter Schäfer, Jürgen Rose, Martin Feinstein, Georgette Tsinguirides and (on his departure from Stuttgart to become director of the Frankfurt Ballet) Egon Madsen. Since 1978 the society has also published a yearbook of the company's work and personalities.

In New York, friends and admirers of Cranko collected funds for a scholarship that enabled a young black dancer, Christopher Boatwright, to go to Stuttgart to study; afterwards he joined the company and soon became a leading member. An appeal in London for a memorial fund permitted the construction of a much-needed additional ballet studio at Sadler's Wells, named the John Cranko Room and opened by Princess Margaret on 22 September 1977.

Far more influential in keeping his name alive, however, has been the wide dissemination of his ballets. The two Royal Ballet companies at Covent Garden and Sadler's Wells, the Joffrey Ballet in New York, the Royal Swedish Ballet, the Scottish Ballet, the Australian Ballet, the Hamburg Ballet and the Ballet de l'Opéra in Paris are only the most prominent of many companies that have received examples of Cranko's choreography into the repertory, ranging from the big narrative works (*Onegin, Shrew, Romeo and Juliet, Swan Lake*), which are inevitably the ones most in demand, through distinctive smaller ballets like *Brouillards* to miniatures such as *Beauty and the Beast*. Ten years after his death, John Cranko's ballets are more widely and more frequently performed than in his lifetime. Because so many dancers have experienced them, including inevitably some who will eventually find themselves running companies, the prospect is high that some of them will be numbered among those few ballets which survive indefinitely the changes of fashion.

Even more important, perhaps, is the way his example inspired a new generation of choreographers, and continues to do so. Besides those who worked with him and learned directly from him, others have gained their knowledge only from his work. One of them, Uwe Scholz, a bright hope of the present Stuttgart Ballet, and one whose cheeky originality and wit often recall the young Cranko, wrote for the first of the Stuttgart Ballet Annuals:

> The essence of Cranko's art is that we re-encounter the archetypes of the whole range of human emotions in the steps of his ballets. ... What I admire in Cranko is that he is so great a poet in that universal language that is not confined to words, and therefore cannot be misinterpreted. For example, the genius with which he translates Shakespeare into movement, so that — in my opinion — a deaf person could understand without the help of music. Or the ability to create characters as a poet does. Carmen, for instance: it is not Marcia, Birgit or Lucia, it is Carmen, however much the various interpretations may differ. ... I never met Cranko, so it is possible for me to love him without restriction or bias. I have also been spared the panic and suffering of physical loss. The way I know him, I love him.

John Cranko's earthly remains lie on a hillside overlooking Stutt-

232

gart. His spirit is alive in Stuttgart, London, Cape Town, and throughout the world of ballet. There was never enough time for him to do everything that his great heart wanted or his quick mind imagined, but thanks to him, others are still trying.

Appendix A
_____THE NAME CRANKO_____

THE volumes of the _Cape of Good Hope Almanac and Annual Register_ from 1843 (the earliest I have seen) until 1846 record Theunis Krankoor, tailor, occupying premises in Keerom Street, first number 40, then 14. After his death, his elder son is listed at the same address; in 1847 as James Krankoor, from 1848 as James Kranko. In 1850, James has two entries, as Cranko and Kranko (the listed being arranged alphabetically, not by streets). His will, written in October 1850, calls him Cranko. He reverts solely to Kranko in the _Register_ for 1851 and 1852, the last time his name appears, when his address is given as Primrose Hill; but when registering his death in 1852, his widow wrote the name Cranko and retrospectively changed his father's name to match. She also recorded that he died "at his lodgings in Keerom Street". The 1852 volume of the _Register_ also includes the name William Cranko (so spelled) at the Keerom Street addresss. In 1853 he becomes Willem Kranko, and for that year only James's widow, named as Christiaan Kranko, is shown at the same address. The _Register_ again lists Willem Kranko in 1854 and 1855, moving in the latter year to Longmarket Street, but an official Post Office street directory was also published in 1855, giving him under the more English-seeming version of William Cranko and, incidentally, listed his sister's husband, Hermanus Dempers, carpenter, among the other occupants of 21 Longmarket Street.

The next _Register_ entry I have seen is for 1859, when William (no longer Willem) Kranko is shown as living in Canterbury Street, with a separate entry under the name William Justavius (_sic_) Cranko for a shop in Shortmarket Street. By 1878, the only other _Register_ entry I have seen, he has become firmly William Justavus Cranko and is described no longer as a tailor but as a general outfitter, with premises in Adderley Street, the main shopping street of Cape Town. That volume also has an entry for his late brother's son Frederick as F. Cranko, clerk, of Long Street.

JOHN CRANKO'S
NOTES FOR TRISTAN

Scene 1 — The Beach
1 The overture intoduces the sea theme. As the curtain rises, the lament grows in bits and pieces out of the sea music (a little like the opening of *Sacre du Printemps*). The people assemble and start a ritual dance of grief. King Mark enters with attendants and joins in the dance. The victims are brought on, either tied to poles or else in cages, but must look very ritualistic. The lament reaches a climax which is suddenly cut off and we hear Tristan's harp in the distance.
2 The harp grows stronger (lamento di Tristano?). Tristan appears in a boat, foreground (as if the orchestra is the sea). The boat moves without oars or sail (do you know the Böcklin *Tödeinsel*? This feeling). Tristan is wrapped in his cloak like the figure in *Tödeinsel*. He comes on shore, and as he approaches the people they turn away from him, too grieved to talk. He finds Mark prostrate on the ground and lifts him up. Tristan, Orpheus-like, starts to play his harp. The people lift their heads and draw towards him, attracted by the music. Tristan puts down his harp, which continues to play, magically, and dances a very serene and beautiful solo. This is interupted by the arrival of Morholt's ship.
3 Morholt and attendants descend from ship (I imagine Morholt like the Minotaur in Fellini's *Satyricon*, not with a bull's head but a huge closed helmet and corselet-like scales, and built-up shoes and grieves). Morholt's music very bestial, like pigs and rhinoceroses. He stomps forward and demands tribute. Everybody recoils including Mark. The attendants lift up the victims. Tristan comes forward and challenges Morholt.
Fight between Morholt and Tristan.
Morholt has a huge two-handed sword. Tristan, in contrast, strips off his tunic and has only a dagger. The music should be like a fight between a rhinoceros and a bee. Morholt wounds Tristan with his sword (a black wound appears in his side). Tristan does not notice and finally stabs Morholt through the scales of his armour. Morholt stands still as if amazed, the blood runs out from between the chinks of his armour. He falls rigidly to the floor. His attendants carry him back to the ship.
4 General rejoicing, the victims are unbound, laughing, weeping, etc. Suddenly, this is cut short by them seeing Tristan's wound, they crowd round him. Tristan's wound begins to bleed red blood, which changes to poisonous green, staining his body and legs. With the green, the people register a terrible stench by covering their noses and mouths with their hands and garments; one by one they shrink away, only Mark is left holding Tristan. Tristan comes to himself and leaves Mark. Slowly and painfully he picks up his cloak, which stains with the green blood. He climbs into the boat and starts to play his harp, but the tune is twisted and broken. The boat moves off of its own accord.

Scene 2 — The Sea
This is a corps de ballet number, the dancers being water in which we see Tristan's voyage over the sea (sea motif again).

236

Scene 3 — Ireland, a room in the castle open to the sea. Morholt's armour and sword stand on one side.

1 The Queen, Iseult and Brangien at their weaving. I would like their witch-like quality stressed. They should suggest the triple Goddess; i.e. Brangien, the virgin, in white; Iseult, the woman in full glory, in red; and the Queen, the hag and the death-goddess, in black. Their weaving should be magic, and I think we could find a trick-effect so that they are weaving light (maybe laser beams).

2 The weaving dance stops, and we hear Tristan's harp getting louder. The boat reappears with Tristan lying rather like a mummy in it. Tristan painfully climbs out, short solo, Tristan appealing to the three women, who lift him up. I would like this scene to be reminiscent of pietas or the descent from the cross.

3 See drawing 1. At the back is a huge perspex tank, about 250 cm by 200 cm. This is filled with water and lit from the back. Right and left staircases go up to a rostrum, level with the top of the tank.

The three women carry Tristan up the steps on to the rostrum. They take strange objects which look like stones and throw them in the water. The stones open under water, like those Japanese water-flowers, and mysterious waterplants grow up. Next they take a cord and wind it around Tristan's body, putting the end into his mouth (this should be reminiscent of the umbilicus, but is in fact a breathing tube) and lower him into the water. Tristan sinks like a stone, his wound begins to bleed green (this is oil and floats upwards in great globules). Then his wound starts to bleed red (this is a water colour which mixes with the water in the tank, making it all one red). The women pull Tristan out of the tank, they search his wound and the Queen draws out a piece of metal, the shape of a half-moon. Immediately, Tristan magically starts to recover. They come downstairs.

4 Tristan has a "recovery" solo. While he is dancing, the Queen fits the piece of metal into Morholt's sword, and realizes that Tristan is Morholt's killer. She takes the sword, which is much too heavy for her, and tries to kill Tristan. Struggle, Tristan with the three women. He jumps into the boat and escapes.

Scene 4 — Mark's tent (see drawing 2) — the tent is open in front but closed at the sides and back, so that we can make back and side projections on it.

1 Formal dance of Mark's courtiers. During the dance Mark tries to get Tristan to join in (Tristan has been sitting at the side, Hamlet-like). Tristan starts a solo, but breaks down.

2 Mark calls in jugglers who dance but do not move Tristan.

3 Mark sends the court away and comes to Tristan. Pas de deux, Mark and Tristan, in which we see Mark's love for Tristan and Tristan's indifference. The music changes and Tristan tells Mark about Iseult, the audience sees this by projections, back and from both sides, of Iseult, laughing, dancing, etc. These need not be realistic but should be in beautiful colours, very psychedelic. The projections stop and we see Mark is now jealous. He takes an inner crown from inside his own crown and gives it to Tristan, ordering him to go. I think this will convey the meaning to the public.

Scene 5 — Same as 3

1 Iseult and her maidens are washing tweed in the sea. There are lines with great bits of coloured cloth drying in the sun. I have seen this in the Hebrides, the tweed is wet and beaten on stones. To the slap slap rhythm of the beating the women sing and dance. This whole scene should be very lyrical.

2 Tristan enters, disguised as a fool. The maidens are curious. Fool's solo dance for Tristan.

3 Tristan plays his harp, the maidens dance, solo for Iseult and then all together (dance of the princesses, *Firebird*).

4 The Queen enters and recognizes Tristan. Now should follow an episode in which Tristan saves the women from danger — but I have not thought of it yet. The main thing is he puts the women in his debt.

Iseult is obviously pleased to go with Tristan. At this moment, an over-lifesize projection of King Mark appears and Tristan shows the crown. Iseult thinks that Tristan does not love her. He leads her off.

Scene 6 — The Voyage to Cornwall

1 Iseult, dressed very richly, lies on furs. The ship is suggested by sails moving, and is not realistic. Tristan stands apart. The courtiers dance, but Tristan and Iseult are distracted and will not join in. The courtiers leave.

2 When they are alone, Tristan and Iseult are drawn together. The lighting, which until now has been fairly normal, becomes fantastic. I think of the *Bâteau ivre* of Rimbaud. This is their great pas de deux, but I do not want it to be a "fuck" pas de deux, it should be their mounting passion in which ship, sky, sea, sails, all become hallucination. It should end with them sinking down on Iseult's furs, exhausted. The lighting becomes normal and we are on the ship again.

Scene 7 — Mark's Palace in Cornwall

1 A great ceremonial dance of the people (*Noces* or *Sacre* in Celtic, if you get me). Mark, a jewelled static figure, in the middle. Tristan leads Iseult in. Ritual tableau of Iseult, loaded with jewels and clothes, then crowned — very like an icon, she takes her place on the throne beside Mark. At the end, all the lights go down, except spotlights on Tristan and Iseult; they exchange a look — curtain.

Appendix C

—————— John Cranko's——————
—————————— Ballets——————

THE names in brackets following each title are those of the composer and designer. Next comes the company for which the work was created, and the date of premiere, followed by information about companies for which the work was later remounted. Incidental dances for plays, revues and television are not included, and opera-ballets are included only where they were of a substantial nature.

1944

The Soldier's Tale (Stravinsky/Hanns Ebensten) Cape Town Ballet Club, 24 November
1945

Suite, Opus 3 (Grieg/Ebensten) University of Cape Town Ballet, 3 October/Cape Town Ballet Club (as *Suite "Aus Holbergs Zeit"*) 3 December

Primavera (Debussy/Ebensten) University of Cape Town Ballet, 3 October
1946

Tritsch Tratsch (J. Strauss/Ebensten) University of Cape Town Ballet, 1 March/ Sadler's Wells Theatre Ballet, 1947/Henley 1952/Royal Ballet 1959/Stuttgart Ballet 1963 and many concert or gala programmes
1947

Adieu (Scarlatti/Hugh Stevenson) Vic–Wells Ball, January/SWTB 19 May

Morceaux enfantins (Debussy/Ebensten) RAD Production Club, 15 June/ SWTB (as *Children's Corner*, designs Jan Le Witt) 1948
1948

The School for Nightingales (Couperin/Ebensten) St James's Ballet, 20 September
1949

Sea Change (Sibelius/John Piper) SWTB, 18 July/University of Cape Town Ballet, 1952

Beauty and the Beast (Ravel/Margaret Kaye) SWTB, 20 December/Henley (des. Piper) 1952/University of Cape Town Ballet, 1952/Wuppertal Ballet, 1965/Western Theatre Ballet, 1966/Northern Ballet Theatre (des. Farmer), 1977
1950

The Witch (Ravel/Dorothy Tanning) New York City Ballet, 18 August *Pastorale* (Mozart/Stevenson) SWTB, 19 December/Stuttgart Ballet (as *Divertimento*, des. Richard Beer) 1961
1951

Pineapple Poll (Sullivan, arr. Mackerras/Osbert Lancaster) SWTB, 13 March/Borovansky Ballet, 1954/Covent Garden Royal Ballet, 1959/National Ballet of Canada, 1959/Cape Town Univ. Ballet, 1960/Joffrey Ballet, 1970/Noverre Ballet, 1972/Oslo Ballet, 1975

Harlequin in April (Richard Arnell/Piper) SWTB, 8 May/Covent Garden R B, 1959

Dances in *The Fairy Queen* (Purcell/Michael Ayrton) Covent Garden Opera Ballet, 3 July
1952

Bonne-Bouche (Arthur Oldham/Lancaster) Sadler's Wells Ballet, 4 April

Umbrellas (Lanchbery/Piper) Henley, 21 July

239

The Forgotten Room (Schubert/Lancaster) Henley, 21 July

Paso Doble (Spanish music arr. Lanchbery) Henley, 21 July

L'Après-midi d'Emily Wigginbotham (Lanchbery/Piper) Henley, 21 July

Dancing (Shearing/Piper) Henley, 21 July

Reflection (Gardner/Keith New) SWTB, 21 August

1953

The Shadow (Dohnanyi/Piper) SWB, 3 March/Munich (des. Sylvia Strahammer), 1969

Dances in *Gloriana* Britten/Piper) Covent Gdn Opera Ballet, 8 June

1954

The Lady and the Fool (Verdi, arr. Mackerras/Richard Beer) SWTB, 25 February/SWB,
     1955/Stuttgart (des. Werner Schachteli), 1961/Australian Ballet, 1962/ Deutsche
     Oper, West Berlin, 1965/CAPAB Ballet, Cape Town, 1965/Royal Danish Ballet,
     1971/Houston Ballet

Variations on a Theme (Britten/Kenneth Rowell) Ballet Rambert, 21 June

1955

Ritual Dances in *The Midsummer Marriage* (Tippett/Barbara Hepworth) Covent Gdn
     Opera Ballet, 27 January

La Belle Hélène (Offenbach, arr. Aubert & Rosenthal/Marcel Vertès) Ballet de l'Opéra,
     Paris, 6 April

Dances without Steps (Casella) London Ballet Circle, 30 September

Corps, Cous, Coudes et Coeur (Stravinsky/Desmond Heeley) London Ballet Circle, 30
     September

1956

No new ballets

1957

The Prince of the Pagodas (Britten/Piper & Heeley) Royal Ballet, 1 January/Ballet of La
     Scala, Milan, May/Stuttgart, 1960

The Angels (Arnell/Heeley) Royal Ballet Touring Company, 26 December

1958

Romeo and Juliet (Prokofiev/Nicola Benois) Ballet of La Scala, Milan, 26 July

Secrets (Poulenc/Piper) Edinburgh International Ballet, 25 August

Cat's Cradle (Addison/Heeley) International Ballet of the Marquis de Cuevas, 28
     October

1959

La Reja (Scarlatti/Carl Toms) Rambert, 1 June

Pièce d'Occasion (Delibes) Concert tour by Merle Park and Gary Burne — adagio only,
     9 July/complete (costumes Toms) Festival Ballet, 10 September/Royal Ballet 18
     September

Antigone (Theodorakis/Rufino Tamayo) Royal Ballet, 19 October/Stuttgart (des.
     Schachteli), 1961

Sweeney Todd (Arnold/Alix Stone) Royal Ballet Touring Company, 10 December

1960

No new ballets

1961

Familienalbum (Walton/Beer) Stuttgart, 16 March

Intermezzo (Shearing/Beer) Stuttgart, 16 March

Katalyse (Shostakovitch/Schachteli) Stuttgart, 8 November/National Ballet of
     Washington, 1964/Deutsche Oper am Rhein, Düsseldorf-Duisburg, 1965/Munich
     1968

1962

Scènes de ballet (Stravinsky) Stuttgart, 10 June

Coppelia (Delibes/Max Bignens) Stuttgart, 10 June

Die Jahreszeiten (The Seasons — Glazunov) Stuttgart, 15 July/Autumn duet — Western Theatre Ballet, 1963/revised version, Stuttgart, 1971

Daphnis and Chloe (Ravel/Nicholas Georgiadis) Stuttgart, 15 July/Munich, 1969

Romeo and Juliet (new version — Prokofiev/Jürgen Rose) Stuttgart, 2 December/ National Ballet of Canada, 1964/Munich, 1968/ Australian Ballet, 1974/Frankfurt Ballet (des. Elisabeth Dalton) 1981/Scottish Ballet, 1982/Ballet de l'Opéra, Paris, 1983

1963

Wir reisen nach Jerusalem (Musical Chairs — Stolze/Wilfried Gronwald) Stuttgart, 27 April

L'Estro armonico (Vivaldi) Stuttgart, 27 April/Deutsche Oper, Berlin, 1964

Variationen (Trade) Stuttgart, 13 July

Swan Lake (Tchaikovsky/Rose) Stuttgart, 14 November/revised version, Munich, 1970/revised version, Stuttgart, 1972

1964

The Firebird (Stravinsky/Rose) Ballet of Deutsche Oper, Berlin, 4 March/Stuttgart, 20 May

La Source (Pas de deux — Delibes/Philip Prowse) Stuttgart, 30 May

Hommage à Bolschoi (Pas de deux — Glazunov) Stuttgart, 30 May

Concerti grossi (Handel) Ballett der Bühnen der Stadt Köln, 8 November

1965

Bouquet garni (Rossini, arr. Britten) Stuttgart, 22 January

Jeu de Cartes (Stravinsky/Dorothee Zippel) Stuttgart, 22 January/Royal Ballet, 1966/Royal Danish Ballet, 1967/Cologne, 1967/Ballet of Komische Oper, East Berlin, 1969/Hamburg Ballet, 1971/Norwegian Ballet, 1973/Sadler's Wells Royal Ballet, 1973

Onegin (Tchaikovsky, arr. Stolze/Rose) Stuttgart, 13 April/revised version, Stuttgart, 1967/Munich, 1972/Australian Ballet, 1976/Royal Swedish Ballet, 1976/London Festival Ballet, 1983

Raymonda (Pas de deux — Glazunov) Stuttgart, 3 June

Jeux de vagues (Pas de deux — Debussy) Stuttgart, 3 June

Carmina burana (Orff) Stuttgart, 10 July

Opus 1 (Webern) Stuttgart, 7 November/Berlin, 1968/Frankfurt, 1970/Royal Danish Ballet, 1971/Düsseldorf, 1975

1966

Brandenburg 2 & 4 (Bach/Zippel) Royal Ballet, 10 February

Concerto for Flute and Harp (Mozart) Stuttgart, 26 March

Pas de Quatre (Glinka) Stuttgart, 6 April

The Nutcracker (Tchaikovsky/Ralph Adron) Stuttgart, 4 December 1967

Die Befragung (The Interrogation — Zimmermann/John Neumeier) Stuttgart, 12 February

Oiseaux exotiques (Messiaen/Neumeier) Stuttgart, 5 May

Quatre images (Ravel/Alan Beale) Stuttgart, 13 May/Royal Danish Ballet, 1971/Munich, 1972

Holbergs Zeiten (Pas de deux — Grieg) Stuttgart, 13 May/Heidelberg, 1969/Eliot Feld Ballet, 1976–7

1968

Begegnung in drei Farben (Stravinsky) Munich, 23 February

Song of the Nightingale (Stravinsky/Zippel) Munich, 23 February/Noverre Ballet, 1972

Fragmente (Henze/Zippel) Stuttgart, 30 May/Munich, 1969

Présence (Zimmermann/Jürgen Schmidt-Oehm) Stuttgart, 30 May/Noverre, 1972

Kyrie eleison (Bach-Stolze) Stuttgart, 30 May

Suite from "Salade" (Milhaud/Dalton) Stuttgart, 1 June
1969
The Taming of the Shrew (Stolze after Scarlatti/Dalton) Stuttgart, 16 March/Royal
   Ballet, 1977/Royal Swedish Ballet, 1978/Hamburg, 1979/Sadler's Wells Royal
   Ballet, 1980/Joffrey Ballet, 1981
Triplum (Fortner/Sylvia Strahammer) Munich, 18 May
Grund zum Tanzen (Grund/Strahammer) Munich, 23 May
Fête Polonaise (Chabrier, Dalton) Munich, 23 May
Französische Suite — Une Fête galante (Egk/Strahammer) Munich, 28 November
1970
Brouillards (Debussy) Stuttgart, 8 March/Sadler's Wells Royal Ballet, 1978/Joffrey
   Ballet, 1978
Poème de l'Extase (Scriabin/Rose) Stuttgart, 24 March/Royal Ballet, 1972
Orpheus (Stravinsky) Stuttgart, 6 June/Munich, 26 July
Cous, coudes, corps & coeurs (Pas de quatre — Stravinsky) Stuttgart, 17 June
Ballade (Fauré) Stuttgart, 17 June
Ebony Concerto (Stravinsky/Strahammer) Munich, 26 July/Stuttgart, 24 October/
Batsheva 1971
1971
Carmen (Bizet-collages by Fortner and Steinbrenner/Jacques Dupont) Stuttgart, 28
   February
Ami Yam Ami Ya'ar (Song of my people — Ben-Zvi, Sternberg and spoken
   words/Ya'akov Sharir & Yair Vardi) Batsheva Dance Company, 12 October
Into the Cool (Getz) Noverre Ballet, 19 Decmeber
1972
Initials R.B.M.E. (Brahms/Rose) Stuttgart, 19 January
Legende (Pas de deux — Wieniawski) Stuttgart dancers in Munich, 11 March
– 1 + 6 (Haydn) Stuttgart, 29 June
Ariel (Chabrier) Stuttgart 29 June
Children's Corner (Debussy, new version) Stuttgart Ballet School, July
1973
Green (Debussy) Stuttgart, 7 April
Spuren (Traces — Mahler/Rose) Stuttgart, 7 April

Appendix D

_____SOURCES AND_____
__ACKNOWLEDGEMENTS__

MANY of the people who supplied information or comments used in the preparation of this book spontaneously offered their help on hearing that I was working on it. Some of them, and others whom I approached, were previously strangers to me; yet nothing, it seemed, was too much trouble for them in helping to commemorate John Cranko's life and work. The bare thanks I can offer seem inadequate.

A primary source of information, of course, was my own observation of his work since 1946, and discussions with him throughout that period, ranging from casual conversations to formal interviews. However, the book could not have taken its present form without the help of John's mother, Mrs Grace Martin, who wrote many long letters in response to my enquiries, and entrusted me with precious photographs of her son; also from three of John's closest friends at different periods of his life. Hanns Ebensten provided photocopies of the letters he received from John between 1944 and 1948, wrote down his recollections for me, answered many written enquiries and supplemented that orally when I visited him in New York. Frank Tait obtained for me John's own scrapbook and other personal papers, together with the notebooks and typescripts left behind by John's father, Herbert Cranko; he put me in touch with other friends of John's, and spent many hours discussing his own memories, besides lending me a tape recording of *Cranks*. Dieter Gräfe talked at length about John's Stuttgart days, lent me copies of correspondence, allowed me to reproduce the quotations from *Cranks* and the portrait of John by Dorothee Zippel which has never previously been published. To all of them, my gratitude is deep.

Special thanks are due also to Robin Cranko, for making available the results of his researches into the Cranko family history; to David Poole and Marina Grut for putting me in touch with many other helpful people as well as themselves providing valuable information about the South African background and about John's early days; and to Fritz Höver for his helpful comments and for allowing me to hear his own recording of a conversation with John immediately after the Stuttgart Ballet's first American tour.

All those mentioned so far also read and commented on appropriate parts of the typescript. So, too, in addition to providing information orally or in correspondence, did Mrs Gertrude Pitceathly (daughter of William Johan Cranko); Dr Dulcie Howes, Cecily Robinson (Mrs Hattingh), Pamela Chrimes and Lionel Luyt, on John's South African career; John's former schoolmaster John Parry, and John Wright, the puppeteer; Peter Darrell, Leo Kersley, Maryon Lane, Henry Legerton, Mr and Mrs John Piper and Jane Shore (Mrs Nicholas) on John's London career; Reid Anderson and Marcia Haydée on John's Stuttgart days.

Others who provided information in discussion or correspondence were Richard Arnell, Kenneth Barlow, Ray Barra, Alan Beale, A. V. Camroux, Petrie Cranko, Dudley Davies, Martin Feinstein, Dorothy Grummer, Anne Heaton, Dick Hendricks, Michael Hobson, Jonathan Hurwitz, Marilyn Jones, Oleg Kerensky, Ashley Killar, Cara Lancaster, Charles Lisner, Laura Luyken, Sir Charles and Lady Mackerras, Kenneth MacMillan, Egon Madsen, Patricia Miller, John Neumeier, Joanne Nisbett,

243

Deirdre O'Donohoe, Galina and Valery Panov, Jann Parry, Gunther and Leslie
Petzold, Peggy van Praagh, Domy Reiter-Soffer, Gert Reinholm, Judith Reyn,
Rahamin Ron, Clover Roope, Harold Rosenthal, Peter J. Rosenwald, Paul
Sanasardo, David Scott, Margaret Scott, Jan Stripling, David Sutherland, Veronica
Tennant, Georgette Tsinguirides, Yair Vardi, Ilse Wiedman, Anne Woolliams, Fred
Ziegler and Dorothee Zippel.

I am particularly grateful to Horst Koegler for hospitality in Stuttgart and the free
run of his extensive collection of press cuttings about the Stuttgart Ballet. The Dance
Collection of the New York Public Library was most helpful; Mrs D. B. Strand kindly
went to the British Library at Colindale on my behalf; and I received help in
correspondence from the City of Johannesburg Public Library, the Huguenot
Memorial Museum at Franschhoek, South Africa, and the Gemeentelijke Archief-
dienst van Amsterdam.

Valuable material was provided by interviews with John Cranko in *Ballet Today* (by
Elisabethe Corathiel, July 1956), *The Stage* (Eric Johns, 27 February 1958 & 10
February 1966), the BBC *Monitor* programme (Huw Wheldon, 24 April 1960), *Adam*
(Jonathan Pollitzer, Nos 304–6, 1966), *The Observer* (John Gale, 26 May 1968),
Newsweek (10 June 1968, 23 June 1969, 18 July 1971), *The New Yorker* (21 June 1969),
the *New York Times* (Murray Schumach, 25 June 1969, Anna Kisselgoff, 19 April &
26 July 1971, Hubert Saal, 18 July 1971), *Opera News* (Jane Boutwell, 11 October
1969), the *News Tribune*, Woodbridge, New Jersey (Mirko Tuma, 8 July 1971) and *The
Guardian* (15 February 1972). I consulted *Dance and Dancers* for interviews, news and
background information throughout. John Cranko's own writings in *Ballet Annual*
(1953), *The Sunday Times* (13 & 20 January 1957, the Noverre Society's Tenth Anniversary programme, 1968 and the Stuttgart Ballet's programmes and souvenirs were invaluable, as were Koegler's *Werkstattgesprach mit John Cranko* in *Ballet in Stuttgart* (Belser,
Stuttgart, 1964), the essay on Cranko in John Gruen's *The Private World of Ballet* (Vik-
ing, New York, 1975) and the posthumous *John Cranko Über den Tanz* (Fischer,
Frankfurt, 1975). Wilhelm Killmayer's interview with Cranko and Bernd Alois Zimmermann's article *On the Future of the Ballet*, both in *International Ballet on German Stages*
(Prestel, Munich, 1968) provided useful information; so did several of the tributes in
the memorial volume *John Cranko* (Belser, Stuttgart, 1973) and Walter Erich Schäfer's
Bühne eines Lebens (DVA, Stuttgart, 1975). Hanns Ebensten's account of four South
African ballets appeared in *Ballet Today*, July 1947, and Myfanwy's Piper's *Portrait of
a Choreographer* in *Tempo* No 32, Summer 1954, which also contained Joan Cross's ac-
count of the Rhodes Centenary celebrations at Bulawayo. The best accounts of
Cranko's collaboration with Britten are to be found in the essays by Basil Coleman,
Colin Graham and John Piper in *The Operas of Benjamin Britten* (ed. David Herbert,
Hamish Hamilton, London, 1979).

Index